J P GRAHAM

POPPAEA SABINA

The Power of Myth

p. 111 Nero
use of masks
(regia)
Josephus
p.

The E

Published by Lulu.com 2016

ISBN: 978-1-326-95227-3

Cover photo Poppaea Sabina
Archaeological Museum of Olympia (Greece)
© Konstantinos Tsakalidis

For the women of Ancient Rome

CONTENTS

	Foreword	i-iv
	Introduction	v-xiii
1	"A cruel and devious woman"	1-13
2	Child to woman	14-36
3	Education: To form her character	37-58
4	Images: Real or imagined?	59-82
5	In the company of witches	83-104
6	A woman of property	105-128
7	Marriage: "I am Gaia":	129-179
	(i) Rufrius Crispinus	130-150
	(ii) Marcus Salvius Otho	151-165
	(iii) Emperor Nero	165-178
8	A politician's wife	180-211
9	The spectacle of death	212-237

≈≈ 000 ≈≈

| 10 | Chroniclers of Ancient Rome | 238-264 |

Appendix I:
A very Roman problem with parentage   265-271

Appendix II:
Women of antiquity as writers   272-283

Bibliography   284-300

Foreword

This is a work of non-specialism. In this, it does not follow the accepted route of history books, more especially those concerned with ancient Rome: it has not been born and bred in a centre of learning. The Encarta Dictionary defines 'born and bred' as "*Coming from a particular place or background and usually having the qualities or character regarded as representative of it.*" This book does not qualify – nor does its writer. A number of points, therefore, call for explanation.

The vast body of work that already exists on ancient Rome, that most fascinating of cities, is sufficient to keep scholars and historians happily occupied into the next millenium and beyond. Such is the nature of the place: an endless source of pleasure and discovery – imposing, humbling, awe-inspiring.

A primary aim of this work is to attract a general readership: those who did not have the opportunity to study Latin, or to access those renowned centres of learning, spending countless hours in libraries, legitimately soaking up the atmosphere of ancient Rome and the lives of its people. Those who did are to be envied.

Texts emanating from those institutions are often abstruse and intimidating, unreachable and – usually – prohibitively expensive. No one should be deprived of the stories of Rome because of this.

An attempt has been made to make the language accessible (as far as it can be, given the sources). If the result is seen as reducing the text to an elementary level, so be it. Aiming at a wider readership than the fortunate residents of those august (There he is already![1]) establishments perhaps makes this inevitable. If the subject draws in those who are fascinated by ancient Rome and its women, but who, for whatever reasons, have never studied them in any detail, then the aim is achieved.

Latin words and phrases are, for the most part, briefly defined – with apologies to those for whom this is unnecessary. It becomes apparent when exploring the subject that those who do not speak Latin do not write books about ancient Rome; the subject is colonised by those who do.

Translation of Latin texts is a 'vast body' unto itself. The weight and influence of the translator's interpretation cannot be overstated. In Chapter 21 of *"A Companion to Perseus and Juvenal"*[2], Gideon Nesbit refers to *". . . the prestige of the translator as a source of cultural authority and*

---

[1] This is of course the Emperor Augustus (63 BCE-14 CE), who would see no need for further explanation.
[2] Blackwell Publishing Ltd (2012), (eds Susanna Braund and Josiah Osgood), USA/UK

arbiter of style . . . "; no more needs to be said. It therefore seemed essential to examine the issue. The original draft included a chapter on what the attraction is of such a daunting task, who does it[3], and why. However, firmly rooted as it is in academe, such an immense and complex subject is well beyond the scope of this book.

While names of well known figures of the Imperial Roman era[4] will be more than familiar to those spending their academic careers studying them, the same cannot necessarily be assumed of any general reader. Brief explanations are therefore included for the benefit of those who might appreciate help with working out who everyone is.

The most well-known roles and occupations – of the ruling élite – are defined to avoid those same assumptions being made. That they apply with few exceptions to Roman men reflects the fact that it is overwhelmingly about them that Roman history is written.

*

[3] A cursory look indicated that it is overwhelmingly men, as will be clear from the footnotes and Bibliography. This state of affairs seems to demand a book of its own – a statement that will be seen to crop up from time to time in the following pages, with particular reference to gender issues.
[4] Accepted to have begun in 27 BCE, when the Emperor Augustus was anointed as *Princeps* (first citizen), ruling the Roman Empire until his death in 14 CE with a skilled combination of republican and monarchical traditions – while pretending to be upholding neither.

The subject, Poppaea Sabina, is far from the most famous of Imperial Roman women. However, as with Cleopatra VII, the lack of information about her early life results in an abundance of myth, rumour and conjecture as to her true character.

Myths, especially about women, always benefit from being questioned. When they are found wanting, they should be blown away.

This results in a level of speculation being necessary to the text, inevitable in the absence of known detail. Statements are qualified; many questions go unanswered. To state as fact that which is unproven is unacceptable. *All* the women of antiquity deserve better, more particularly those of insalubrious reputation.

For those of us engaged in seeking out the lives of Roman women in order to learn more about who they were, and how they lived, it is a matter of regret that so little can be found of them. It is to be hoped that this book will shift the balance, and help to bring them out of the shadows, and into the light.

*

Introduction

The women of ancient Rome do not, by and large, enjoy very positive press. This unhappy situation sits uneasily alongside the fact that, in a part of the ancient world so intriguing, significant and influential, women did, and do, exert a fascination that is undeniable.

Such inconsistency is shown to good effect by the recording of their lives: scanty at best, heavily biased at worst. The 'stars' in the historical narrative do not, of course, need any illumination. In sheer volume, and as might be expected, the extensive writings on the emperors – their triumphs, their strengths and weaknesses, their friends and their enemies – greatly outweigh the exposure afforded Roman women of rank. (In fairness, however, the same imbalance might be applied to any grouping of citizens who had the misfortune not to be an emperor.) This disparity in the record only becomes apparent when attempting to uncover the stories of, in particular, those high-ranking women.

However, in considering the *content* of this disproportionate coverage, some historians see the matter differently:

> *But these* [Edward Gibbon, Theodor Mommsen,
> Michael Rostovtzeff, Ronald Syme] *were great
> historians whose insight, learning, and passion have
> illuminated for all the experience of the Roman people.*[1]

Such a sweeping collective commendation calls for a closer look, since it is manifestly untrue.

The comparative lack of illumination of the lives of Roman *women*, of any status, is clearly not something the writer recognised. (The age-old problem of 'people' meaning 'male people' is mentioned further below.)

The "passion" ascribed to those sources, if real, deserves recognition. However, the "insight" that results in the exclusion of the presence and experience of half the population cannot be applauded. These "great historians", in short, have a lot to answer for.

Of the second charge, the negative bias directed at women, examples are too numerous to count. While providing some small measure of that elusive illumination, close scrutiny will be both provoking and disheartening. It will uncover the same invective, the same damaging stereotypes, accepted as often as not without question and enshrined in the literature of ancient history.

---

[1] R Mellor, *Tacitus* (1993), Routledge, New York, NY, USA and Abingdon, UK

It is indisputable that Rome's high-status women were severely restricted in public activities: political, military, educational. Almost without exception they had no public face, nor was any such feature expected of them, and certainly none was approved of by the conservative ruling élite.

Nonetheless, their notable absence from so many texts claiming to describe life in the capital of the Roman Empire is to be deplored. In being treated as barely worthy of mention they seem to embody some kind of lesser species, living in the shadows of its menfolk: insignificant, often close to invisible.

Whether or not this properly reflects the reality is open to question. Credible evidence that Rome's male population vastly outnumbered the female is hard to find. While many women did not survive childbirth and its after-effects, many men died in battle; and both succumbed to infectious diseases that were often little understood.

Estimating the size of the female population, however, poses a challenge (though less so, it appears, than counting the slave population at any point). In coming up with numbers, later writers can fairly be charged with raising arbitrariness to an art form.[2]

---

[2] See, for example, L H Friedländer, *Roman Life and Manners Under the Early Empire*, Vol. IV (1913), George Routledge & Sons Limited, London

The ancient sources were hardly any better. Historian Cassius Dio (see Chapter 10), quoted in Friedländer below, "*. . . expressly states that the free* [i.e. not slave] *female population of Rome was considerably smaller than the male . . .*". No evidence is provided in support. Elaine Fantham et al[3] suggest that this "female population" may have meant women of child-bearing age, although there is still no justification of why this should be.

The lack of clarity as to when women first appeared in censuses is unhelpful. This may have begun with the Emperor Augustus' first census in the late Republic[4] (though sources are unclear about dates). However closer examination offers an early hint of the Emperor's well known, and impressive, propaganda skills. It suggests that his primary objective seemed not so much aiming at a reasonably accurate recording of citizen numbers, but rather making clear that Rome was a much improved place under his reign.

At all events, gender considerations in censuses were clearly not an issue. A much higher priority for the censors was the rank of the (male) denizens of Rome, with women continuing to inhabit the shadowy background.

---

[3] Elaine Fantham, Helene P Foley, Natalie B Kampen, Sarah B Pomeroy, H A Shapiro, *Women in the Classical World: Image and Text* (1994), Oxford University Press Inc, New York, NY, USA

[4] The ancient period predating Imperial Rome, commonly accepted to have run from 509 BCE, when the last of the Etruscan kings was vanquished, to 27 BCE, when Imperial Rome began under Octavian, later the Emperor Augustus.

In fairness, though, two of the primary purposes of counting heads, military and taxation, excluded women anyway – the latter slightly less so. Demographic information, such as property assets, further clouded the results, with the censors assigning far greater importance to property criteria than to gender. A problematic offshoot: were properties owned by women, and these certainly existed, to be included with the rest?

Counting methods generally were somewhat capricious. One example used the size of the grain distribution to the citizenry, with an attempt – surely no more than that – to calculate how much men, women and children ate in a day. Another counted houses (*domus*) and tenements (*insulae*), with no apparent reference to the numbers of heads inside them; and what about those heads inside properties owned by women?

Finally – and predictably – the language employed by those writing on matters of population has for too long assumed 'people' to mean 'male people'. This string of problematic factors clearly did not set an especially helpful standard in looking at the population as a whole.

Whatever their numbers, it is indisputable that women have historically received only passing mention in the record – and even that is subjective. Eve D'Ambra[5] confirms:

> *The tenuous traces* [they] *have left did not originate with themselves . . . but were filtered through the gaze of the men who held the power . . .*

How deeply do we need to dig to challenge this, and allow women an authentic and respected presence in the depiction of life in ancient Rome?

Even when women of status are mentioned, many are not even afforded the dignity of being named; there can be no more effective means of ensuring invisibility. Julia Agricola, for example, who married the venerated historian Tacitus in 77 CE, seems to suffer this fate more than most. The reasons are not clear, but it is remarkable considering the fame of both her father and her spouse. The former was Gnaeus Julius Agricola, long-term governor of the conquered colony of Britannia under the reigns of the Emperors Vespasian (69-79 CE) and Domitian (81-96 CE). Her mother, Domitia Decidiana, receives barely a mention.

Should this be thought a one-off example of their very real cloak of invisibility, the revered historian Livy proved otherwise. In a footnote to the article entitled

---

[5] *A History of Women in the West: From ancient goddesses to Christian saints* (1992), Harvard University Press, Cambridge, MA, USA

"Women in Livy's History" mentioned elsewhere, Smethurst[6] notes:

> *Of the twenty-one passages where women are specifically mentioned or play some active part . . . nine occur in the first two books, and in each case the women are named. In the other thirty-three books women are named only five times.*

Historical bibliographies tend to illustrate that male scholars and historians predominate in the recording and interpretation of events (in the Roman Empire and elsewhere). On the face of it, they therefore constitute the majority of those purporting to teach us about history in all its many aspects. They are the writers whose books line the shelves.

The revival of feminism in the 1960s and 1970s saw a long-overdue increase in the visibility of the work of female historians; the subsequent application of women's studies, later gender studies, to the world of antiquity was a welcome sight. One of the most valuable messages of feminism must be that the male version of history is not the only one.

A belief in the existence of two world views rather than one is all very well. However, in the visibility of women's contributions to a more balanced view of *any* history, there is still some way to go. On the Goodreads

---

[6] S E Smethurst, *Women in Livy's* History in *Greece and Rome*, Vol. 9, Issue 56 (1950), Cambridge University Press, Cambridge, UK

Inc website (accessed January 2015), a first page selection of thirty quotes about history, not necessarily from scholars or historians, contained entries from twenty-seven men and three women.

Curiously, the same 27:3 ratio appears in a 2011 paper by Walter Scheidel, *"Updated citation scores for ancient historians in the United States"*.[7] He records the *". . . relative impact of scholarship . . ."* in academic journals of thirty of the most frequently cited ancient historians. What does that say about the impact of that minority of three in competition with the twenty-seven majority?

This clear imbalance has profound implications for the recording, and publication, of ancient Roman lives. The consequences are both enlightening and disturbing. When they do appear, mothers and wives, sisters, daughters, nieces and aunts are all at risk of being commonly portrayed as unscrupulous and scheming, ambitious and ruthless. Throw in shameless, licentious and immoral, and the reader can hardly miss the drift.

The pictures commonly painted of the women of antiquity can go well beyond unflattering, a practice that has haunted history books for a very long time. Challenging such wholesale disparagement of those high-status Roman women is imperative if their reputations are to be salvaged. They did of course help to populate the

---

[7] *Princeton/Stanford Working Papers in Classics*, Stanford University, Stanford, CA, USA

Empire, but they did *not* bring it down. Examining the evidence, repainting the portrayal and redressing the balance is the least they deserve.

The last word should go to Amy Richlin[8], who reminds us that the term 'Roman women' does not include slaves. This is easily forgotten, though slaves vastly outnumbered women of rank. Nonetheless they too deserve to be remembered; Rome would not have functioned, or survived, in any form without them.

*

---

[8] *Arguments with Silence-Writing the History of Roman Women* (2014), University of Michigan Press, Ann Arbor, MI, USA

CHAPTER 1

" . . . a cruel and devious woman . . . "[1]

It is a disquieting fact that scholars and historians – ancient and modern – share an apparent enthusiasm for defaming the characters of Roman women in the historical narrative. Sandra Joshel[2] rightly notes:

> . . . *adulterous, ferocious, deceitful women populate the ancient Roman sources and modern images of Rome . . .*

She goes on to pinpoint those responsible with unswerving accuracy:

> [they] . . . *belong to a popular imagination about the Roman empire nurtured by Baroque opera, Enlightenment history, French revolutionary literature, and Robert Graves's novels . . .*

---

[1] M A Armstrong, *Poppaea 2nd Wife*, in *Monetary History of the World* (undated website), Armstrong Economics, Wilmington, DE, USA, a company ostensibly concerned with global economics. How Poppaea Sabina's supposed character defects illuminate the global financial picture is not clear.

[2] *Desire, Empire and Tacitus's Messalina* (2013), University of Chicago Press, Chicago, IL, USA

1

The effects of this comprehensive disparagement are both far-reaching and regrettable: not illuminating the lives of the women of antiquity, but rather distorting the record. In this it undeniably does the women of ancient Rome a disservice. Those of high status, in particular, suffer the worst effects; a handful of the more infamous of them is listed at Chapter 5.

Furthermore, the frequency with which these unflattering portrayals appear, both in historical texts and other general media, is cause for suspicion. However shaky its basic premise might be, the law of averages should tell us that so many women cannot have been *that* bad, all of the time; being immoral, unscrupulous and scheming requires a lot of energy.

Given this, and the gender imbalance in the sources (see Chapter 10), this continuing denigration should be treated with a healthy dollop of scepticism.

*

One longstanding victim of this historical vilification is Poppaea Sabina. The second wife of the Emperor Nero (reigned 54-68 CE), she is known as Poppaea the Younger to avoid confusion with her mother of the same name.

In the big picture of the narrative of Imperial Rome, Poppaea more usually figures as a relatively minor character. It is not so fanciful to think that had she not married one of Rome's more notorious emperors, she might never have appeared at all. Though she does not rightly belong in the 'A list' of Rome's wicked female stereotypes, her unsavoury reputation ensures her a place in the top ten.

In spite of the dearth of writings on Roman women generally, certainly when compared to Roman men, Poppaea by and large receives greater than average exposure. It cannot be said to be a lot, but it is more than many. While on the face of it this might seem encouraging, there is an inevitable downside, which disappointingly follows the established pattern.

What is most striking is that the common portrayal of her character is so malign. Though almost nothing is known of her early life (see the chapter following), this does not lead to even a hint of restraint in the degree of negativity she attracts.

Sources old and new write confidently of her objectionable nature as if they had known it firsthand. (Notably, Josephus of Jerusalem (37-c. 100 CE) is the only ancient source known to have actually met Poppaea – see Chapters 3 and 8.) Malevolent intent is ascribed to her every move, topped by steaming piles of iniquity. Remarkably, no writer admits to any degree of speculation or doubt as to her true character. All are apparently in full possession of the 'facts', and these, Josephus excepted, do her no favours at all.

The level of hostility Poppaea invites is startling, and the language employed in describing her often brutal. Tacitus, probably the most revered of ancient sources, supplied an early example.[3] Allowing no room for misinterpretation, she is *superba paelex*; she is 'the Imperial whore'. By no likely coincidence, Messallina, third wife of the Emperor Claudius (reigned 41-54 CE), is similarly described by Tacitus' contemporary, the satirist and poet Juvenal (50-127 CE). Poppaea might thus be elevated to the highest levels of reviled Roman women – which can be no cause for celebration.

Latin speakers will recognise an issue with translation in Tacitus' description of her. However the message at its core is unmistakeable, at least as far as Poppaea is concerned. Disturbingly, that message is incorporated into a thousand textbooks, to be read by countless thousands of students absorbing the history of ancient Rome – and the portrayal of its women.

This scathing treatment of the more notorious of them is not limited to the ancient sources. Modern historians, taking their lead from those whose texts have taught them everything they know, can be similarly virulent. For example, in Desmond Seward's 2008 *"Jerusalem's Traitor: Josephus, Masada, and the Fall of Judea"*[4], Poppaea Sabina is both "ferocious slut" and "sinister

---

[3] *Histories*, Book I.13 (trans. W Hamilton Fyfe/David S Levene, 1997), written c.109 CE – more than forty years after Poppaea's death.
[4] Da Capo Press, Cambridge, MA, USA

termagant". Language such as this from a popular historian (as described by *Wikipedia*) is shocking in its animosity. Can such hostile language truly be said to benefit students of ancient history?

We might also ask where this level of hostility stems from – and why. Whatever the explanation, a crucial question arises for anyone intent on shedding light on the lives of the women of antiquity: should we prefer to have negative portrayals of them rather than none at all?

Alongside the vitriol, Poppaea bears a heavy weight of responsibility in the historical narrative. The indirect despatch of her would-be mother-in-law Agrippina with cold-hearted resolve, for her own ends, is perhaps the most common charge levelled against her:

> *Nero's passion for Poppaea was* probably [emphasis added] *the immediate cause of his mother's death.*[5]

However recent scholarship has begun to dispute this contention, bringing her 'guilt' into question. Historians now incline towards the belief that Nero had been considering despatching Agrippina before he and Poppaea had even met, such was the level of his resentment of her meddlesome behaviour. Nero had already been Emperor, under his mother's 'guidance', for four years before he is thought to have become

---

[5] *A Dictionary of Greek and Roman biography and mythology* (2005), William Smith ed., University of Michigan, Ann Arbor, MI, USA

enamoured of Poppaea, in around 58 CE. Sandra Bingham suggests that his patience with his mother was already being sorely tested as early as the first year of his reign (54-55).[6]

Suetonius (c. 70-c. 130 CE), another acclaimed ancient writer, was clearly committed to emphasising Nero's brutality.[7] Nonetheless, his lengthy list of Nero's purported crimes against his mother is damning: more than one attempted poisoning, a planned collapse of her bedroom ceiling, and the scuppering of her boat while she was on board (before the final fatal attack by guards, in 59). When considering the truth of all of these charges, the above caveat concerning Suetonius' detestation of him should be kept in mind. However, they can otherwise be seen as indicative of Nero's increasing desperation.

Such a catalogue of Neronian malevolence cannot credibly be seen as a spur-of-the-moment scheme; it was only the year before Agrippina's death in 59 that Poppaea had become the object of his passion. Instead it looks more like a sustained long-term plan, sinister in its intent. Even Tacitus, no friend to Poppaea, appeared to suggest that Nero's plan to eliminate his mother was of longer duration than his relationship with Poppaea.

---

[6] *The Praetorian Guard-A History of Rome's Elite Special Forces* (2013), I B Tauris Ltd, London
[7] *Lives of the Caesars*, Oxford University Press, Oxford, UK (trans. Catharine Edwards, 2000)

The degree to which Nero was influenced by Poppaea in his scheming, in any sphere, is open to conjecture. No one can truly know who was not a party to their conversations (Tacitus, take note!). Ever-present slaves would have known to keep eyes and ears shut, and repeated anything only on pain of death. No amount of bribery to tempt them to indiscretion can surely have been worth the inevitable savage punishment.

Agrippina's death was one of Imperial Rome's more shocking events (though the region of Campania, south of Rome, rather than the capital itself, was its setting). However the final order for the murderous deed did not come from Poppaea, nor could it have done. That power rested with the Emperor alone. Influence is not to be equated with responsibility, which again was his alone. Nonetheless, scholars and historians continue to use this deplorable act of matricide to illustrate Poppaea's detestable character, still without apparent doubt as to the 'facts', and where responsibility rightly lay.

In the commission of loathsome deeds, Poppaea is claimed to have 'probably' carried out quite a number, with speculation and guesswork frequently standing in for fact. Charges against her are commonly prefaced by the conditional 'must have' or 'most likely', along with the sloppy, but always useful, 'probably'. However as evidence of her innate wickedness they do not stand, since proof is invariably lacking. If she 'probably' committed some heinous crime (the sources would have her knowing no other kind), why do historians or scholars show no inclination to establish the existence, or otherwise, of proof?

Examination of the issue of proof in the literature is conspicuous by its absence. On the face of it, evidence appears unnecessary to condemn one whom the sources have already decided is guilty, if only by implication. This want of rigorous scholarship makes a statement about all of those historians and scholars who profess to be telling the 'true' story of Imperial Rome – as far as it can be known. For the most part, the charges against Poppaea, by their nature, should not be lightly made. The apparent lack of enthusiasm for close scrutiny of them is telling. As important, it is of no assistance to the historical record.

These presumptive claims are of course linked to Nero, whose reputation needs no recounting here. His true character – uncontrollable megalomaniac or weak and besotted pawn – is covered extensively in the literature. However Poppaea does not escape vilification. Married to him (or else his mistress), she *must* have insisted that he kill his mother/eliminate his wife/flaunt his extravagance. How could she not? Once again, supposition is strong, evidence rather less so.

We do not lack for examples of the vices that she and Nero reputedly shared. Ancient sources were prone to attributing the negative qualities of certain Imperial Roman men to their women – as noted elsewhere, a device often associated with Tacitus. Such an insidious practice should properly be acknowledged, since it has important consequences, more particularly for Poppaea. Her portrayal in the record is greatly affected by the damning reputation of Nero since she was, briefly, married to him. The effect of this tradition on the representation of other Roman women, particularly those of 'questionable' character, is discussed at Chapter 8.

Linked to the suggestion that evil goes hand-in-hand with evil is a school of thought that calls for robust challenge. The hypothesis suggests that the true targets of the invective aimed at women such as Poppaea were actually men. Women, the argument goes, simply provide a handy conduit through which writers – Tacitus is a good example – can make plain their dislike of certain Roman men: Nero once again fits the bill. Jenifer Swindle, for example, contends that there is "*. . . rhetorical use of a woman as a type of a man.*"[8] Given Tacitus' use of women in this fashion, it is argued, and the era in which he lived and wrote (c. 56-c. 120 CE), his consistently hostile treatment of them is not surprising (for which read 'understandable' or 'excusable' – both are unacceptable).

The claim that the denigration of his wife is in fact an attack on Nero's own character is specious and misleading. Poppaea is relegated to being some kind of rhetorical mirror, allowing the writer to direct his venom,

---

[8] *A Rhetorical Use of Women in Tacitus'* Annales in *Studia Antiqua*, Vol. 3 No. 1 (2003), Brigham Young University, Provo, UT, USA

indirectly, at the real target. Spurious rationale such as this hints at a level of cowardice that is unbecoming in a scholar. Are the best known writers of antiquity to be accepted so unquestioningly, and protected so effectively from challenge or criticism?

In comparing literary images of Roman women to their Greek counterparts, it seems that both experience contradictory portrayals of character. Sarah Pomeroy places the wide discrepancies in the depiction of Greek women at the feet of the sources.[9] In a nutshell, the women, the 'heroines', in Greek drama were accorded high status by dramatists, while orators and writers of prose commonly did the opposite. Having a weakness for an actress, it seems, has a long history – even if she was played by a man (as was the case in both cultures). The same reasoning does not necessarily translate to the women of Rome; indeed the whole area of theatre and actors was a source of mixed feelings, and some discomfort, for the Roman élite.[10]

Closer examination is needed to get at the root causes of this tradition of bias; it is hard to ignore and too common to be easily dismissed. Why did, and do, male historians seem so intent on painting the women of

---

[9] *Goddesses, Whores, Wives, and Slaves* (1975), Schocken Books, New York, NY, USA

[10] See Catharine Edwards' *The Politics of Immorality in Ancient Rome* (1993), Cambridge University Press, Cambridge, UK

ancient Rome in such unflattering colours? A number of possible explanations arise.

One stands out as perhaps the most obvious. Can it be that, due to an almost complete lack of records of their own, women could not answer back? It can only have been clear to the ancient sources that any statements they made concerning the characters of Roman women would go unchallenged – an obvious outcome of the general lack of enthusiasm on the part of Roman men for educating them (see Chapter 3). In a comparable modern context, if yours is the only newspaper in circulation, you are free to say whatever you like.

Perhaps a more significant factor is that those ancient sources were, almost without exception, men of status, usually of senatorial rank, with all the prejudices of their time. Those attitudes were embedded in the texts that were handed down to be absorbed, seemingly without question, by subsequent generations of scholars and historians. (See Chapter 10 for further discussion.)

This subjective representation of half the Roman population is unhelpful and damaging. By writing as they did, those revered ancient sources were establishing a tradition of recording 'history' that was to last until the present day.

It is intriguing to wonder how Poppaea might have presented herself in writing had there been opportunity, or inclination, to do so. In a more benign and fantastical world, we might dream of the discovery of an ancient autobiography, or better still her diary: an unimaginable treat. Either might go some way towards helping to set the record straight, perhaps bestowing on her some measure of dignity not to be found in the language of Tacitus (or Seward). In the absence of such potential treasures – along with virtually every other Roman woman of rank – what we have instead are (mostly) male historians, lining up to disparage her.

Poppaea had, and has, no voice – aside from a couple of imagined conversations with Nero, contrived by Tacitus to enhance his narrative. This was another of his common practices, and its purpose is acknowledged by modern historians. In one of these, as he would have it, *"Tearfully directed with the artfulness of an adultress . . ."*[11], Poppaea berates Nero for his recalcitrant behaviour, and taunts or threatens him, depending on the reader's disposition towards her. The term 'harpy' springs to mind – but it may be lost in translation.

As noted, detailed depictions of the women of ancient Rome are generally in short supply. However Poppaea's notoriety ensures that descriptions of her, overladen with malice, dislike and disapproval, are not hard to find. This is disquieting when attempting to redefine the common portrayal, and paint her as someone more edifying than 'the Imperial whore'.

---

[11] *Annals*, Book 14.1, Oxford University Press, Oxford, UK (trans. John C Yardley, 2008)

For someone who has been at the receiving end of such invective for so long, Poppaea's historical treatment is unjustifiable. With its striking lack of evidence, any modern-day defence lawyer would take it apart with ease on that ground alone. Nonetheless the portrayal of her character is well-entrenched: she is in large measure damned, and likely to remain so in the absence of any challenge to those much lauded writers of antiquity – or those who follow them.

Despite that pervasive negative image, Poppaea's presence in museums, historical sites and popular culture has lasted for almost two thousand years. Statuary, coins, temples and inscriptions were dedicated to her. Like her 'sister-in-crime', Cleopatra VII, she left a legacy that will outlast the most vociferous of her critics.

What might Poppaea think of the reputation she left behind if she were alive today? Her (all but) undisputed reputation suggests that she would not care. More charitably, we might be surprised to find her shocked; it can safely be assumed that she is unlikely to be flattered. So it is to be hoped that her thoughts on the matter would be sufficiently robust in her own defence, pointing up the lack of evidence against her, and laid down in a few pithy entries in her diary.

CHAPTER 2

Child to Woman

Born, most likely, in Pompeii in 31 CE (some sources suggest 30 or 32), Poppaea seems to have been an only child. Single-child families were not common in the period; the more usual numbers hoped for, at least by high-born families, would have been two or three survivors out of, perhaps, six or seven births. Alarming infant mortality rates, according to the sources, suggest that one in four babies did not survive their first year. Rome was not an especially healthy place for even the wealthy to give birth.

Poppaea may therefore have had siblings who did not survive; we are unlikely ever to know. It is also possible that, had her father lived longer (see below), the family might have gone on to produce male children. However his early death meant that the common practice, in both Imperial and high-ranking families, of adopting a son where none had been born or survived, in order to ensure continuity of the line, could not have applied in Poppaea's family.

Most accounts describe her as intelligent, witty, charming and a great beauty – as was her mother before her, Poppaea the Elder. A statue from what is thought to be the younger Poppaea's villa, in present-day Torre Annunziata, south of Naples, is revealing. It suggests that Poppaea was red-headed, and slightly taller than Nero, her third husband (see Chapter 7, (iii)) and more notorious by a considerable margin than either of his predecessors.

Poppaea's father was Titus Ollius (b.?-31 CE); little is known of his origins or family. He was a quaestor (an elected junior magistrate with primary responsibility for finance) in the reign of the Emperor Tiberius (14-37 CE), which suggests a birth date early in the 1st century CE. Had he completed his term of office, he might have gone on to join the ranks of senators. However, aside from marriage to a woman of beauty and distinction, records show that the most noteworthy act he managed to commit, in what must have been a fairly short life, was to die in somewhat discredited circumstances.

His one claim to fame – much good that it did him – was to become a friend and associate of Lucius Aelius Sejanus, administrator and Prefect (Commander) of the Praetorian Guard, the military body responsible primarily for the protection of the Emperor Tiberius and his family. This proved to have been a bad decision.

*

Most sources are unremittingly negative concerning Sejanus' character. None, however, disputes his closeness to the seat of power:

> ... *praetorian prefects, whose very appointments testified to the emperor's confidence in their loyalty and friendship, were among the most influential figures in imperial circles.*[1]

In his *Roman History* (Book LVIII), Cassius Dio claimed that Sejanus' escalating power derived from the weak and indecisive nature of Tiberius' behaviour towards him. Such unpredictability would have served to create an unsettling atmosphere, ensuring that the Senate and the people remained wary and nervous. Sandra Bingham, conversely, suggests that Sejanus was by no means the Emperor's only adviser, and that any threat arose from the *possibility* of plots against Tiberius rather than the actuality.[2] The reasons for his downfall can therefore only be speculative.

Sejanus lobbied successfully for new barracks – the *Castra Praetoria*, in the city's north-east – to house the entire military presence, said to number not less than 10,000 men. With soldiers no longer scattered throughout the city, or camped outside it, they could be more quickly marshalled in large numbers should the need arise, no

---

[1] R P Saller, *Personal patronage under the early Empire* (1982), Cambridge University Press, Cambridge, UK

[2] *The Praetorian Guard: A History of Rome's Elite Special Forces* (2013), I B Tauris & Co Ltd, London

doubt adding to the levels of general apprehension. It also consolidated a major change in historical precedent: under the Republic, the presence of large numbers of soldiers within the city had not been allowed.

Sejanus was executed in October 31 CE following a charge of treason arising from an alleged plot to overthrow Tiberius. Whether or not such a plot existed seems debatable. Cassius Dio, who commonly displayed particular relish in gory detail, spared none of it in describing Sejanus' gruesome death, and how the people rejoiced – he had been deeply unpopular.

The Emperor's revenge, exacted upon anyone he thought implicated in the plot, however slightly, was swift, savage and protracted. (Tacitus noted continuing reprisals three years after Sejanus' death.) However the record here is somewhat murky: sources disagree about whether the persecution and despatch of suspects could be ascribed to the Emperor's own design or that of the Senate. However it is not disputed that the Senate was responsible for Sejanus' *damnatio memoriae*: expunging from history in disgrace, including the destruction of public images.

As for Tiberius himself, he is said to have left the city in 27 CE, never to return – though he did come close. Whether in Rome, however, or bolting to his hideaway at Caprae (modern Capri), he is painted throughout these events in colours far from flattering.

*

It is unclear how Ollius' fateful association with Sejanus, with its significant impact on Poppaea's early life, came about: who initiated it, and in what circumstances? Whatever the explanation, most sources agree that it would have been instrumental in his own ignominious death before that same year was out. This timing was unlikely to have been a coincidence. Ollius had seemingly made no attempt to distance himself from a connection that looked increasingly out of favour. As a result, he stood to be swept up in the Emperor's purge of suspected conspirators.

The image of Ollius' wife, still young, and possibly the mother of an infant daughter, watching from the sidelines while this drama played out is an affecting one. We cannot know her thoughts on her husband's choice of political patron; however she might well have prayed to the gods that his death would not mirror that of Sejanus in being both grisly and shaming.

At all events, his death left her, and her baby, in a vulnerable position. To add final insult to fatal injury, Ollius is generally portrayed as little more than a minor character in the proceedings, whose truncated career left barely a mark on Rome's political map. We might wonder who was responsible for promoting the idea that she should marry him in the first place; he had ultimately been a most unfortunate choice.

What Poppaea was to know of these fateful events before her mother's death, more than a decade later, cannot be known; likewise how the story of her father's demise might have influenced and affected her. Whatever she was eventually to learn, and from whatever source, these same events are thought to explain her name.

Roman women were named after their fathers, on the eighth day after their birth. Thus Poppaea's birth name would have been Ollia, after her father Titus Ollius. Rarely is she so named in historical records, although an early mention appears in a genealogical chart in jurist J H Heineccius' 18th century *Commentarius ad legem Iuliam et Papiam Poppaeam*. According to him, Poppaea was "*Ollia quae dici maluit Poppaea Sabina*", which might loosely translate as 'preferred to be called'. Exactly when the change of name took place, however, remains far from clear.

Most sources record that Poppaea herself 'took' the name of her maternal grandfather, Gaius Poppaeus Sabinus, some time after his death in 35 CE. However Poppaea then being only a small child, we can assume that a number of years would have passed before the change took place. Precocious she might well have been, but renaming herself at five years of age, or six, or seven for personal enhancement or political expediency seems rather a stretch.

Though it cannot be ruled out with certainty that her father *was* alive at her birth, if not for very long, other family members might have influenced an early name change:

(i)   *Poppaea the Elder* (her mother)

Logic points to Poppaea's mother being instrumental in making the decision to change her daughter's name, perhaps consulting with family members, more particularly if she was widowed by the time of the birth.

Her husband's reputation can only have been badly tarnished by that ill-fated connection to the notorious Sejanus; and at his daughter's birth Ollius may already have been dead, or close to it, depending on the accepted birth date for the baby Ollia/Poppaea. Dacre Balsdon[3] offers some light-hearted speculation:

> *Her father, an undistinguished Knight called T. Ollius, shared in Sejanus' disgrace in 31; and died perhaps before her birth. That enabled her mother to spare the child the dreadful name of Ollia, and to call her Poppaea Sabina instead.*

We are left to wonder: did Ollius ever see his baby daughter, or simply leave behind a pregnant wife? Might the change of name have been more easily effected by her mother if the child's father was no longer alive? Regrettably the records provide no clarification. However, the likelihood is strong that her mother was the one to

---

[3] *Roman Women: their history and habits* (1963), John Day Co/Barnes & Noble Inc, New York, NY, USA

choose not to keep Poppaea's rightful birth name, though at a point that remains unclear. Other pertinent factors might also have played a part:

Her own background. From a wealthy and distinguished family, the elder Poppaea was accustomed to life in an élite environment. This cannot have sat easily alongside the likely unfavourable circumstances of her husband's demise. Unhelpfully, no historian seems inclined to mention her mother in any context, so her feelings on the matter of her granddaughter's name cannot be taken into account.

The worth of connection. In a family of some prominence, its daughter would have been well aware of the value placed by high-status Romans on attachment to a name of rank and reputation. Such awareness was the very bedrock of the way in which élite Romans saw themselves, and wished others to see them.

Her father's career. At around the age of twenty, Poppaea the Elder would have known that by the time of her father's death, at a good age by Roman standards, he had distinguished both himself and the family name. It is perhaps as well that no family members remained to learn of Tacitus' later opinion of him[4], the ancient Roman equivalent of damning with faint praise:

---

[4] *Annals*, VI.38, (trans. Michael Grant, 1956-96)

> *Humbly born, he had owed his consulship and honorary*
> *Triumph to the friendship of emperors. He had been*
> *retained as imperial governor of important provinces for*
> *twenty-four years – not for any outstanding talent, but*
> *because he was competent and no more.*

The family would hardly have thanked him for that.

Roman convention. It was not uncommon for children to take the name of a grandparent:

> *. . . in the imperial period there was a growing tendency*
> *for children to incorporate their mother's name as well as*
> *their father's into their own name, or to adopt simply the*
> *maternal name . . .* [5]

(ii) *Publius Cornelius Lentulus Scipio* (Poppaea's patrician[6] stepfather – see further below)

Scipio would have understood better than most the disadvantage of connection to a tainted reputation: that of his wife's former husband, his stepdaughter's father. Here, however, the law intervened:

> *. . . no legal relationship between a stepfather and his*
> *wife's children from a previous union was established by*
> *a remarriage . . . nor did these stepchildren fall under his*
> patria potestas [power of a father]. *These*

---

[5] Beryl Rawson, *The Family in Ancient Rome: News Perspectives* (1993), Cornell University Press, Ithaca, NY, USA

[6] The wealthy aristocratic ruling class of Republican Rome

> *responsibilities came only with the adoption of his*
> *stepchildren, not remarriage to their mother.*[7]

We do not know if Scipio adopted the young Poppaea, or why he might have done so if he did. A common reason was to allow stepfathers to position themselves closer to their stepchildren's assets, an unnecessary consideration for the high-born Scipio – he was unlikely to have needed the money.

Likewise, it is not known if he became her official guardian (*tutela impuberum:* guardian of children below the age of puberty). Guardians of children who lost their fathers at an early age were commonly the closest male relative: in Poppaea's case, her maternal grandfather (at least until his death in 35 CE), since we know nothing of the paternal one.

However it is unclear which occurred first: the death of Poppaea's grandfather or the remarriage of his daughter, Poppaea's mother, to Scipio. This leaves the position of the child Ollia/Poppaea somewhere in a hazy limbo as far as the legal record is concerned. Furthermore, in such a politically and militarily volatile environment, Poppaea would have been far from alone in losing her father at an early age, leaving a mother who might perhaps have been keen to remarry, more especially having an infant daughter.

---

[7] Sabine R Hübner and D M Ratzan (eds), *Growing Up Fatherless in Antiquity* (2009), Cambridge University Press, Cambridge, UK

Nevertheless, Scipio was well placed to emphasise the desirability of a reputable name – having an exemplary one himself – and to exert his influence accordingly. Exceptions to the laws enacted by the Emperor Augustus in 18-17 BCE (known as the *lex Iulia* – see Chapter 7) would doubtless have existed, expressly for the purpose of the élite classes using them to their own advantage. The high-ranking Scipio could effectively have used his status to achieve whatever desired end result might be sought. In the absence of adoption or guardianship, though, his *lawful* influence on the young Poppaea's life would have been somewhat circumscribed.

As a daughter, Ollia/Poppaea legally belonged to her father's family, the Ollii, hence her birth name. Regrettably we know virtually nothing of them: how extensive the family was, where they lived (though Pompeii is suggested – see Chapter 6), the standing of the relationship between them and Poppaea the Elder, widow of their deceased son Ollius. Did they have a legal claim to the 'ownership' of the child Ollia? If so, how might it have been exercised? The gap in our knowledge of the Ollii leaves these questions unanswered.

The fate of both mother and child in the immediate aftermath of Ollius' death would have rested to a large extent on the length of the interim between his death and his widow's marriage to Scipio. Negotiations may perhaps have been necessary to settle a number of important matters: the question of the child's name, where and with whom she should live, and the issue of the customary return of the elder Poppaea's dowry to her since her husband was no longer alive. Given her father's lengthy and relatively elevated career, this latter point could not have been lightly dismissed.

A more intriguing question is how much her new husband was involved in all of this. Once again, it is not hard to imagine the weighty opinions of the aristocratic Scipio being brought to bear in such discussions – along with any necessary pulling of strings.

As for Scipio himself, information about his effect on Poppaea's life is entirely lacking. How did his marriage to her mother come about, and how welcome was a stepdaughter to him? It can be assumed that his new wife and stepdaughter moved into his home on the remarriage, rather than he into theirs; any competition between the Scipiones and the Ollii in the ownership of prestigious properties would surely have seen Scipio the clear winner. Discussions on the important matter of residence would have been fascinating, if perhaps short. However, since no records describe this second marriage of the elder Poppaea, once more all is speculation.

(iii) *Rufrius Crispinus* (Poppaea's first husband – see Chapter 7, (i))

Poppaea the Younger married him when she was around thirteen or fourteen, in 44 CE. As a knight, Crispinus belonged to a wealthy élite – though not in the same league as Scipio – another stratum of Roman society keenly aware of the importance of a valued family name, along with a knight's dedication to upholding it.

On marriage, Poppaea may have come under his *manus* (because her father was dead), giving him legal control over her, although this custom was increasingly uncommon in the wake of Augustus' newly enacted laws. At all events, a fourteen-year old wife would undoubtedly have been subordinate to an older spouse (though we do not know his age at marriage) in the matter of significant decisions.

As with her mother's remarriage to Scipio, we have no helpful information about this marriage as it might have related to the timing of Poppaea's name change. However it is hard to imagine her mother and stepfather allowing the proposed marriage to approach without taking steps, if they had not already been taken, to regularise her name and remedy any damage caused by her father's tainted one. No family of status would have settled for any less.

If it was the younger Poppaea's decision to take her grandfather's name, it is reasonable to assume that she was near adulthood when she did so. However 'adulthood' in the period does not equate to the present day, with high-status Roman women, Poppaea among them, commonly marrying at thirteen or fourteen.

The possibility of Poppaea changing her name of her own volition before marrying at thirteen – or even earlier? – hardly deserves serious consideration. While most sources claim that she 'took' her grandfather's name, none questions how this might have been achieved by a child; indeed the finer points on the issue are passed over by every historian or scholar with something to say on the matter.

Poppaea's unflattering reputation was established early by the ancient sources. Following their lead, it appears that the truth behind her change of name is insufficiently salacious, indeed so mundane that it barely attracts the attention of modern writers. However if the majority opinion prevails, we are to believe that Poppaea's allegedly designing nature emerged when her grandfather died, and she was no more than five years old.

Given all of this, then, we cannot know with any certainty how long Poppaea was an 'Ollia' before she became a 'Sabina'.

Most writers are neither subtle nor flattering in their references to the matter. The hypothesis goes like this: by not wanting, in contemporary terms, to align herself with a loser, Poppaea calculatingly dropped her father's name, sullied as it was, taking up instead her grandfather's more honourable one:

> *Whether being opportunistic or otherwise, there is no sign that Poppaea Sabina ever acknowledged her*

> *patronymic* [a name deriving from father or other male ancestor], *choosing instead to* flaunt [emphasis added] *the proud name of her maternal grandfather . . .*[8]

'Flaunting' here has undeniable negative connotations; where is the evidence of it? Once more Poppaea's self-serving reputation is underscored. Butterworth and Laurence[9] add to it:

> *Even the name she bore . . . had been taken out of necessity, to disguise the identity of an overreaching father.*

This comment does not place Ollius in a flattering light, nor is Poppaea much better served by it. The authors continue in similar vein:

> *When Sejanus was caught plotting to seize the throne, and executed, Ollius had been plunged into disgrace and had struggled to regain his footing; his daughter clearly preferred not to be tainted by association.*

The temptation to direct caustic comments towards Poppaea in any context seems too hard to resist. This applies even to her name, a relatively innocent area of misdemeanour compared to most other charges levelled against her.

---

[8] P Kragelund, *The Temple and Birthplace of Diva Poppaea* in *Classic Quarterly*, Vol. 6, Issue 2 (2010), Cambridge, UK
[9] *Pompeii: The Living City* (2005), Orion Books Ltd, London

For example, on Nero conferring the title of 'Augusta' (= venerable or great) on both his wife and their daughter Claudia on her birth in 63 CE, Owen and Gildenhard[10] remark:

'Poppaea' sounded (gob-smackingly?) [sic] incongruous when yoked to the austere yeoman ethnic 'Sabinus'; tacking on holy 'Augusta' completed the effect.

What effect? Presumably this observation is intended as a criticism of Nero's undeniable excess. However, what comes across instead is a spiteful comment on the origins of what is, after all, her grandfather's name. Buried within it is the implication that the disreputable Poppaea does not deserve 'yoking' to such a distinguished connection.

The title of 'Augusta' had a dignified history. First bestowed on Livia, Augustus' wife (though not until after his death), no more celebrated honour could be conferred upon an Imperial wife since it connoted divinity.

Nero's 'tacking on' the title to Poppaea's name was undoubtedly a demonstration of his reverence of his wife, and his exaggerated expression of it. Nonetheless, this passage manages somehow to reflect badly on her; somewhere in there is the subliminal notion that the self-aggrandising Empress was likely to have been responsible for the high-flown title, properly reflecting her exalted (for which read 'undeserved') status. Nero's besottedness with

---

[10] *Tacitus, Annals, 15.20-23, 33-45*, Latin Text, Study Aids with Vocabulary, and Commentary (2013), Open Book Publishers, Cambridge, UK

his wife was well known, with its implicit assumption that he could refuse her nothing.

The authors do note Tacitus' stern disapproval of the title's overuse, given its exalted history. However this is not without another jibe: *"Here the honorands are a new-born baby – and a concubine-turned wife."* This needlessly acerbic description makes clear the true target: there is no subtlety here. Nero's excess is overshadowed by Poppaea's insalubrious character.

The relentless criticism of both Poppaea and Nero in this text echoes the practice ascribed to Tacitus of defaming by association those closely connected to characters of whom he has already expressed his dislike. It might be seen as another manifestation of 'evil going hand-in-hand with evil.'

*

Although Tacitus was clear in his disdain for Poppaea, in his *Annals* (Book XIII.44) he described her mother Poppaea the Elder as *". . . the loveliest woman of her day . . ."*. She fared somewhat better in the historical record than her infamous daughter, at least in her earlier life. Though of humble birth, her father Gaius Poppaeus Sabinus' career was noteworthy, if not outstanding – as Tacitus helpfully describes above. As already noted we know nothing of her mother, not even her name.

It seems likely that her family, the *gens Poppaea*, rather than that of her husband Ollius, owned the impressive Pompeian properties excavated in the aftermath of the volcanic eruption of Vesuvius in 79 CE (see Chapter 6). Although the Ollii name does appear in Pompeian records[11], no information about them is offered to enlighten us further, or point to a direct connection to Titus Ollius if one exists.

As mentioned above, the precise date of the elder Poppaea's remarriage following her husband's early death is unknown. Roman custom dictated a year's mourning (later extended) before any subsequent marriage of a widow could take place, unless there were extenuating circumstances.

Augustus' moralising legislation, the *lex Iulia*, meant that widowed women were caught in a bind. There was an expectation on them to remarry in order to procreate, thereby increasing the declining population, more particularly of the élite; the plan was never to have the plebeian class overrunning the city – Jupiter and Juno forbid!

However there was also the pre-existing model of the *univira*, the dutiful wife who would not remarry as a display of devotion to the memory of her (one) husband. Poppaea the Elder therefore stood to be subjected to

---

[11] See, for example, Mary L Gordon's *The* Ordo *of Pompeii* in *The Journal of Roman Studies*, Vol. 17 (1927), Cambridge, UK

pressure both to remarry or not to remarry. Where might such pressure have come from? Once more, frustratingly, we cannot know. The existence of her infant daughter may well have been one of the deciding factors, a desire for further offspring another.

A revealing example of 'extenuating circumstances' applying to widows was the marriage of the widowed Octavia, sister of Octavian, to Marc Antony in 40 BCE – a political marriage if ever there was one. It was brought forward by senatorial decree, no doubt at Octavian's instigation, so eager would he have been to cement his position of power by shrewdly marrying off his sister to his arch-rival. It is unlikely that he would even have considered the possibility of the parties detesting each other; more likely he relied on his sister's unquestioning obedience.

Any such extenuating circumstances that might have existed for Poppaea the Elder can only be guessed at. (We might also imagine Scipio being well able to deal with any obstacle placed in the way of his marriage to "the loveliest woman of her day".) An estimate for the date of this second marriage of hers, then, is c. 33-34 CE, when the child Ollia/Poppaea would have been three or four years old. What did this tiny creature think of her new father?

Whatever the timing, her mother's second husband appeared an eminently suitable match for a woman of rank. Publius Cornelius Lentulus Scipio was descended from the Scipiones, a branch of the distinguished patrician *gens Cornelia* which dated back to the early Republic. It is even suggested[12] that the face of a recent ancestor (of unknown name, but a suffect consul[13]) makes a possible appearance on the *Ara Pacis Augustae*[14]; acclamations in Rome did not come much higher. Scipio had a noteworthy military/political career, becoming a suffect consul himself in 24 CE (suggesting a birth date, though unconfirmed, of c. 15-10 BCE) and later a senator. His marriage to Poppaea the Elder produced a son, named after his father, though the child's birth date can only be estimated.

Though her date of birth is likewise unclear, Poppaea's mother can only have been in her thirties when she was driven to suicide in 47 CE. The instigator was Messallina, Emperor Claudius' third wife. The elder Poppaea was never going to be in a position to contend with Messallina's own powerful position and emerge the winner; few would have had the courage even to try.

---

[12] See G Stern, *Women, Children, and Senators on the Ara Pacis Augustae: A Study of Augustus' Vision of a New World Order in 13 BC* (2006), ProQuest LLC, Ann Arbor, MI, USA

[13] Appointed to replace a consul (a chief civil and military magistrate) who did not complete his term of office

[14] The Augustan Altar of Peace, commissioned by the Senate in 13 CE to honour Augustus on his return to Rome after successful campaigns in the provinces. Ironically, it was originally sited in the Campus Martius (the Field of Mars), a decidedly military location for an altar of peace. It is covered in carved marble friezes, and is one of the most impressive of all Roman monuments.

Her husband Scipio was less than voluble by way of assistance to his wife in these extraordinary and dramatic events (see Chapter 7). In his *Annals* (Book XI.4), Tacitus appeared alone in quoting Scipio's one comment in the matter – which was, to say the least, unhelpful – as well as adding his own opinion. When asked in the Senate to comment on events, Scipio was said to have cautiously replied:

> *'Since I feel the same as everybody else about Poppaea's offences, just assume I say the same thing as everyone else' – an elegant compromise between conjugal love and his senatorial obligation.*

One might also call it covering his back. "Conjugal love" in Rome appeared of limited use, at least to his wife; clearly "senatorial obligation" ruled. Did he really believe her to be guilty of these alleged misdeeds? His rather coy comment suggests that he did. In a harsh light, and a very Roman one, it could be said that this diplomatic response to his senatorial colleagues, and his apparent reluctance to plead on Poppaea the Elder's behalf, protected his career but lost him a wife, and Poppaea a mother. And where was he while his wife was being threatened and hounded towards suicide? The sources are silent.

It is unfortunate that Poppaea the Elder's thoughts on the level of her husband's support go unrecorded; likewise the manner in which she took her life. However, in her last moments, it can be imagined that she might have been less than impressed. One hopes that one of her final acts, before plunging in the knife or downing the poison, was to let him know in no uncertain terms what she thought of his "conjugal love" – sufficient to rip his ears off. No source tells us who was with her when she died. It may well have been one or more loyal slaves; it is to be hoped that it was not her daughter, now aged seventeen. Given his comment in the Senate, it strains credibility to believe that it would have been her loving husband.

Poppaea the Younger was three years into the first of her marriages at her mother's death. It can only be imagined how, as an only child, she might have been affected by the loss of her mother, to say nothing of the disturbing circumstances surrounding it. She was certainly old enough to grasp what was going on. It seems unlikely that those dramatic events at court, with the Emperor's wife centre-stage, would have been unknown to her, the more so since her husband Crispinus, as co-Prefect of Claudius' Praetorian Guard, was necessarily near the centre of court circles.

Poppaea the Elder had seen her daughter enter this first marriage, in 44 CE; indeed she and her new husband Scipio were likely to have been responsible for engineering it. However it seems that she did not live to see the birth of young Rufrius Crispinus, her first grandchild.

As for Poppaea the Younger's early life, details are tantalisingly scarce. For a woman who garnered so much negative opinion in her adult years, it is a great pity that we know so little about the earlier circumstances that might have contributed to making her the woman she was.

We do know that she was born to a woman admired for her beauty and refinement, and a hapless father fatally lacking the political nous that might have kept him alive (though see Appendix I for an intriguing alternative theory regarding her parentage). As an infant she inherited a stepfather descended from the ruling élite of Republican Rome. Her only known sibling was a half-brother born, perhaps, not many years after she herself, who followed his father in a political career. In a family of such high rank, it can be assumed that their residence, wherever it was, would have reflected the family's status, with a retinue of slaves very much a part of the early lives of both children.

However no record confirms where and in whose company Poppaea lived out her early years, and if those years, and her relations with her new family, were happy ones.

CHAPTER 3

Education: To form her character

As with the majority of high-ranking Roman women, we are unlikely ever to know the extent of Poppaea's education, if any. Emily Hemelrijk[1] lays out the matter without preamble: *"The education of Roman women is veiled in obscurity."*

It was Seneca (4 BCE-65 CE), philosopher, Stoic and leading Roman intellectual, who advised his mother Helvia on the education of his niece, her grand-daughter Novatilla, who had recently lost her mother.[2] Novatilla's father was, in fact, still alive, but presumably not seen as fitting the role of educator; once again, his deceased wife, whose absence was the cause of Novatilla's educational deficiencies, goes unnamed.

Exhorting Helvia to guide Novatilla by her own virtuous example – we might be forgiven for reading it as rather closer to a lecture – Seneca urged that the formative years were the time in which Novatilla's character could,

---

[1] *Matrona Docta: Educated Women in the Roman Elite from Cornelia to Julia Domna* (1999), Routledge, London
[2] *De Consolatione ad Helviam*, 18.4

and should, be formed, and that Helvia should unquestionably be the one to do it. Regrettably, this was not a model that seems to have been generally laid down for the daughters of Rome.

The sources are not in agreement as to how much education daughters of the Roman élite received in reality – in anything, that is, unconnected to the running of a household. In mentioning the fortunate educated few, Hemelrijk asks:

> *Were they the proverbial 'exception to the rule' that women usually lacked an education, or do they represent, so to speak, the 'tip of an iceberg', implying that there were many more educated women who are unknown to us?*

She is right to wonder, and the problem comes down once more to the scarcity of in-depth information about the lives of Roman women. We simply lack sufficient detailed examples from which to draw useful conclusions, which results in a level of speculation that can at best be described as unhelpful. A comment on the education of Cicero's[3] daughter Tullia provides a frustrating example of the vagueness so often evident on the subject:

---

[3] Marcus Tullius Cicero (107-44 BCE), renowned orator, lawyer, writer and politician, whose career might have been expected to encourage him to advance the cause of education, at least in his own family. It appears it did not.

> *. . . her father's later praise of her intellectual qualities*
> *suggests that she probably had as much literary training*
> *as was usually given to daughters in the upper classes.*[4]

We are not much better informed.

Not uncommonly, sources supply contradictory information on the matter. The general consensus seems to be that girls, in the main, were largely excluded from advanced education. Augustus' legislation, the *lex Iulia*, ensured that their new marriageable age of twelve would effectively cut off any education they might have been receiving up to that point. We might assume that the education of Novatilla was being proposed at an age, her 'formative years', that was too young for marriage – otherwise, why bother with it? Excelling in the academic arena would not have helped to find her a husband.

Paradoxically, however, high-status Roman women did freely accompany their husbands to social events, without apparent difficulty or objection. This must have required a level of education sufficient to enable them to string an informed and coherent sentence together without embarrassment to anyone present. Élite girls and women were therefore effectively placed in something of an educational bind, with the two positions seemingly irreconcilable.

---

[4] Susan Treggiari, *Terentia, Tullia and Publilia: The Women of Cicero's Family* (2007), Routledge, Abingdon, UK

Élite Roman wives were largely held responsible for their children's early education. However, in order to be able to apply themselves to the task, sufficient both to satisfy their husbands and maintain family status, they of course needed education of their own.

High-ranking husbands generally were likely to have been far too preoccupied with public affairs (Novatilla's father may have been an example) to devote much time to teaching their offspring. It is hard to imagine men of, for instance, senatorial rank gently leading their young children through chorus after chorus of the alphabet, or holding the abacus while they learnt how to count. While having no quarrel with the importance of their children imbibing ancestral values, who should be responsible for ensuring that they did was another matter.

Furthermore, in the process of socialisation it is apparent that mothers were not the only female relatives to be given responsibility for the education of the children of the family. With Seneca's pressure on his mother Helvia to take on her grand-daughter Novatilla's education and moral development, he clearly saw her in the role of mother-figure.

The educational responsibility resting with Roman wives, then, might simply have meant overseeing Greek tutors employed for their children at an appropriate age, and ensuring that lessons proceeded as they should. This may well have presented the opportunity to learn (quietly) alongside their children for those women with an interest in doing so.

Most descriptions of Poppaea presume that she would have been well-educated insofar as the restrictions on daughters, as opposed to sons, allowed. Hemelrijk reveals that Poppaea's cleverness is confirmed from a surprising source:

> *The reference to her learning in the last line* [of Leonidas'[5] poem] *agrees with Tacitus' grudging remark that she possessed a lively intelligence.*

Note the "grudging", Tacitus having consistently made plain his dislike of her. This, it seems, was as positive as he could bring himself to be on the question of her character.

In speculating on the matter of Poppaea's education, a brief chronology might assist. We know that she lost her father to political machinations around the time of her birth, married at about thirteen, and by seventeen was an orphan. She acquired a stepfather some time after her father's death in 31 CE, and a possible stepmother[6] following her mother's death by suicide in 47. In present-

---

[5] Leonidas of Alexandria was a poet popular in Nero's reign, said to have written Poppaea an epigram accompanying a gift for her birthday c. 63 CE.

[6] According to *Wikipedia*, her stepfather Scipio is thought to have remarried an unnamed woman and produced another son, Publius Cornelius Scipio Asiaticus, who became suffect consul in 68 CE. It is an odd coincidence that Asiaticus was also the name of the man who allegedly was instrumental in the downfall and subsequent suicide of Poppaea's mother.

day terms, her early life would therefore be considered a fairly fractured one, though no sources comment on this. The emotional damage resulting from those early life events can only have affected any education she might have received.

It should be borne in mind that the education of Roman women *at all* was far from universally approved. To draw them away from the *domus*, their traditional and rightful place, made Roman men nervous. At the heart of that nervousness was the fear – no exaggeration – that an education would enable women to move closer to the political arena, wherein lay the power to shape events.

As alarming, it would encourage 'masculine' behaviour in wives and daughters, sending a shudder down the collective spine of those men comprising the ruling élite. For all but a few true exceptions, this could not be countenanced. How in the name of the gods could it be otherwise?

Marilyn French[7] neatly encapsulates their problem:

> *It is an obvious fact . . . that the dominator . . . must spend his life devising controls, silencing mechanisms, and motivations to keep the dominated in line . . .*

The barriers to the full education of girls and women should remain firmly in place; there could be no argument

---

[7] *Beyond Power: On Women, Men and Morals* (1986), Jonathan Cape Ltd, London

with that. To be thought of as unwomanly by virtue of being educated was unacceptable, and significant numbers of Roman men publicly said so.

Perhaps the most outspoken on the subject was Juvenal, contemporary of Tacitus. Often accused, not without cause, of misogynistic ranting against women (see also Chapter 5), in Book II of his *Satire VI* he stated that he found educated women repulsive: the *"most intolerable of all"* – in a long list.

Basic education differed greatly in purpose for high-ranking girls and boys. Daughters were being trained for the roles of housekeeper, wife and mother, sons for a role in public life. However, generally it would have included, along with reading, writing and numbers, such matters as religious observance, morality, virtue, modesty and respect for ancestors and Roman values.

With even a modicum of understanding of these, and taking into account her acknowledged intelligence, Poppaea would have been well prepared for a life beyond that of spinning and weaving, near the top of the Roman *matrona*'s list of essential skills.

Moreover, it is significant that boys' education could continue long after their sisters were waylaid by early marriage. So that while élite Roman sons were conquering grammar, and graduating towards the study of rhetoric and a possible career in politics or the law, or the study of philosophy in Greece, their married sisters might already have produced – or lost – more than one child. Many, after all, were giving birth at an age when they themselves might not yet have finished growing; it would have been cause enough for celebration if both mother and baby survived. If they did, these child brides would in all likelihood have been steeped in maternity and family long before reaching the age of twenty, whatever their own personal preferences might have been.

The opportunity for women to continue their education in later adulthood, while feasible, was not without obstacles. It required a spouse who approved the idea, and perhaps parents willing to encourage it, along with the employment of tutors for the task. Most importantly, it would have depended largely upon the resources, and inclinations, of the individual family.

Educational opportunities for Imperial women were somewhat different. The wife of an emperor, for example, was surrounded by courtiers, assumed to have included teachers, poets and philosophers, all of whom would have been literary and educated men. This might have seen learning passed on without appearing to be seeking it overtly – rather like the Roman *matrona* learning alongside her children.

Agrippina the Elder, Nero's grandmother, provides an enlightening example of the education allowed to Imperial daughters. In an incident claimed to have come from her daughter's memoirs (see Appendix II), she is addressed by Tiberius in Greek, which he presumably knew she would understand.

The possibility does exist, though perhaps a slight one, that Poppaea's stepfather Scipio may have had some influence on her education, having entered her life by the time she was around five years old.

His aristocratic background would have ensured that he himself received the education enjoyed by the sons of patrician families. In addition, his forebears, the Scipiones, were thought to have greatly respected Hellenism and the Greek way of life, even down to encouraging the learning of Greek by Roman women and children – though this is likely to have excluded girls. It seems plausible that his educational grounding could have filtered down to Poppaea's generation, so that she might, to some unknown extent, have benefited. Her half-brother, Publius Cornelius Lentulus Scipio (II), would doubtless have received the same patrician education as his father, culminating in his becoming a consul.

Another element in Roman education was the existence of libraries. Rex Winsbury[8] explains:

> *They can be more usefully seen as being in the direct line of tradition of the large libraries that leading Roman generals acquired . . . in the main through looting Greek cities – except that they were owned and managed by the emperor and his minions and successors.*

---

[8] *The Roman Book* (2009), Gerald Duckworth & Co Ltd, London

And crucially:

> *In both republic and imperial times, libraries were for the elite, and were about power, wealth and prestige, and the display of all three.*

Tragically, Rome was not only a dangerous place for its citizens:

> *The city's great conflagration of A.D. 64 (during which Nero supposedly fiddled as the city burned[9]) claimed the Palatine Library.[10]*

The Palatine Hill was the grandest of the seven hills of Rome, being the home of the great and the good – and the rich. Anyone of any note, be they would-be emperors or mere mortals, lived there. The library would therefore have been large, prestigious and well equipped. Disturbingly, the high fire risk generally prevailing throughout the city, made worse by overcrowding and flammable building materials, meant that this disaster cannot have been a one-off event.

In his *Lives of the Caesars*, Suetonius claimed that Julius Caesar wanted Rome to house a comprehensive collection of both Greek and Latin texts in public libraries, employing Marcus Terentius Varro (see below) to take on the task.

---

[9] A matter of considerable controversy and debate; it is more commonly thought that he didn't.
[10] M Battles, *Library: An Unquiet History* (2004), Vintage Books, London

His successor Augustus, no slouch in the propaganda department, set up more than one Imperial library, and some of his successors – Tiberius, Vespasian and Trajan among them – followed suit. Winsbury confirms: *"An inventory of Rome made in the time of Constantine* [it is unclear which one is meant here] *counted 28 libraries in all."*

That is an impressive number of educational resources for the use of the literate minority. As to who might have benefited from these institutions – public or private – Rena Van den Bergh[11] conjectures:

Fundania must have used her husband's impressive library if she were actually to read some of the treatises on agriculture he advised her to consult . . .

Her husband Varro was a scholar and prolific writer. Fundania had purchased an estate, and Varro composed three books, *De Re Rustica*, in the form of a dialogue addressed to her, as an instruction manual for its management. She can only have benefited from access to such an extensive library as Varro would have owned; we can assume that other wives, and daughters, of literary men would have been similarly fortunate.

Closer to home, for Poppaea at least, Lorne Bruce reveals the discovery of a library in the excavated House

---

[11] *The Role of Education in the Social and Legal Position of Women in Roman Society* in *Revue Internationale des Droits de l'Antiquité* XLVII (2000), University of South Africa, Pretoria, RSA

of Menander (*Casa del menandro*) in Pompeii, dated to the early part of the Emperor Augustus' reign (27 BCE-14 CE).[12] This villa was named after the Greek dramatist and poet, and is thought to have belonged to the *gens Poppaea* (see also Chapter 6). The last-known owner before the 79 CE eruption of Vesuvius is suggested to have been Quintus Poppaeus Sabinus, an aedile[13] in the reign of the Emperor Claudius.

Sources writing of the excavation describe a luxurious property with four main areas: atrium, peristyle, living and domestic quarters. However Bruce notes that the key area is designated separately:

> *There is sufficient space in room 21 [the library] for a small desk or a reclining chair. But it seems more plausible that a rectangular alcove (room 23) was used for study, where the portrait of Menander reading from one of his own compositions is found.*

The house is decorated throughout with multiple references to literary and classical figures. Ivan Varriale[14] suggests that the presence of a library reinforced the

---

[12] *Palace and Villa Libraries from Augustus to Hadrian* in *The Journal of Library History (1974-1987)*, Vol. 21, No. 3 (1986), University of Texas Press, Austin, TX, USA

[13] Junior magistrate responsible for public buildings and their maintenance; useful for the acquisition of property

[14] *Architecture and Decoration in the House of Menander in Pompeii* in *Contested Spaces-Houses and Temples in Roman Antiquity and the New Testament* (2012), D L Balch and Annette Weissenrieder (eds), Mohr Siebeck, Tübingen, Germany

cultured presentation of the whole by its owner, whoever he may have been; he is wanting visitors to see and appreciate his civilised and artistic tastes.

The alcove was south-facing, with plentiful natural light. Given its overall splendour, it is likely that, at some point, a high-status family occupied the house and enjoyed the use of the library and its sunny alcove. Given the suggested family connection, might one of its fortunate earlier users have been Poppaea Sabina?

As noted, Rome's public libraries held both Latin and Greek texts, though they could not have competed in size or scope with, for instance, the great library of Alexandria. None of this is to suggest, however, that Poppaea – or any other woman of rank – ever had access to them. Indeed, information is relatively scarce on the ease of access to these esteemed institutions for educated men as well.

Librarians in Rome were persons of status, managing a team of assistants and copyists, and no doubt jealously guarding their privileged position. Sextus, believed to have enjoyed the presumably coveted role of Palatine librarian in the reign of the Emperor Domitian, is said to have possessed " . . . *intelligence approaching that of a god."*[15] Gods employed as keepers of the keys does not sound

---

[15] Quoted in Alex Wright's *Glut: Mastering Information Through the Ages* (2007), Cornell University Press, Ithaca, NY, USA

hopeful for library doors being swung open freely to admit women.

Astonishingly, the situation had hardly improved for women by the 1920s. Virginia Woolf, in *"A Room of One's Own"*[16], wrote, in a spirit of irony, of being denied admission to a Cambridge University library as she had neither a letter of introduction nor a Fellow of the College accompanying her (what on earth did they think she would do without such restraints to control her?). If the reasons for the exclusion of women then were recognisably similar to the Roman model, this would be one of the Empire's less praiseworthy legacies. As a continuing example of restrictive practices designed to curb the education of women, Woolf's story has a distressingly familiar ring.

The picture drawn of those Roman institutions is of a decidedly male domain: somewhere to meet with friends of similar class, with like interests, and to spend leisure hours in pleasant social discourse and philosophical discussion. In this they sound not unlike bathhouses (*thermae*), some of which were large enough to incorporate libraries; the spectacularly luxurious Baths of Caracalla in the south-east of Rome, completed early in the 3rd century, had two. Having to take time out to improve one's knowledge along the way in such a leisured environment almost begins to sound like an afterthought.

---

[16] The Hogarth Press Ltd, London (1929)

Pleasing as the fantasy is of Poppaea and her friends whiling away their time at the library, accompanied by slaves and a flagon of wine, it sounds unlikely. So where did she learn about what she knew?

One apparent feature of her later life was Judaism, and numerous sources note her interest. The primary one is Jewish historian Josephus[17], who travelled to Rome in 64 CE where he met with Poppaea through Aliturius, whom Josephus claimed was a Jewish actor in Nero's favoured inner circle.

Poppaea famously assisted with, amongst other matters, Josephus' mission to free a number of Jewish prisoners incarcerated there, and he therefore held her in high regard (see also Chapter 8). For present purposes Josephus' existence should be highlighted, since he is alone of all the sources in his positive presentation of Poppaea's character.

Michele Murray states that he described her as a 'pro-Jewish' Gentile[18] (though much scholarly debate surrounds the intended meanings in Josephus' usage of Greek in his descriptions of her). There is no suggestion that she considered conversion to Judaism; the renouncing

---

[17] See *The Works of Flavius Josephus* (1820), (trans. William Whiston, London); *The Life of Josephus*, (2001), *Brill Josephus Project*, E J Brill, Leiden, Netherlands (trans./ed. Steve Mason)
[18] *Playing a Jewish Game: Gentile and Christian Judaizing in the First and Second Centuries, CE* (2004), Canadian Corporation for Studies in Religion (website)

of the worship of all idols but one would alone have put paid to that. Rather, she showed sympathy for Jewish causes, and used her knowledge to persuade Nero to act favourably towards Roman Jews. How Poppaea might have understood the position of Jews, in Rome or anywhere else, without some education in the matter is intriguing; even more so, where any such education might have come from and what might have instigated it.

Poppaea was not the only high-status Roman woman shown to have had a connection, proven or not, to Judaism. Murray mentions the following:

- **Fulvia**, wife of Saturninus, who converted to Judaism in the reign of the Emperor Tiberius;

- **Pomponia Graecina**, wife of Aulus Plautius, 'conqueror of Britannia' on behalf of the Emperor Claudius in 43 CE;

- **Julia Severa**, wife of Servenius Capito, who build a synagogue in the mid-1st C. CE in Akmonia in Phrygia (modern Turkey), her home;

- **Berenice**, great-granddaughter of Herod the Great and mistress of the Emperor Titus (reigned 79-81 CE); and

- **Flavia Domatilla**, wife of Flavius Clemens, cousin to the Emperor Domitian.

As women of rank, their interest in Judaism is likely to have been common knowledge in their social circles. If so, it would suggest that it was acceptable to be open about one's interest in the subject without fear of censure.

Rodney Stark[19] suggests a possible explanation for the attraction of Judaism, or indeed any other religion:

> *Typically people do not* seek *a faith; they* encounter *one through their ties to other people who already accept this faith.*

Lacking any enlightening records, relating this theory to Poppaea's dealings with Josephus is problematic. Likewise we do not know the identities of any women having an expressed interest in Judaism, and with whom she might have discussed it. How much credence it warrants as a plausible explanation of her interest is therefore arguable.

In her attention to Judaism, Poppaea predictably has her detractors. Ancient and modern, they posit that her 'support' for Jewish causes was simply an aspect of her personality, faddish and superficial:

> *As far as most of our ancient authorities were concerned, Poppaea was nothing if not obsessed with fashion.*[20]

---

[19] *The Rise of Christianity: A Sociologist Reconsiders History* (1996), Princeton University Press, Princeton, NJ, USA

> *She also took a fashionable interest in Judaism . . .* [21]

As a slave to fashion, it is implied, she could have had no more serious interest in the subject than anyone else inclined to attention-seeking behaviour. Aside from the uncomplimentary tenor at work here, the position of Roman Jews in antiquity was tenuous at best. This would seem to be at odds with the inference that only on some frivolous whim of fashion might anyone of influence have lifted a finger to help them.

An earlier source suggests another reason for Poppaea's inclination, one that is no less acerbic:

> *Agrippina and her friends had oppressed the Jews. Poppaea* of course [emphasis added] *favoured and protected them.* [22]

Though her behaviour might otherwise be thought commendable, Poppaea's motives are once again questioned. This time her supposed interest in Judaism is little more than a means to best the reputation of a rival: Nero's mother Agrippina. Her actions are therefore implied to have been no more than shallow pretence; it seems she cannot win. (It is worth noting that Josephus,

---

[20] A reference to both Pliny's *Natural History* and Juvenal's *Satires* by Margaret H Williams in *Jews in a Graeco-Roman Environment* (2013), Mohr Siebeck, Tübingen, Germany

[21] E Champlin, *Nero* (2003), Harvard University Press, Cambridge, MA, USA

[22] T Burgess, *Tracts on the Origin and Independence of the Ancient British Church* (1815), London

quoted in Barrett[23], wrote positively of Agrippina, in direct contrast to the above claim: another example of the contradictory portrayals of Rome's 'wicked women' – see Chapter 5.)

Astrology was another of Poppaea's apparent interests, and one that lit a fire under her critics. Tacitus, in particular, had strong views on the matter, as he demonstrated in Book I.22 of his *Histories*:

> *Many of these men* [astrologers] *were attached to the secret councils of Poppaea and were the vilest tools in the employ of the imperial household . . .*

Quite what it was about the subject that set him off is not clear. Astrology was far from unpopular in Imperial Rome, as he must have known. In discussing soon-to-be-Emperor Otho's[24] gullibility in the matter, he made a comment that was both revealing and striking in its condescension: ". . . *human nature always likes to believe what it cannot understand.*"

Tacitus appeared most comfortable looking back to Rome's halcyon days rather than forward to a Rome increasingly mired in degeneracy and moral collapse. Might it therefore have been his own fear of astrology, stemming from *his* lack of understanding of it, that was

---

[23] *Agrippina-Sister of Caligula, Wife of Claudius, Mother of Nero* (1996), B T Batsford Ltd, London
[24] See Chapter 7, (ii) for discussion of the relationship between Otho and Poppaea.

the source of his disapproval? For a people as unwaveringly superstitious as the Romans, it seems disingenuous to have roundly dismissed astrologers and not also, for instance, augurs – or soothsayers, portents, magic, omens (such as comets), and dream interpretation, all of which featured largely in the Roman belief system.

However well-founded – or not – Tacitus' criticisms might have been, he was outvoted at very senior level, as John Michael Greer[25] notes:

> [Emperor] *Augustus found astrology useful as a propaganda tool in his quest to legitimize his rule over the former republic . . . His patronage and that of his successor Tiberius made astrology the most prestigious of divination systems . . .*

The Emperors Gaius (Caligula – reigned 37-41 CE), Nero and Vespasian were similarly on record as fervent believers in astrology, which ought to have given Tacitus some pause in his scornful dismissal of it. Yet none of them invites the level of invective on the subject that Poppaea does. Given their elevated status this is perhaps understandable. No emperor, of any period, stood up well to criticism; and those historians writing so many years after the lives of their subjects would have been conscious of the need to tread warily in criticising present, as well as past, rulers with impunity (see Chapter 10).

---

[25] *Secrets of the Lost Symbol* (2010), Llewellyn Publications, Woodbury, MN, USA

In fact Tacitus veered between outrage and acceptance according to the thread of his narrative, his own inconsistency being no bar to criticising others. He continued:

> *Poppaea had always had her boudoir full of these astrologers, the worst kind of outfit for a royal marriage.*

It might have been enlightening to learn what kind of 'outfit' was *beneficial* to a royal marriage; not to mention the identities of the implied spies in her bedroom, who presumably went on to publish their memoirs.

This is an excellent example of Tacitus' commonly accepted guilt in imputing behaviours to people whose intimate lives he – or his sources – cannot have personally witnessed. More predictably, however, the topic simply becomes another stick with which to beat one of his most derided targets.

The true extent of Poppaea's intellect, then, sadly eludes us. Her recorded intelligence and wit point towards sufficient education to enable her easily to hold her conversational end up in social settings. It is unlikely that this particular image of her would have been promoted by the sources had her conversation been known to have consisted solely of in-depth discussions of hair and makeup.

Whatever else is written about her, nowhere do we uncover a hint of a Poppaea who was beautiful but brainless, decorative but no more. We can assume, then, that those descriptions in the record of her lively mind, even from Tacitus, were accurate. This makes the character of 'Poppaea the Person' still more intriguing.

Once more we are left to wonder how she might have dealt with the imbalance in educational opportunity that existed for women and girls. Was the lack of advanced education that was her lot, along with the overwhelming majority of her sex, a source of frustration? Did she resent the fact that the education traditionally open to her (younger) half-brother Scipio (II) would never be hers? For a girl, and woman, of acknowledged intelligence, it would have been both understandable, and to be expected, if she did.

Whatever means Poppaea might have had at her disposal in her later life to broaden that lively mind and increase her worldly knowledge, to do so without access to some degree of education, somewhere along the line, would have required considerable effort, and determination. It is disheartening to think that, in any such struggle against the constraints placed upon her sex, she would have been far from alone.

CHAPTER 4

Images: Real or imagined?

For a woman so seemingly unpopular in the historical record, Poppaea's image left a lasting impression, both on the world of antiquity and in popular culture. Though not as widely disseminated as, for instance, that of Livia, wife of the Emperor Augustus – and certainly not in the same class as Cleopatra – her image can nonetheless be found on statues, busts, coins and cameos, and she receives mention in innumerable inscriptions to be found in her assumed home territory of Campania.

This assortment of images naturally results in a variety of different descriptions of their subject. However, as with so many events in her later life, it is hard to imagine that the young Poppaea would have envisaged any of them as she embarked on the first of her marriages, in 44 CE.

These surviving images of course come to us through the interpretations of the artists who produced them. How many knew, or had even seen, the real Poppaea? What existing images can they have used as a 'model'? Sadly, and frustratingly, we cannot know. As if seen through layers of glass (or a veil, as Tacitus would have it[1]), her true identity remains hazy and indistinct. Though she can have played no part in how her later images were presented, they nonetheless encourage the use of the word 'tantalising' to describe her.

By contrast, and at a more general level, the display of images of the rulers of ancient Rome was both clear in purpose and weighted with significance. As in ancient Egypt, the majority of its citizens were likely to have been illiterate. Pronouncements nailed to the doors of the Roman Senate might therefore have gone over their heads, but statues thrown up in the Forum gave them something to stare at, symbolically above them in every sense and intended to inspire awe.

The size of some of these was staggering: the colossal statue of the Emperor Constantine (reigned 306-337 CE), more than forty feet high, the head more than six; Nero's gilded bronze statue, built for his *Domus Aurea* (see Chapter 6), over one hundred feet high. Bronze was particularly expensive – never a consideration for Nero – often melted down in later periods for use as weapons of war. However some exquisite examples can still be seen in the National Archaeological Museum of Naples and the Capitoline Museums in Rome.

---

[1] *Annals*, 13.45 (trans. John C Yardley, 2008)

Whatever form these monuments took, and wherever they were sited, they reflected the wealth and status of those who commissioned them. Their function as disseminators of the party line was without equal. One imagines Augustus, long the undisputed King of Propaganda, crotchety and impatient in his old age, grumbling from his exalted position in the company of the gods while he surveyed his bronze statue atop his Mausoleum in Rome's Campus Martius: *"Well,* that *should have made some of them sit up and take notice."* He would doubtless be less than impressed to note that it took until 2016, two years after the 2000th anniversary of his death, for major restoration of the site to begin.

Statues – of marble, stone and terracotta as well as bronze – had particular cultural signficance. Those displayed in Rome required the approval of the reigning emperor, and were used as models for reproductions in far-flung provinces. That so many still survive in, for example, eastern areas of the former Empire indicates that their propaganda value was considerable, even so far from 'home'. Nothing emanating from the Empire's capital could more effectively have demonstrated to the people, wherever they might be, the locus of power, and to whom they should give obeisance, even unto death. Such solid tangible monuments, of the highest quality and so often larger than life, were eternal reminders of the place of each and every class in the rigid hierarchy of ancient Rome.

Statues were often painted in the original, and rare examples showing traces of colour can still be found. We are so used to white marble, or pale-coloured stone, that the technicolour impact of the original is lost. Frescoes in surviving élite properties such as the Villa Oplontis in Campania (see Chapter 6) illustrate the vividness of the original colours, and the skill of craft workers in ensuring that they did not fade. This is a talent that cannot be said to have survived intact into the present day; the Romans seemingly knew something about dyes and colours (unaided by technology) that we do not.

It is a great pity that we have no lasting examples of Poppaea and her 'amber-coloured tresses'; Pliny the Elder (23-79 CE) claimed in his *Natural History*, written shortly before his death, that Nero wrote of them in poetry. Dazzling amber, in all its multifarious shades, somehow fits the popular image of a woman of striking appearance; and it was imbued with all kinds of mystical properties centuries before the time of ancient Rome.

Two images, both 'said to be' of Poppaea Sabina, remain probably the most widely disseminated, perhaps because they are the largest.

(i)   Palazzo Massimo alle Terme, Rome

This marble bust is remarkable, and of high quality. She presents as serene, beautifully coiffed, wearing a diadem, the ornamental crown denoting royalty: very much the 'queen' – as indeed she was, as Empress of

Rome in the brief portion of Nero's reign during which they were married. Though its origins are unclear, it cannot fail to impress. Rosaria Ciardello suggests a connection to the Villa Oplontis.[2] The National Museum of Rome dates it no more precisely than c. 54-68 CE, the period of Nero's reign. The wearing of a diadem suggests a production date following the Nero/Poppaea marriage in 62 CE.

(ii)   Archaeological Museum of Olympia, Greece

This full-length statue is complete but for the loss of the hands, though it can be imagined that some sacred item(s) of significance might have been held in either or both of them. Though the face is slightly different in shape it is no less striking, and the quality of the work is again very high.

Poppaea wears the characteristic garment of a priestess; Joan Connelly points to a possible intended link to Eirana, Priestess of Artemis.[3] Margarete Bieber's extensive work is useful in examining the clothing worn by both Greeks and Romans, its significance as it was 'copied over' from Greece to Rome, and the implications

---

[2] *The Villa of Poppaea at Oplontis: decorative frescoes from Republic to the Empire* in *Apolline Project Vol. 1: Studies on Vesuvius' North Slope and the Bay of Naples* (2009), eds F de Simone, G de Simone and R T MacFarlane, Napoli, Italy
[3] *Portrait of a Priestess: Women and Ritual in Ancient Greece* (2007), University of Princeton Press, Princeton, NJ, USA

of that for Roman women, for example symbolically dressing Poppaea as priestess.[4]

The statue was found in the 1st century CE in the cella (inner room) of Olympia's Temple of Hera. The cella was the main repository of statues of the deity to whom the temple was dedicated: in this case Hera, wife of Zeus and 'queen of the gods'.

Connelly further suggests that two other similar statues of women at Olympia, dressed identically, were produced by the Athenian sculptors Eros and Eleusinios, and dated to the period of Poppaea's adulthood. Were these two sculptors also responsible for 'Poppaea as Priestess'?

Many more of Poppaea's images from antiquity are thought to have been lost, although Susan Wood suggests that Nero's appreciation of the unpopularity of their relationship may have accounted for the relative scarcity of surviving images.[5] The machinations he engendered in 62 in veering between Claudia Octavia, his popular first wife, and Poppaea, his much-desired second, are likely to have contributed, though the resulting losses of Poppaea's statues cannot have been his intention.

Following his disgraceful treatment of Octavia (see Chapter 7, (iii)), of whom he wished to be free in order to

---

[4] *Ancient Copies* (1977), New York University Press, New York, NY, USA
[5] *Imperial Women: A Study in Public Images, 40 BC-AD 68* (1998), Koninklijke Brill NV, Leiden, Netherlands

marry Poppaea, the people protested angrily, storming the streets. The upshot was an alleged swift volte-face on Nero's part, with him 're-embracing' his marriage to Octavia. According to Tacitus:

> *Then the people joyfully climbed the Capitol . . . They threw down Poppaea's statues, lifted effigies of Octavia on their shoulders, scattered flowers over them, and set them up in the Forum and temples.*

However events in Rome could famously move swiftly. Troops of the Praetorian Guard moved in to control the protesting crowds that invaded the Imperial palace. Tacitus continued: *"The changes they had brought about with the riot were reversed, and Poppaea's honours were re-established."*

Whether Poppaea's *statues* were also re-established is not clear; nor do we know their numbers, or how badly they were damaged. Their location is likewise unexplained: were they placed "in the Forum and temples", as were those of Octavia? They are gone before we can even see them. At all events it is clear how precarious was the existence of monuments to those whose fortunes might, for the moment, have been riding high.

Eric Varner[6] notes the significance of the verb *reponere* (= to set up again) for statues ostensibly removed

---

[6] *Mutilation and Transformation-Damnatio Memoriae and Roman Imperial Portraiture* (2004), Koninklijke Brill NV, Leiden, Netherlands

by Imperial edict but carefully stored, to reappear at a later time. This suggests that those responsible were aware, perhaps even instructed, that their removal might not necessarily be permanent:

> Reponere *is also used by Tacitus in conjunction with the statues of Poppaea which were returned to public display under Otho* (Hist 1.78) *as part of the emperor's campaign to rehabilitate the memories of Nero and Poppaea.*

Once again we are not told how many there were, or where they might originally have been located.

Christina Kokkinia[7] contributes further:

> *The preservation of an inscription* [at Sebasteion; Greek Sebastos = Augustus[8]] *in honour of Poppaea Sabina* . . . *does not provide secure evidence that her statue remained in place, two centuries after that of her disgraced husband had been removed* . . .

She notes the further anomaly of the survival of Poppaea's image in a location not apparently intended for it:

> . . . *an explanation must be sought for the preservation of Poppaea's statue for so many decades, and even centuries, in an architectural context in which apparently there was no space to spare.*

---

[7] Kera: Institute for Greek and Roman Antiquity,*Survey results in Boubon (Cibyratis, northern Lycia) 2004-2006*
[8] 'Augusteum' in Latin; an Imperial cult temple discovered in Turkey, rich in finds from the Julio-Claudian era.

The mystery of where, and under whose control, images of Poppaea survived continues. Furthermore, since she and Nero were inextricably linked by marriage and children it is remarkable, given her unpopularity, that her image appears from this text to have outlasted his.

The accuracy of visual images, however, can be unreliable. Anthony Barrett[9] notes:

> *Sculpture must be used with some caution, since Roman sculpted heads are very rarely found with inscriptions and are identified largely on the basis of resemblance to coin types.*

Frustratingly, statues were more likely to bear the name of the sculptor than the subject. Added uncertainty stemmed from the convention of idealised portraits retaining their popularity long after production. Augustus was an example: it is a rare surviving face – and there are many – that portrays him as ageing any further than his twenties. It is therefore a generous stretch to describe them as 'accurate', with such a youthful face belonging to someone who died in his seventies.

A further example of problems of identification is the reworking of originals, where portraits of Imperial family members began life as someone else entirely. Emperor Claudius' bust in the Vatican Museums, for example, is thought to have been reworked from one of his

---

[9] *Agrippina - Sister of Caligula-Wife of Claudius-Mother of Nero* (1996), B T Batsford Ltd, London

predecessor Caligula: one of similar instances of Roman ingenuity impelled by political pragmatism. This practice might seem to suggest Roman eccentricity at work until we consider that later artists are known to have painted over canvases of 'original' subjects in creating new ones.

In addition, Wood suggests that images of Octavia and Poppaea, Nero's first two wives, share such similar features that they could be mistaken for each other, though this does not seem to be an opinion generally shared. It is, however, one more frustrating example of the problems inherent in attempting to 'read' images from antiquity, whether jewellery, statues, or fragments of buildings. Romans produced *nothing* that was not weighted with significance.

Given all of this, we cannot know which of Poppaea's surviving images is closest to the real thing. The Imperial family were of course well positioned to commission artists skilled enough to produce the requisite images in praise of Imperial virtues. These were by no means 'warts and all'; it would be a brave soul who produced an unflattering image of an Imperial personage.

One striking exception is the Emperor Caracalla (reigned 198-217 CE). Virtually all images of him on busts and coinage are extraordinarily unappealing, his threatening scowl seeming to confirm just what an abhorrent character he was generally held to be. Perhaps he thought them flattering.

Roman sculptures, at least those favoured by the upper classes, veered between realism and idealism, according to fashion. However, comparison alongside their Greek counterparts makes clear that the latter invariably went for beauty. It is even thought that Romans, with impressive resourcefulness, replaced the heads of generic 'body beautiful' Greek statues with Roman ones.

Claudius provided a variation on the theme: he is thought to have removed the face of Alexander the Great from paintings, replacing it with that of his great-uncle, the Emperor Augustus.[10] The head of Nero's gilded bronze *Domus Aurea* statue was altered by a succession of Flavian emperors after his death, as if to eradicate the worst memories of him and his reign. Whether commissioning objects of hero-worship or propaganda, or erasing reminders of iniquitous Imperial behaviour, Romans were nothing if not inventive.

Although less striking in appearance than those described above, Poppaea's image, often with Nero, appears on a number of existing coins, in silver, gold, bronze and copper. As expected, they are usually heavily symbolic.

Coins clearly had a role to play in the images they portrayed that statues did not. They embodied messages

---

[10] K W Arafat, *Pausanias' Greece: Ancient Artists and Roman Rulers* (1996), Cambridge University Press, Cambridge, UK

loaded with significance: the Emperor Augustus ('good') versus the Emperor Caligula ('bad'). In addition, while much easier to produce in great numbers, coins might not have remained in circulation as long as originally planned before being superseded.

Interpretation of their markings reveals a wealth of detail about subject and status. They were also important in disseminating portraits of the Imperial family to commemorate significant events. However, whether or not those events were as meaningful to the population at large as to the Imperial family themselves can only be guessed at.

The appearance of deities on the reverse of coins was clearly meant to connect both sides, imbuing Imperial personages with the virtues of gods and goddesses. As a variant form of propaganda, they could hardly be bettered. However, we cannot know how much store Roman people set by this shrewd promotion of moral ideologies and behavioural ideals. We might also wonder what they thought of an Imperial face on a coin markedly different from that same face atop a statue; one imagines it producing no more than a weary Roman shrug.

Sébastien Aubry[11] describes a slightly different sample from the Cabinet des médailles in Paris:

---

[11] *Inscriptions on Portrait Gems and discs in Late Antiquity (3rd-6th centuries AD)* in *Gems of Heaven: Recent Research on Engraved Gemstones*

> *A 1st century AD sardonyx . . . representing a crowned*
> *bust of Poppaea, the wife of Nero, shows the use of*
> *initials and symbols . . . which are put together in order*
> *to specify the status of the engraved figure.*

More significantly:

> *The two letters O P apply to Ollia Poppeia, and the*
> *miniature cornucopia to the symbol of* Fecunditas
> [fertility], *as on some imperial silver coins.*

If this reading is correct, it is another rare appearance of Poppaea's birth name, Ollia – now long out of use – though why it appears on such an object, and who ordered that it should, is a mystery. We can assume that the reference to Poppaea's fertility marks the production date as 63 CE, commemorating the birth of baby Claudia, the short-lived Imperial child.

Both gold and silver coins depicting Emperor Nero and his 'Augusta' can be found in the British Museum in London. Though unspecified, the assumed date of production, 64-65 CE, indicates that Poppaea is his Augusta since they married in 62.

A bronze coin from a mint in Phrygia (now western Turkey) dated 63-65 CE depicts Poppaea – without Nero – in the company of Greek goddesses Artemis (childbirth, the moon and the hunt), and Nike (victory). Artemis

---

in Late Antiquity, AD 200-600 (2011), C Entwistle and N Adams (eds), British Museum Company Ltd, London

might reasonably connect to the birth in 63 of Claudia, though she lived for less than four months. Nike's significance, however, is less clear. The coin shows wreaths and palms, both symbols of victory, and no historical record connects Poppaea to any battles, victorious or otherwise. Joining Roman women, whoever they were, to a political theme rather than those more commonly associated with women, such as fertility (*Fecunditas*) or marital harmony (*Concordia*), was highly unusual.

Other sources of extant coins showing Poppaea alone or with Nero are traced to Alexandria in Egypt, Galatia (Asia Minor, modern Turkey), Perinthos (Marmara district of Turkey), Tavium (central Turkey), Caesarea Paneas (ancient Roman city now in the Golan Heights), and Ephesos (Anatolia, Turkey). This list is in all probability incomplete; Susan Wood suggests that such coins were minted from fifteen provincial cities, with a total of eighteen issues.[12] Archaeologists will no doubt continue to unearth more with the passage of time. The excitement they generate, more particularly those depicting such well-known figures, understandably seems never to fade.

One coin stands out from the many still in circulation. Bronze, said to have been minted in Caesarea Paneas, exact year unclear, it depicts a temple of Diva Poppaea ('*DIVA POPPAEA AUG*') and another of Diva

---

[12] *The Incredible Vanishing Wives of Nero*, lecture as part of *Tyranny and Transformation*, USA/Canada/Chile (2000-2005)

Claudia (*'DIVA CLAUD NER F'*), their baby daughter. The locus of discovery connects it to Jewish historian Josephus, who would doubtless have thought himself a friend to Poppaea; perhaps less so to Nero, since it is not clear that they ever met. The 'Diva Poppaea' temple is thought to represent that decreed by Nero (or the Senate – both are claimed) in 63 CE to celebrate Poppaea's fertility, though whether the temple was actually built seems less certain. It would be no surprise to discover that its building was overtaken by the death of baby Claudia before four months had passed.

Though not all sources agree, Poppaea is linked specifically to the goddess Venus, the patron deity of Pompeii and 'mother of the Roman people'. It is suggested that Pompeii's original cult of Venus sprang from the worship of the goddess Venus Physica, who ruled over life and death, rather than the goddess Venus more familiarly known to represent love and beauty. According to Salvatore Nappo[13], it was the dictator Sulla[14] who 'converted' the subject of worship from life and death to love and beauty, possibly connected to his founding a colony there in 80 BCE.

However, by Poppaea's time the city was clearly linked to Venus as we know her. Her association with

---

[13] *Pompeii* (2004), White Star S.r.l., Vercelli, Italy

[14] Lucius Cornelius Sulla (138-79 BCE), "a soldier and a politician, a dictator and a reformer" (*Encyclopaedia Britannica*), who played a significant, if controversial, role in Republican Rome.

Pompeii's favoured goddess should be no surprise since the *gens Poppaea* have been shown to have had strong connections with the city. The citizens of Pompeii had clearly taken the goddess of love and beauty to their hearts:

> *When the sanctuary of Venus was built at the time of Caesar* [i.e. c. 50 BCE] *it was the largest of all temple precincts in the city, and it remained so throughout the rest of Pompeii's history . . .* [15]

Carroll goes on to highlight its historical importance:

> *. . . it is one of the earliest temple groves in the Roman world for which there is archaeological evidence.*

The National Archaeological Museum of Naples contains a golden oil lamp from the Sanctuary of Venus, said to have been an offering to the goddess by Nero and Poppaea. Carroll again:

> *Graffiti from the* House of Iulius Polybius [in Pompeii] *suggest that costly gifts of gems, pearls and significant amounts of gold had been donated to the sanctuary of Venus by Nero and his wife, Poppaea Sabina.*

Similarly Stefano De Caro:

---

[15] Maureen Carroll, *Exploring the Sanctuary of Venus and its sacred grove. Politics, cult and identity in Roman Pompeii*, Papers of the British School at Rome, 78 (2010)

> . . . *a graffito in the* House of Julius Polybius . . .
> *reports a gift by Poppaea (Augusta) of a beryl*[16] *and two*
> *pearls to the same goddess* [Venus] . . .[17]

However Carroll makes the point that such Imperial gifts should not be seen as constituting state-sponsored financial support for the Sanctuary's restoration post-earthquake, but rather as an example of Imperial largesse. It is also suggested that the story of Nero's gift of "significant amounts of gold" was not mentioned by, for example, Tacitus since it did not support his well-entrenched detestation of the Emperor. Indeed he could not apparently bring himself to mention Nero's visit at all.

The destruction of the Sanctuary of Venus by Campania's February 62 CE earthquake would have been a shocking event for Pompeians to come to terms with, since Venus was their patron goddess, revered above all others. Like countless other buildings in Pompeii, restorative work was interrupted by the 79 volcanic eruption of Vesuvius, and the Sanctuary was never completed. The people must have been badly shaken by this unremitting wrath of the gods; twice they had suffered the destruction of their sacred monument to the divinity they worshipped. What could they have done to deserve this?

---

[16] Beryls are beryllium-aluminium-silicates, said to originate from India; morganite (pink), emerald (green) and aquamarine (blue) are all examples of beryls (International Coloured Gemstone Association).
[17] *Sculpture found at the Villa Oplontis* in *Ancient Roman Villa Gardens* (1987) (ed. Elisabeth B MacDougall), Trustees for Harvard University, Washington, DC, USA

Post-antiquity, the image and character of Poppaea still hold sway in the public imagination. Why this should be is a matter for conjecture, although images of women that have attained iconic status have a long history. Though not all entirely predictable, she has made a considerable number of appearances in popular culture.

It might be seen as ironic that both Poppaea and Agrippina, unlikely to have been the best of friends, are the subject of much-acclaimed operas. *L'incoronazione di Poppea* (The Coronation of Poppaea), by Claudio Monteverdi, was produced in 1643, and considered by some to be his greatest work. Even non-opera lovers might be converted by *Pur ti miro*, the final duet between Poppaea and Nero, thought by many to be the most romantic in the entire operatic canon. However the plot requires a generous suspension of disbelief, perhaps even more so as it was said to have been produced for performance at Venice's *Carnevale*. Nonetheless it is described as the first opera to have been based on historic events.

George Frideric Handel's *Agrippina* was first performed in 1709, when he was only 24 years old. Described as a 'comic opera', it is regarded by some as a 'true operatic masterpiece'. As might be expected Poppaea also has a role, although once more the plot requires a similar suspension of disbelief as to historical 'facts' and final outcome. Interestingly, from a choice of Claudius,

Nero and Otho, she ends up with the latter, portrayed as her 'true love'.

In the musical modern-day, and as far removed from the two above as it is possible to be, a song entitled "Poppaea" was performed by the Norwegian gothic metal band Theatre as Tragedy in 1998. Unsurprisingly the lyrics, written in early English, are not easy to interpret. As evidenced by an early line, *"Thine feral grith with me, Poppaea, be Hell's hap"*, one sees the problem.

The catalogue of Poppaea's cinematic appearances is impressive, running almost from the beginnings of cinema to the first decade of the current millenium. Predictably, her character echoes the familiar, with diaphanous costumes and a record as a former prostitute (Where did *that* come from?) thrown in for added titillation. She is lascivious, sensual, jealous, seductive, sexually aggressive, manipulative, *ad nauseam*. Something about the populist medium of film, perhaps encouraged by the imagined licentious, no-holds-barred setting of ancient Rome, seems to encourage screenwriters to let loose with their own interpretations of dramatic licence.

The first historical cinematic marker to Poppaea's credit is the dubious honour of appearing in an early blockbuster, the 1913 Italian version of "Quo Vadis?". Written and directed by Enrico Guazzoni from the novel by Henryk Sienkewicz, in it she was played by Olga Brandini.

In a demonstration of the power of the box office – even in 1956 – "Mio Figlio Nerone" (My Son Nero), an Italian-French co-production described by *Wikipedia* as an "historical comedy", was radically altered for its later US release. From Agrippina, played by Gloria Swanson, aged 57, its focus shifted under the new title of "Nero's Mistress" to Poppaea, played by a young Brigitte Bardot (aged 22).

At the time of writing, Poppaea's last screen portrayal was by Catherine McCormack in the 2006 BBC docu-drama "Ancient Rome: The Rise and Fall of an Empire". In some forty productions on the IMDb film website (though IMDb do not acknowledge authorship), perhaps the most bizarre is Kay Patrick's 1965 portrayal of Poppaea in "Dr Who"! One imagines Poppaea, open-mouthed in amazement, too stunned even to be flattered by all this cinematic attention; she might also understandably be somewhat bewildered by her connection, historic or otherwise, to Dr Who.

Unsurprisingly, however, all is not truth and beauty. In *"The Ancient World in the Cinema"* (2001)[18], Jon Solomon presumably means to be seen to be taking a light-hearted look at the women of antiquity on film. However, what he succeeds in doing is reducing the text to a level that is both insulting and unacceptable in a professor of classics. For example, in discussing the 1922 Italian-American production of "Nero":

---

[18] Yale University Press, New Haven, CT, USA

> *Nero's infamous and sexy wife, Poppaea, whose name to this day in modern Italian means 'chesty', is perhaps more evil than either history or drama demands.*

It is not clear which dictionary gives him such a translation. In writing of a 1951 production, "Nero", he comments: "*And Nero's wife, Poppaea (Patricia Laffan), is a real lizard.*" He carries on in similar vein in describing another 1951 production, "O.K. Nerone". After commenting on the exterior location of the film (in the Mussolini-designed EUR district in Rome's south-east), he continues: "*The sexy Silvana Pampanini (Poppaea) fills out the interior shots . . .*".[19]

It seems that cinematic portrayals of Poppaea, and those who play her, are not so very different in flavour from those literary ones, ancient and modern, we have come to know.

Poppaea's other contemporary appearances cover a wide range. She appears in Terence Riley's text (quoting Jean Starobinski) on contemporary architecture surveys at the Museum of Modern Art in New York. His 1989 essay entitled "Poppaea's Veil: the hidden fascinates" mentions her alleged propensity for wearing a veil (as does Tacitus, noted earlier, whose observations border on the spiteful). He metaphorically compares this image to walls that keep out spectators while ensuring that they hunger for what is

---

[19] Poppaea does not suffer alone from such offensive descriptions; Messallina is ". . . *one of the most notorious aristocratic sluts in history . . .*".

hidden behind the facade. Poppaea could hardly have failed to be impressed by being compared to a wall.

She is also credited with beauty masks based on supposed extracts from donkey's milk.[20] In addition, Juvenal is alone in claiming that a facecream was named after her, with a none-too-subtle connection to her supposed obsession with her looks. However, a note of warning is offered by Andrew Wallace-Hadrill[21] regarding the satirist's credibility:

> *For attitudes as well as for facts, the historian would be well advised to . . . give a very wide berth indeed to Juvenal.*

The cosmetic allusion is a slight variation on the many she-asses Poppaea is alleged to have needed at her disposal – along with Cleopatra, her legendary sister in crimes of extravagance – in order to bathe in their milk. On this latter charge, Annelise Freisenbruch[22] makes a useful point concerning female extravagance and negativity:

> *The fact that the same bathing habit* [as Cleopatra's] *was said to have been shared by later Roman women who were regarded as profligate and corrupting, such as Nero's second wife Poppaea, may suggest that the*

---

[20] Article by Irina Chassiotou on Health website of environmental news (2014)
[21] *Patronage in Ancient Society* (1989-ed.), Routledge, London/New York
[22] *The First Ladies of Rome: The Women Behind the Caesars* (2011), Vintage, London

> *practice was commonly attributed to any woman who*
> *was seen to offend morality.*

On a more frivolous note, the logistics are nowhere explained of where the asses were kept, or what became of them after Poppaea's death. (Did she keep five hundred, a number often bandied about by the sources[23], in both Rome and Antium, or was it two hundred and fifty in each?) It is difficult to imagine them inhabiting their own quarters close to her bathing rooms, even for the sake of convenience – five hundred is a lot of asses. An entire legion of slaves must have been employed solely for the purpose of milking them. No source assists in clarifying these details in a matter of such gross profligacy; where are Tacitus, or Pliny, when we need them?

This connection to extravagance is significant when examining the way in which the lives of such purportedly decadent Roman women were recorded, and how they are stereotypically linked together. The practice is easily extended to encompass other unfavourable examples:

♦ The supposed propensity of certain women to use poison as weapon of choice in clearing the way of obstacles – examples too numerous to cover;

---

[23] Pliny the Elder, in his *Natural History*, claimed that Poppaea always travelled with such a number. No source is named. Cassius Dio made a similar claim. A more extensive search among the sources reveals that the number varied from fifteen to seven hundred. It is unfortunate that such crucial historical detail cannot be more accurate.

- The pleasure they allegedly derived from seeing rivals' heads paraded before them after beheading, for example Poppaea and Agrippina (see Chapter 7 for further discussion); and

- The desire to own beautiful gardens being sufficient reason to eliminate anyone who stood in the way of their acquisition, for example Messallina and Agrippina.

This last extraordinary example of alleged unbridled female wickedness is hard to take seriously (though the five, six or seven hundred asses is a worthy competitor). Are there no depths to which the high-ranking women of Rome would not have sunk in order to get their hands on a pretty plot of land? Freisenbruch suggests that ". . . [it] *implies some recycling of stereotypes across the centuries.*" It is difficult to argue otherwise.

As far as is known, Poppaea is innocent of dastardly deeds committed in cold-blooded pursuit of someone else's garden. If ever she was ambitious enough to covet one, it would appear that she kept it to herself.

Whatever the intentions behind them, the variety of representations of her in both ancient and modern cultures ensures that Poppaea has not been forgotten. If her aim was to create a lasting impression, she succeeded.

We might imagine her and Mona Lisa, across the centuries, sharing a smile.

CHAPTER 5

In the company of witches

For the purpose of clarification, the word "witches" in the title above is carefully chosen. It is intended to draw an analogy to 'wicked women', rather than to suggest that iniquitous Roman women spent their days stirring powerful potions ('eye of newt, and toe of frog' – with thanks to Shakespeare), cackling and casting spells. It is undeniable, however, that ancient Romans, the most superstitious of people, habitually engaged in rites that might now seem close to sorcery.

Nowhere in ancient history did the stereotyped witch have a positive image, though some might equate her with ancient goddesses and their cults. However, much later literature exists that portrays witches as wise and knowledgeable women. It should not need mentioning that men's fear of witches over the ages is the subject of another book entirely.

*

As noted in the Introduction, the history of Rome's highborn women comes to us through the eyes of men, of whatever period. A clear line in the recording of Roman lives separates the public – male – domain from the private – female – one. Crucially, that line assists in sending out a clear message:

> *When the women do enter the world of public action, their stature in the public world of political power cannot match that of the males, because . . . they do not belong there . . .* [1]

The half of the population who are members of that 'unbelonging' may find such a statement shocking. This denial of belonging had profound implications for the way in which the behaviour of Roman women was judged – and recorded. Any public action they took was not history, it was aberration. Allen *et al* continue:

> *. . . the women who stride across those established borders* [of prescribed female behaviour] *appear as perversions of good women, as either domineering dowagers or scheming concubines.*

This latter role, the 'scheming concubine', strikes a familiar chord: it is one that might be said to have been monopolised in the record by Poppaea Sabina.

---

[1] *Stereotypes of Women in Power: Historical Perspectives and Revisionist Views* (1992), Pauline Allen, Barbara Garlick, Suzanne Dixon (eds), Greenwood Press, Westport, CT, USA

As discussed at Chapter 8, the focus of her assumed ambition is far from clear; likewise her alleged quest for power, and how it might accurately apply. She was no Fulvia or Agrippina (Elder or Younger) – see further below. She seems not to have hankered after strapping on a sword and rallying the troops; nor did she appear interested in devoting her life to placing her offspring on the throne at any cost (see Appendix I for a discussion pertinent to this last point). Alongside the most overtly 'political' of Imperial women, Poppaea seems a different breed entirely.

This can be explained in part by her birth. We know that she was not born to the 'blue blood' of the Julio-Claudian dynasties. As far as we know, no role models inhabited her world who could shine a light on where her destiny lay. Given this, and the dearth of information about her early life, historians' enthusiasm for continually focusing on the intensity of her ambition involves, at best, a mixture of loose interpretation and guesswork.

The connection commonly made by sources between looks and behaviour, at least when discussing women, is hard to avoid. Anthony Barrett supports this in highlighting ". . . *an ancient stereotype that links physical charms to moral degradation.*"[2] The power of the myth of 'Beauty = Vice' should not be underestimated; it goes a long way back – and sadly a long way forward too.

---

[2] *Agrippina-Sister of Caligula-Wife of Claudius-Mother of Nero* (1996), B T Batsford Ltd, London

We can only speculate about how much women of non-Imperial lineage, such as Poppaea, knew of their infamous predecessors. Did she know, for instance, anything of the life of Livia, wife of the Emperor Augustus, who died just before she was born? Or Augustus' daughter Julia, who died more than ten years before that? Or Marc Antony's wife Fulvia of the previous century? For all we know, they, and those other women with whom Poppaea shares the wicked pigeon-hole, might have left a trail that was afterwards carefully covered.

There were no history books, as we now know them, from which to learn. As stated elsewhere, no historian of senatorial rank appeared minded to ensure that important historical details concerning women were recorded for posterity; still less was any concern shown for accuracy. As noted at Chapter 3, education for women and girls, if it happened at all, was likely to have been rather patchy.

We might imagine the following scene, of an educational nature:

The location is the sumptuous domus *of Publius Cornelius Lentulus Scipio, aristocratic stepfather of Poppaea the Younger. It is in a suitably prestigious part of Rome: the Palatine Hill would not surprise.*

Poppaea, aged about nine, is curled up in the lap of her mother Poppaea the Elder, who is probably in her twenties. The notorious women of the recent past have, to her mother's chagrin, managed to find their way into the conversation.

'They were all wicked, my darling, wicked – you must never be like them. Never.'

'What did they do, Mama?'

'Oh, my honey – too – too dreadful to talk about! Think about something nice – would you like a peach? Shall we feed the fish?'

'But Mama, you haven't said. What did they DO?'

Poppaea's mother, if indeed she herself knew, might have struggled to explain.

Such playful fantasy cannot have been what Roman men of rank intended their wives to cover in educating their children. Sons might reasonably be supposed to have learnt of battles, and conquests, and the superiority, might and rightness of Rome.

But what, if anything, did high-ranking daughters learn about those trail-blazing women who had gone before? They were, after all, famous in their own ways. Though we might wish to describe those ways as diverse, we are prevented from doing so by the largely stereotyped portrayals of them; the usual list of alleged defects will apply.

The answer to the question concerning Poppaea's knowledge of her predecessors would in all likelihood have been 'very little'. Augustus' daughter Julia's alleged promiscuity in the Forum and elsewhere, and her seeming desire to test her father's tolerance to its limit, can hardly be regarded as 'imbibing the values of ancestors', a high priority in the education of élite Roman children. Were all of these women, with their variously scandalous reputations, simply airbrushed from the early records?

The loss of so many ancient texts, or large parts of them, of course affects the extant records of women's lives. Julia's fate in 14 CE, for example, had to wait almost one hundred years before Tacitus first recorded her in his *Annals*. He noted that her father had been driven to having her imprisoned "for immorality". A further decade or more passed before Suetonius is thought to have begun writing. Livy died three years after Julia did (and more than ten years before Poppaea was born).

It is clear, then, that any airbrushing of the histories of these most notorious of women that might have gone on in the years immediately following their deaths did not continue. Allen *et al* remind us of the treatment meted out to women who had the audacity to display signs of independence: " . . . [they] *call forth the most vitriolic condemnations from the men who record their activities.*"

Those lengthy gaps between the appearances of the more famous of the writers of antiquity point up the considerable degree to which they were obliged to rely on earlier sources. For the most part they were not writing contemporaneously and their styles reflect the fact.

Tacitus' narrative style, for instance, is one that is mentioned by numerous modern writers. Marc Kleijwegt[3], for example, notes:

> [it] . . . *is condensed and occasionally puts effect before historical accuracy. The emphasis is on a rapid sequence of events, glossing over the fact that these were the result of long-term processes.*

The lack of acknowledgement of those "long-term processes", and their importance in the recording of history, can only have affected the way in which, in particular, Imperial women were portrayed. With the exception of Augustus' wife Livia, none had lengthy lives. That those relatively brief lives so often earned only passing mention, and that compressed, plausibly explains the heavy reliance on stereotypes.

Put another way, if the teacher of Roman history is struggling to uncover early details of a Roman woman's life, it is a simple matter to scatter about those prevailing stereotypes. Who is to protest? Which of his students might be bold enough to question the truth of the story, or of the reputation under discussion? Or, for that matter, the lack of detail that caused the struggle in the first place?

Furthermore, that public arenas were largely closed to women naturally ordered their lives – as was the undoubted intention (see also Chapter 8). In challenging

---

[3] *Nero's Helpers: The Role of the Neronian Courtier in Tacitus'* Annals in *Classics Ireland* Vol. 7 (2000), University of South Africa Pretoria, RSA

the restrictions of the ruling élite, the only constraint on women was their own courage. Those aspiring to any role beyond that of the ideal *matrona* were perforce required to operate behind the scenes, predictably feeding into the notion that they were 'devious', 'cunning', 'scheming', 'conniving', *ad infinitum*. The most cursory examination of the records will show historians over the ages embracing this sinister image with relish, heaping opprobrium onto the heads of those wily women in large dollops. Thus is a stereotype born . . .

However, it is gratifying to note that increasing numbers of scholars and historians are questioning this unjust treatment of Roman women in the historical narrative. It has been a long time coming.

That same cursory examination will also find that the most popular stereotyped representation is the 'wicked woman'. In modern populist terms, she is the female equivalent of the male 'monster'. As such, she effortlessly garners the most publicity. Perhaps more importantly, she is also the one that lasts:

> . . . *men's vitriol proves as powerful a historical preservative as does their desire.*[4]

There is manifestly no shortage of vitriol directed at Poppaea by her detractors. Their desire is, once again, the subject of another book entirely.

---

[4] J Holland, *A Brief History of Misogyny-The World's Oldest Prejudice* (2006), Constable & Robinson Ltd, London

By contrast, at the lower end of the spectrum of evil, the women who did *not* suffer the poison pen treatment, and about whom we know, are so few in number that they might easily be covered in a couple of paragraphs.

These paragons of virtue clearly posed no threat to the *status quo* as they demonstrated the kind of behaviour expected of the virtuous *matrona*. (If they harboured any untoward inclinations these have regrettably been kept from us.[5]) They are trotted out with tedious regularity by writers intent on displaying their objectivity in the portrayal of Roman women. The same small handful of names reappears, time and again; one imagines a Tacitus or a Cato the Elder[6] exclaiming: *"And thank the gods that they do!"*.

Idealisation of the Roman *matrona* was common for the times, indeed for centuries back into the Republic. She was homemaker first and foremost, her behaviour prescribed to a degree that, to modern eyes, seems almost suffocating. She was required to be dignified, modest, pious, obedient, moderate in all things and supportive. A

---

[5] Although even the saintly Cornelia, the so-called mother of virtue, was suggested by at least one source – Appian of Alexandria (c. 95-c. 165 CE) – to have had a hand in poisoning her son-in-law Scipio Aemelianus, married to her daughter Sempronia, in 129 BCE, for political reasons: see *Roman Women* (1994), originally *Roma al femminile*, ed. A Fraschetti, G Laterza & Figli S.p.a., Roma-Bari, Italy

[6] Marcus Portius Cato (234-149 BCE), also known as Cato the Censor, was a Roman statesman, arch-conservative and self-styled guardian and judge of morality.

high priority in her day-to-day activities was spinning and weaving (and making the household's clothes).

With his propaganda machine at full throttle, the Emperor Augustus is said to have insisted that all the women of his household learnt to spin and weave – so that he could boast about it (though this story may, of course, be a product of the Augustan rumour mill). This can have been no one's idea of a fun *pater familias*, although achieving the undoubted aim of reflecting well on the head of household. It is to be hoped that, by way of silent objection, looms and wheels were deserted for bathing quarters or garden as soon as he left the house.

As one who showed no known inclination towards spinning and weaving, Poppaea has nonetheless been repeatedly vilified, with far worse conduct attributed to her than a disinclination to spend her days patiently working at her wheel.

As for the rest, names already familiar – Tacitus, Cassius Dio, Livy, Juvenal – were of one mind in their dedication to supporting the traditional role of Roman women. Any who did not conform were to be deplored: their non-compliance was shocking and unwomanly, therefore unacceptable. Most importantly, they threatened the *status quo*, which could not be tolerated. Public judgements of such women were cruel and unforgiving.

The traditional role worked in tandem with the portrayal of women as appendages, reflective only of the men to whom they were attached, be they husbands, fathers, brothers or sons. The ideal *matrona* was not expected to have an independent life of her own, nor indeed to want one. Her *raison d'être* was to keep an exemplary house, a creditable kitchen, and a tight rein over her slaves. In addition, she should at all times display to the world a suitably demure (but attractive) appearance. Finally, of course, she should produce healthy, hopefully male, heirs.

All of this required that her true personality, her natural inclinations, be subordinated to those qualities exemplifying the role she had assumed. In addition, all of these daunting expectations were required to be absorbed at an appropriately early age (see Chapter 7). Any woman who did not fit, or did not want to fit, the model would doubtless call forth the wrath of the gods. One envisions whole swathes of intelligent women spending much of their time not in spinning and weaving, but in biting their lips and holding their tongues (rolling of eyes might also be expected).

Perhaps the most notorious example of this requirement to reflect well on the menfolk of the house is Julius Caesar (100-44 BCE). He divorced his second wife Pompeia on suspicion of improper behaviour, though declining to say whether or not he believed the charge to be true: the possibility was enough. Caesar himself might helpfully have clarified the matter: it was *his* reputation at stake, as he saw it, rather than Pompeia's, and he would not risk its being tarnished. So great were the reach and influence of Gaius Julius Caesar that the phrase 'Caesar's wife must be above reproach' (or others similarly worded) has passed into modern-day idiom.

A very select few were allowed to stray outside the prescribed boundaries of female behaviour, for example the Vestal Virgins (see also Chapter 8). Their sacrosanctity removed any requirement to conform similarly to women of rank, although they had their own rules and regulations that were strictly enforced.

They lived well in luxurious surroundings in the Forum, at a cost of maintaining their virginity for the 30-year period of office. Travelling in special transport, they enjoyed privileges such as seating by the emperor at games. Lictors (non-military bodyguards) escorted and protected them when they made public appearances. Their obligatory vow of chastity removed the concern with producing male children, or indeed any children. Their virginity symbolically belonged to the Roman state, therefore its deliberate loss was tantamount to treason. Punishment for any sexual transgression meant being buried alive.

An inherent contradiction exists in the portrayal of Imperial women and others of high status. As noted, their identity derived from their attachment to a man: if not 'mother of' or 'wife of', then 'daughter of'. Thus the present subject is not 'Poppaea', she is 'Nero's wife'.

In contrast is the common representation, *in their own right*, of those high-ranking women who exhibited 'unacceptable' behaviours as they defied the constraints imposed upon them. They are not difficult to find; any modern cinematic depiction of Ancient Rome will have them cast as principal female characters. These are not demure women, modest of demeanour, with eyes downcast. Rather, as often as not, they leap out of the screen, eyes flashing, faces shining with malevolence, morals scattered to the winds. For a revealing look at Poppaea's screen appearances, see the previous chapter.

As the crimes of these women are gleefully trotted out, usually in salacious detail, it seems irrelevant to which illustrious Roman they were connected. There appears little need to reference the men who validated their existence and circumscribed their lives. Suddenly, with the occasional exception, they seem quite capable of misbehaving on their own.

These contradictory depictions are not easily reconciled: high-status *matrona* alongside immoral schemer; accessory versus woman of (relative) independence. Without question, however, all were firmly attached, metaphorically, to a toga, the one permitted exception being widows.

The prospect of a woman wearing a toga – should any have ever wished to do so – was so appalling that it was unimaginable. Only prostitutes did, and they were so far beyond the pale as to have lost sight of it altogether.

Eve D'Ambra suggests that, in wearing male dress, they may have been openly declaring their bodies to be 'in the public domain' by virtue of their profession.[7]

This striking duality of representation of Roman women – prostitutes excepted – is unhelpful, and a rational explanation somewhat elusive. Had all of these women suffered the long-term effects of often complex, and conflicted, upbringing? (see Chapter 2 for Poppaea's); or was it, perhaps, a series of borderline cases of personality disorder? Did they eat different food, or was it something in the water? As noted elsewhere, the suspicion is irresistible that this treatment reveals more about the writers portraying these contradictory images than it does about their subjects. Tacitus, with his legions of devoted followers, laid the groundwork for a master class in inconsistency.

Those infamous Roman women deemed guilty of outrageous conduct are relatively few in number. However, that they are still quoted as illustrations of unpardonable behaviour is evidence of the potent impact they had on the minds of Roman men:

❖ **Clodia Metelli** (b. c. 95 BCE). Savagely ridiculed in a courtroom by the orator and lawyer Cicero for her sins as he perceived them, during a trial of her *brother* (see Chapter 8 for similar treatment of Livia and her husband; the practice of attacking men

---

[7] *Roman Women* (2007), Cambridge University Press, New York, NY, USA

through their women is discussed at Chapter 1). Aside from his other apparent difficulties with women, Cicero seemingly did not care for those who were wealthier than he was, even having married one.

❖ **Sempronia** (1st century BCE). Harshly, and inconsistently, judged by the historian Sallust (see Chapter 10). Having described both Poppaea and Sempronia as 'aristocratic, cultured, clever and beautiful', he went on to spoil things by claiming that both were 'morally depraved'.[8] Once again, such transparent contradiction, often in the same sentence, seems not to have given ancient writers any pause. Perhaps the fact that she was famously said to have been better at dancing than propriety warranted might have pushed him over the edge.

❖ **Fulvia** (c. 80-40 BCE) (See also Chapter 8). Twice widowed, wife of Marc Antony. Roundly accused of meddling in military and state affairs, seen as deplorable behaviour in a woman. If that was not condemnation enough, she was also accused of softening Antony by her overly assertive behaviour. This prepared the way for him to debase himself – and by extension all Roman men – by happily cleaving to Cleopatra's every wish, culminating in, the gods forbid, living like an Egyptian. An assertive

---

[8] Quoted in Emily Hemelrijk's *Matrona Docta: Educated Women in the Roman Elite from Cornelia to Julia Domna* (1999), Routledge, London

woman could, it seems, turn even as masculine a man as Antony to mush.

❖ **Livia Augusta** (58 BCE-29 CE). Long-term wife of the Emperor Augustus, and another victim of blatantly contradictory treatment. Sources concede her considerable influence on Augustus, and his trust in her. In contrast, innumerable portrayals highlight her fondness for poisoning as a means of despatching anyone she found irritating, her interest in the cultivation of plants and herbs being a clear giveaway. There is a lingering charge of her having murdered Augustus with poisoned figs, providing a model for Agrippina (see below) in the alleged murder of her husband Claudius.

❖ **Julia the Elder** (39 BCE-14 CE). Free-spirited daughter of Augustus, who was said to have chosen all three of her husbands. Her reputation for sexual misconduct is her legacy; as a method of protest it was impressively effective in enraging her old-school father. Her behaviour suggested that if she could not prevent the restrictions Augustus placed on her life, she could at least demonstrate what she thought of them. Augustus' response was eventually to banish her to Rhegium, modern Reggio Calabria, a long way from home, where, under the reign of Tiberius (Augustus' successor and her former husband), she is thought to have died of starvation. Her father, unforgiving to the end, withheld his permission for her burial in the family Mausoleum.

❖ **Valeria Messallina** (c. 17/20-48 CE). Third wife of the Emperor Claudius, who seems to have found her rather alarming. She was far from alone in being accused of greed, jealousy, and sexual voracity: familiar vices attributed to Rome's notorious Imperial women. Less than half the age of her husband, one might be forgiven for suspecting that she was simply bored. Reputations such as hers are open to sensationalised depiction; the truth lies buried deep. However her behind-the-scenes power and influence were likely to have been what led eventually to her enforced suicide.

❖ **Agrippina the Younger** (c. 15-59 CE). Mother of the Emperor Nero, itself alone sufficient to consign her to the flames of Hades for all time. Although accused of poisoning her husband Claudius with mushrooms, amongst sundry other crimes, it was undoubtedly her determined and clearsighted political skills that led to her murder by her son (though see Chapter 7 for an alternative theory as to her death). Her greatest crime was clearly ambition: behaviour natural in a man, but not to be tolerated in a woman.

❖ And let us not forget Poppaea, Queen of Immorality!

Innumerable examples exist of the problems for the writers of antiquity with women who would not conform to the ideal. However, the abject disapproval of the sources seems hardly sufficient to justify the ferocity of their attacks.

The language so often employed in describing them has already been touched on. More revealingly, Tacitus' language, in particular, has been equated with that used by him in describing tyrants.[9] It is difficult in all of this not to be drawn towards a suspicion of misogyny, and indeed a number of ancient sources stand accused of it.

Juvenal's vociferous objection to unwomanly behaviour, as he defined it, is well known. His *Satire VI*, mentioned elsewhere, is a vituperative attack on intelligent, educated women in language that is overtly offensive. Todd M Compton[10] gives an indication of Juvenal's reputation:

> *Satire 6 is a massive misogynistic manifesto, Juvenal's longest satire, and, many think, his masterpiece.*

The hint of admiration is undisguised. With this quote as an example, one might wonder how, and why, a 'masterpiece of misogyny' has garnered as much praise in

---

[9] See Alexandra Revell's thesis (Oxford University, UK, undated), A*grippina Maior, Messalina and Agrippina Minor: Tacitus' Female Tyrants*

[10] *Victim of the Muses: Poet as Scapegoat, Warrior and Hero in Greco-Roman and Indo-European Myth and History* (2006), Center for Hellenic Studies, Washington, DC, USA

scholarly texts as it has; the line between satire and insult is a fine one. Juvenal's 'longest satire' is full of complaints. One, for example, strikes a familiar chord: that women – aside from their irritating intelligence – take up too much air-time at the dinner table.

Dale Spender[11], in her research in mixed-sex classrooms, revealed that boys considered their rightful due to be around two-thirds of the teacher's time – regardless of the gender mix of the class. If they did not get it, they complained of discrimination. The parallels are clear.

Along with her modesty, dignity, chastity, virtue, *ad nauseam*, the silent woman was the ideal in Greek society, at least as far as Sophocles (496-406 BCE) was concerned. In his play "Ajax", he intones: "*Silence gives the proper grace to women*". On that principle, a woman speaking *at all* was being too talkative (see Spender above). Juvenal can be heard loudly applauding.

In the wake of mention of Juvenal's diatribe, a brief look at the charge of misogyny is called for. Did Juvenal, or Tacitus[12], or Cato suffer from a pathological hatred of women? Certainly all of them were blatant in their pejorative descriptions of them. If that is the main

---

[11] *Invisible Women* (1982), Chameleon Books, London
[12] See John D Clare's blog (www.johndclare.net) posted 21 January 2013, on *Tacitus's Attitude To Women – His Use Of The Word 'Muliebris'* for a discussion aimed at his history students.

criterion, then they are guilty. The issue is explored further at Chapter 10.

Holland contends that Romans happily perpetuated the damaging female stereotypes existing in Greek culture – as in Sophocles above – without feeling the need to create their own. Interestingly, he also notes that, unlike Greek and Roman cultures, nowhere in ancient Egyptian, Babylonian or Celtic cultures was the belief prevalent that women were the root of all evil.

Joan Smith points to the irony of ancient Greece, the 'cradle of democracy', allowing women the freedom only of certain parts of the house as the right and natural order.[13] Sources commonly highlight the differences between the lives of Roman women and the restrictions placed upon their Greek counterparts (see also Chapter 1). Unspoken is the suggestion that Roman women ought to have been grateful.

Another relevant factor in the attitudes of the men of antiquity towards their women are the unabashed statements from Greek sources on homosexual love being the ideal, the unquestionable higher form. Women fell far short as objects of affection. Eva Cantarella[14] (quoted by Smith) explains:

---

[13] *Misogynies* (1989), Faber and Faber, London
[14] *Pandora's Daughters: The Role and Status of Women in Greek and Roman Antiquity* (1987), The John Hopkins University Press, Baltimore, MD, USA

> *For the Greek man the homosexual relationship was a*
> *privileged outlet for exchange of experience, and he found*
> *in it an answer to his greatest needs. To relegate women*
> *to a purely biological role was perfectly natural.*

The debate concerning the attitudes towards women of those men who believed in the superiority of homosexual relationships stretches far beyond the scope of this book. However the sources already quoted – Smith, Pomeroy and Holland – are useful in any wider examination of those attitudes, and what might have been at their root.

One nagging question remains: given the generally enthusiastic embracing of Greek culture by Romans, to what depth did Roman men imbibe the worst attitudes of Greek philosophers towards women? That Romans took them on board is unquestioned, and there is no shortage of examples. However, some few men argued against, for instance, high-ranking women and girls being denied an education befitting their status. As suggested by Emily Hemelrijk on education in Chapter 3, were they simply examples of the enlightened few?

It cannot be said that male intolerance of a woman who argues politics or is knowledgeable about literature is unheard of. However, such behaviour apparently caused Juvenal to foam at the mouth, even while employing satire. His was an extreme example of the level of disapproval shown by Roman men towards women who behaved in ways deemed unacceptable. We cannot wonder that the majority of them did not care to risk the consequences of their women being educated.

All things considered, it is difficult not to applaud a light-hearted comment by Roberto Gervaso[15] concerning Nero's character. In a 2014 interview for *National Geographic* magazine, he joked that he would much rather go to dinner with Nero than with his later successor, the Emperor Hadrian (reigned 117-138 CE) who was, according to the *Encyclopaedia Britannica*, ". . . not widely mourned".

The same sentiment holds true for the wicked women of ancient Rome. All things considered, their presence round the dinner table would be a delight: amusing, entertaining, above all revealing. We can only dream – and while dreaming, mourn them all.

---

[15] Author of *Nerone* (1978), Editore Rusconi, Milano, Italy

CHAPTER 6

A woman of property

Poppaea's maternal line, and her seemingly undisputed connection to Campania, could be said to earn her the label of 'a woman of property'.

However, no definitive proof emerges to show that Poppaea was in fact born in Pompeii. Instead there are numerous references to the *gens Poppaea* as property owners in the locale, though none mentions specifically either of her parents, Poppaea Sabina the Elder or Titus Ollius:

> *While the connection cannot be established beyond all doubt, both* Poppaei Sabini *and* Ollii . . . *are attested at Pompeii.*
>
> *There was a* gens Poppaea *at Pompeii, and there is evidence that associates it with ownership of various Pompeian properties, however tenuously . . .*[1]

Miriam Griffin[2] records some Pompeian discoveries:

---

[1] *Naked Truths: Women, Sexuality and Gender in Classical Art* (1997), Ann O Koloski-Ostrow and Claire L Lyons (eds), Routledge, London
[2] *Nero: The End of a Dynasty* (1984), B T Batsford Ltd, London

105

> *Inscriptions reveal that the* gens Poppaea *owned at least five houses . . . including the celebrated* House of the Golden Cupids *and the* House of Menander . . . *while recent excavations have revealed that one of the villas at nearby Oplontis belonged to Poppaea.*

She speculates further on the question of origins:

> *It is likely that Pompeii was Poppaea's birthplace, especially as her father's family, the* Ollii, *also owned property and perhaps originated there.*

The 'likelihood' of such a connection seems as far as sources are inclined to go.

*

One of the most productive sources on the ownership of Pompeian properties was Professor Matteo Della Corte (1875-1962), whose major work, *Case ed abitanti di Pompei* (Homes and Inhabitants of Pompeii), was first published in book form in 1954.

He undertook detailed examinations of excavated properties and their inscriptions over a lengthy career, however his work, though extensive, was controversial. His archaeological practice was very hands-on, bringing him into conflict with others whose work was carried out largely in libraries. The inscriptions he unearthed and examined ran into thousands, although he seemed disinclined to share them with his colleagues since he believed himself quite capable of working on his own.

The reliability of his work is now questioned due, in part, to his dedicated intention to assign an owner's name to every excavated Pompeian building. Others working in the field maintained that the necessary scientific evidence to back up his assumptions was often lacking – only one of the sources of conflict.

Post-Della Corte analysis contends, for instance, that the finding of a name such as 'Sabinus' inscribed on a wall, or on an article exhumed from the ruins, is no longer to be considered definitive proof that a 'Sabinus' once owned the property, or even lived there. It can now be as easily interpreted to mean that someone called Sabinus, possibly a slave, might simply have 'made his mark' in the present-day manner of a piece of graffito, with no more serious intention than to show the world that he had once been there.

In any event, it seems questionable that a property owner, particularly one of wealth and status, might have been overcome by the *need* to inscribe his name on a brick. This was surely the behaviour of a common plebeian, or worse, some lowly slave, arguably not of a man – or woman – of distinction.

Koloski-Ostrow and Lyons suggest another possible source of historical misreading:

> *Perhaps the graffiti written on the front walls of the* Amorini dorati [see below], *which proclaim* "Hail Nero!" *and* "Welcome Poppaea!" *were intended to*

> *impress clients and visitors with the prospect of the Imperial couple coming to pay a call, even if they never actually did.*

The same consideration applies; the author of such welcoming inscriptions cannot necessarily be assumed to have been the owner of the property.

Modern historians therefore warn against taking too literally Della Corte's assertions of rightful ownership of Pompeian properties. Nonetheless, he is still considered preeminent in his field, and it is generally accepted that, had he not devotedly carried out such extensive work in the excavations, much valuable information attached to inscriptions on those properties would be lost.[3]

*

Pompeii has been included on the World Monuments Fund's list of one hundred most endangered sites since 1996[4], a reminder, should one be needed, of the continuing vulnerability of the area. This can only add to the ongoing difficulties of establishing beyond question the ownership of Pompeian properties, or any others devastated by earthquake or volcanic eruption.

---

[3] Acknowledgement is due to Ada Gabucci for this valuable information on Della Corte and his work in her 1988 article in the bibliographical *L'Enciclopedia Italiana.*
[4] P W Foss and J J Dobbins (eds), *The World of Pompeii* (2007), Routledge, New York, NY, USA

Scholarship has no doubt advanced considerably since Della Corte's death in 1962. Finds in the ruins of Pompeii and Herculaneum – both buried by the 79 CE eruption of Vesuvius, but otherwise dissimilar – will continue to be uncovered, such is the progressive nature of the archaeological beast, aided by advances in technology. The question of Poppaea's possible ownership of any property in Campania should therefore be approached with caution.

Much has been written about, in particular, the House of Menander and the House of the Gilded Cupids, both very imposing Pompeian properties excavated in the aftermath of the 79 eruption.

House of Menander (Casa del menandro)

As noted earlier, this property was named after the Greek dramatist and poet Menander (c. 342-c. 292 BCE), whose portrait on a wall depicts him reading from what is believed to have been one of his own compositions. Sources suggest that the property was in the process of being renovated when the 79 eruption took place.[5]

Quintus Poppaeus Sabinus is mentioned as a possible owner of the villa at some point (see also Chapter 3). Whether or not a direct connection to Poppaea Sabina herself can be established, it is clear that this was a house

---

[5] See, for example, S C Nappo's *Pompeii* (2004), White Star S.r.l., Vercelli, Italy, which contains many fine colour illustrations.

of distinction, owned by someone of considerable standing.

Excavations around the 1920s-1930s revealed a luxurious villa with sumptuously decorated walls and pavements, as well as priceless furniture and a bronze seal in the servants' quarters inscribed *"Q Poppaei Eros/Erotis"*. The name is suggestive of a freedman of the *gens Poppaea*; some sources suggest a steward of the household (hence his possession of the seal).

In addition, a large hoard of silver plate, more than twenty kilograms in weight and very well preserved, was discovered in the 1930s. This would seem to point to wealth and high status, however the rightful ownership of the Villa, and indeed its contents, remain under discussion. At all events, Foss and Dobbins record extensive refurbishment in the late 1990s, allowing for a description as *". . . perhaps the clearest example of a patrician house in a provincial city of the early empire."*

House of the Gilded Cupids (Casa degli amorini dorati)

Thought to have once belonged to Gnaeus Poppaeus Habitus, a wealthy local figure, this villa was first excavated early in the 20th century. It is named after four gilded glass discs (no longer in place), etched with cupids, that once adorned the walls. The property is exquisitely decorated, and the different period styles are easily recognised.

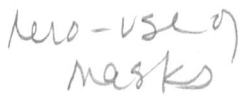

Koloski-Ostrow and Lyons record that intricate theatrical motifs and scenes from drama form part of the decorations of both this property and the one above. These are said to reflect the Neronian influence on properties decorated, or redecorated, in the Imperial period, even if they do not suggest an inarguable connection to Poppaea and Nero.

So publicly insistent was the Emperor on his own artistic and theatrical talents that decorating the homes of prominent citizens to reflect his tastes was almost obligatory. As with his performances, no one would have dared suggest that those tastes were questionable.

Theatrical masks were a dominant feature of Nero's performances and this is reflected in the profusion of them found in this house. Whoever the true owners were, they would have slept easily in the knowledge that the lavish decoration of their *domus* demonstrated their admiration of their emperor. It is unlikely that a family of wealth and standing, who wished to remain so, would ever have seriously considered doing otherwise.

*

The property generally thought most likely to have earned Poppaea the title of 'woman of property' is situated less than ten kilometres from the two described above. It is the Villa Oplontis, sometimes known as Poppaea's Villa.

Villa Oplontis

The origin of the name 'Oplontis' is uncertain. Possibilities include (a) deriving from the Greek *oplon* (hawser), suggesting that Oplontis was Pompeii's former ancient harbour; (b) from the Latin *opulus*, from a tree used to support grapevines; or (c) from the Latin *opulentia*, indicating the sumptousness of local villas.[6]

What seems clear from ancient maps, however, is that Oplontis was originally a seaside town, or perhaps a residential suburb of Pompeii (which was less than five kilometres away), not simply a villa.

The Villa itself is believed to have been first unearthed in the 18th century during construction of the Sarno Canal for the intended provision of a water supply to the present-day town of Torre Annunziata; numerous sources claim that this is the modern name of the ancient 'Oplontis'. In a field of some competition, it is generally held to be one of the best preserved villas in Italy.

Like all properties in the region, the Villa was damaged in the February 62 CE earthquake, and completely buried by the outpourings from the eruption of Vesuvius in the decade following. According to Giubelli, archaeological records indicate that the Villa was covered by both mud (as with Herculaneum) and lapilli and ashes (as with Pompeii). Such a solid mass of

[6] G Giubelli, *Oplontis-The Villa Poppea* (undated), Carcavallo Editore, Napoli, Italy

preservative materials might explain the extraordinarily high quality of the Villa's remains.

Large (c.130 metres x c.110 metres[7]), elegant and richly decorated, this is by any measure an impressive property. The original site dates to the 2nd century BCE, with the initial construction of the Villa believed to be dated c. 50 BCE. It is noteworthy that these dates coincide with those suggested for the Villa di Nerone, in Nero's home town of Antium (modern Anzio).[8]

The Villa Oplontis is for the most part believed to have a more solid connection to Poppaea the Younger herself rather than to the *gens Poppaea* generally. Although a few sources are sceptical, most concede that she was the likely owner.

This is not as surprising as might be thought. Women in ancient Rome, and its environs, enjoyed the right to own property:

> . . . *certain wealthy Roman women of the period* [late Republican/early Imperial], *including Terentia* [wife of Cicero], *Fulvia and Livia . . . are known to have been considerable property owners in their own right.*[9]

---

[7] S De Caro in *Ancient Roman Villa Gardens* (1987), Elisabeth B MacDougall (ed), Harvard University, Cambridge, MA, USA
[8] Annalisa Marzano, *Roman Villas in Central Italy: A Social and Economic History* (2007), Koninklijke Brill NV, Leiden, Netherlands
[9] Annelise Freisenbruch, *The First Ladies of Rome: The Women Behind the Caesars* (2011), Vintage Books, London

Even though these three predate Poppaea, it is clear that the custom of women as property owners was already established before her time. Even lower-status women did not necessarily have to miss out. Freisenbruch continues:

> ... [his mother Agrippina] *was not the only woman to whom Nero had made gifts of property. His freedwoman mistress Acte was the deed-holder of a sizeable amount of real estate in Egypt, Sardinia and Italy, which she could only have acquired through the largesse of the emperor.*

We might therefore discount the possibility that the property was owned by Nero, who permitted Poppaea's occasional use – whether as wife or mistress. Nero's ownership of the villa at Antium is not disputed (though it is thought that Augustus was its first Imperial owner). If the Villa Oplontis was ever acknowledged to have been another of his estates, it would surely be similarly recorded. It is likely, then, that those espousing Nero's ownership are making an assumption: such a grand villa *must* have belonged to an emperor – rather than to his mistress.

How Poppaea came to acquire the property is unclear. De Caro speculates that property inheritance came down to her mother Poppaea the Elder through the *gens Poppaea*, possibly in particular Quintus Poppaeus Sabinus (though he suggests, erroneously, that Sabinus was the elder Poppaea's father). A more logical possibility is inheritance from Gaius Poppaeus Sabinus himself – her rightful father – whose eminent career, bolstered by

Tacitus' sly suggestion of his friendship with emperors, would have given him the means to acquire grand properties. Poppaea's only known sibling, her half-brother Scipio (II) (see Chapter 2) was not in a position to inherit over her because he was not of the *gens Poppaea*.

De Caro connects freedmen named on pottery found there to Scipio (I), as part of Poppaea the Elder's dowry when she married him. An example is "*P. Cornelius Poppaeus Erast(us)*":

> *The name of this person testifies that he or his father was an ex-slave of the Poppaei, adopted by one P. Cornelius: this association is explained by the fact that Poppaea Sabina* mater's *second husband, following her marriage to T. Ollius, was P. Cornelius Lentulus Scipio . . . The slave belonging to the Poppaei, therefore, became the property of P. Cornelius Lentulus as part of his wife's dowry and was freed by him.*

Cooley and Cooley[10] also mention Erastus in describing the sale of a male slave in 63 CE:

> *P. Cornelius Poppaeus Erastus, who is selling the slave, is probably the freedman manager of the clay-pits* (figlinae) [near Pompeii, thought to be owned by Poppaea – see further below].

Given all of this, speculation as to the Villa's ownership strongly suggests that Poppaea may have

---

[10] *Pompeii and Herculaneum: A Sourcebook* (2004), Routledge, Abingdon, UK

inherited through members of the *gens Poppaea*: possibly from her grandfather Gaius Poppaeus Sabinus down to his daughter Poppaea the Elder on his death in 35 CE, and from her down to Poppaea the Younger on *her* death, by suicide, in 47.

De Caro speculates further about the possible involvement of Poppaea's stepfather Scipio (I) in substantially enlarging the Villa's residential (western) areas. He would have been financially better placed than his wife to spend lavishly on the property, which would account for the impressively high standard of decoration, to say nothing of the splendid gardens, swimming pool and sundeck. It might reasonably be assumed that any such works would have predated his wife's suicide – one would certainly hope so.

For the aforementioned doubters of ownership, the possibility must exist that Nero bought the property for Poppaea at some point during their relationship. However as noted, this seems unlikely without it being publicly acknowledged – *cf* Acte above. Poppaea's inheritance through her mother and the *gens Poppaea*, and the possibility of her stepfather's spending on improvements, seems the most probable option, though the timing must remain unconfirmed.

One striking feature of many is the extensive statuary unearthed there, numbering more than forty pieces in the late 1980s. De Caro, writing then, suggested that they were virtually all garden statues rather than those from the Villa's interior. They could therefore be admired, in his words, *"without the pomposity of an exhibition in the* atrium *or a* tablinum *but with the casualness of a walk in the park."* Photographic sources confirm the extensive gardens, and De Caro's use of the term "park" – as opposed to mere gardens – begins to sound closer to the reality.

Wilhelmina Jashemski suggests that the architect of the house was also a *topiarius*, a designer of landscaped gardens: no mere 'gardener' (there may of course have been both).[11] She records the astonishing number of thirteen separate gardens belonging to the Villa. So numerous were they that they required specific individual names, for example "interior garden", "peristyle garden", "sculpture garden" or "courtyard garden" (the latter's walls painted with garden scenes to make the overall area appear bigger).

Excavation of the sculpture garden, by the swimming pool, unearthed ("thus far", in Jashemski's words) an avenue of thirteen trees, each with a statue base in front. If ever time travel were possible, a trip back to the Villa Oplontis in its prime would surely figure high on any architectural wish list.

---

[11] *The Vesuvian Sites Before A.D. 79: The Archaeological, Literary, and Epigraphical Evidence* in *The Natural History of Pompeii* (2002), W F Jashemski and F G Meyer (eds), Cambridge University Press, Cambridge, UK

The size and splendour of the property, both internal and external, is hard to comprehend; it was said to be one of the largest properties in the area, by some considerable margin. The likelihood is that more awaits discovery, making it larger still. Its fortunate visitors, wandering the grounds – it must have taken some time to cover them all – must have marvelled at the profusion of statues of human figures, animals and gods and goddesses carefully, and tastefully, placed throughout. In the wake of Jashemski's fascinating and detailed discoveries, we can only guess at the staggering numbers of workers needed to maintain a property of such size and grandeur.

It is instructive to demarcate the residential (the area Scipio is said to have had enlarged) and service areas of the Villa. The decorations of both are distinctive, and archaeologists seem in no doubt of their differing purposes. A property of this size would have employed vast numbers of slaves, and required large areas specifically designed both for storage and production and slaves' sleeping quarters.

No human bodies were found when the Villa was excavated post-eruption (though it is said that goat bones were exhumed, pointing to their keeping for the purpose of trimming the lawns). However, the finding of substantial quantities of construction materials, as opposed to personal and household belongings, indicates that no one was in residence when the eruption occurred. We can suppose that, like the House of Menander, the

Villa was still in the process of being repaired and rebuilt after the 62 earthquake (or following smaller quakes) before being hit by the 79 eruption.

Giubelli also suggests that restorative work following the earthquake may have been halted on Poppaea's sudden death in 65 (see Chapter 9). Given her status, the tragic news cannot have taken overly long to reach her home location from Rome. The shock, and confusion, that is likely to have affected those slaves and other workers engaged in the repair and reconstruction of their Empress' villa can only be imagined.

By whose authority, though, could tools have been downed and the works discontinued? Someone would have been needed to organise the mourning rituals for Poppaea and her unborn child. Might this have been Polytimus, the loyal steward, in charge of the property in his Empress' absence? (See Chapter 8)

It is hard to believe that, in the territory of the *gens Poppaea*, Poppaea's passing would not have been much mourned. Although Empress of Rome, she was first a daughter of Campania, and inscriptions mentioning her name (see below) attest to her popularity with the local people.

A large nearby property, known as the villa of Lucius Crassius Tertius, was found by chance in the 1970s in the building of a school. The "Oplontis Project", under the auspices of the Center for the Study of Ancient Italy, based in Texas, USA, has designated the two properties Villa A (Poppaea) and Villa B (Tertius).

Both have undergone extensive excavation in the last decade, which is continuing. Villa B may have been devoted to the wine trade, evidenced by the discovery of considerable numbers of amphorae and a great many storage rooms, together with carbonised plant material from vineyards. Unlike its near neighbour, Villa B is confidently assumed to have been a commercial property; tellingly, no gardens have been found there.

By contrast, Poppaea's Villa Oplontis was very much a property designed with *otium* (leisure) and *tranquilitas* (quiet calm) in mind, far from the pressures of politics, business or civil strife. Every aspect of its design and decoration emphasises just those features, no less enviable today than they were then.

*

Domus Aurea

Although unquestionably Nero's project, it seems incongruous not to mention its connection to the 'woman of property'. We have to assume, after all, that Poppaea was intended to share its pleasures alongside him. Nowhere, however, is it described as 'Nero's and Poppaea's *Domus Aurea*'; it seems that it was only ever Nero for whom it was to be made fit for a god.

As the term 'villa' is quite inadequate to describe the Emperor Hadrian's residence at Tivoli, outside Rome (it covers more than two hundred and fifty acres), so 'palace' does not do justice to the *Domus Aurea*, thought to have been of similar size. Neither was simply a collection of grand buildings; parklands, lakes, gardens and vineyards, amongst other delights, contributed to the overall size and splendour of both.

In no sense was the *Domus*, at least, simply a private estate; and as with the Villa Oplontis, workers and artists employed in its construction would have been without number. Lucky was the builder who managed to attach himself and his team to the project for its duration – assuming, of course that his skills were up to such a gargantuan task. The gods must have buckled under the weight of the necessary grateful payoffs.

As noted elsewhere, sources are strangely silent on the level of Poppaea's involvement in the design or construction of the *Domus*, although architect (Severus) and engineer (Celer) receive mention.[12] The painter Fabullus (or Famulus, or Amulius) also receives credit as a major contributor. His swift execution and even touch, all the while supposedly continuing to wear a toga, were essential for the creation of wonderful frescoes, some still surviving.

---

[12] See, for example, W L Macdonald's *The Architecture of the Roman Empire, Vol. 1* (1982), Yale University Press, New Haven, CT, USA

Sceptics might scoff at the possibility of Poppaea's influence on the *Domus* being minimal. While such a claim does seem surprising, the fact that the issue is not mentioned by any of the sources, even in passing, is even more so.

This implied lack of Poppaea's involvement in the *Domus* is more evidence of the contradictory portrayals of her alleged extravagance. Pliny the Elder, for example, seemed intent on emphasising this particular character defect; he was the source for both the five hundred asses supplying Poppaea's bathing milk, and those beasts being shod with gold. (Others suggest that it was her favourite horse who received this honour; are we to believe five hundred shiny-footed beasts, or one?) It is difficult to regard claims of this nature as worthy of serious consideration, or to understand why a naturalist such as Pliny should find them of interest or concern.

Pliny was clearly keen to condemn the rampant levels of profligacy and over-indulgence that he believed had ruled Rome for too long. However, his own 'estate' (which fell to his adopted nephew Pliny the Younger on his death in 79, since he did not marry or produce children) comprised, at the very least, properties in Rome, Comum (modern Como) and Misenum, on the Campanian coast. Ownership of this impressive collection does not suggest that he himself was obliged to live in a shed. One wonders where the line was drawn between abstemiousness and extravagance in his personal lexicon.

Had Poppaea been as profligate as is consistently portrayed, this would surely have surfaced in the repeated mentions of the incredible cost of the *Domus Aurea*. Gold, ivory, marble, mother-of-pearl and semi-precious stones are all cited as materials used in its decoration. It is as if we are to imagine newly plastered walls covered with the combined weight in jewels of its owners, with no thought given to the number of starving plebeians outside them.

However, this lack of mention of Poppaea in any connection with the proposed new Imperial playground is curious. For a woman who allegedly held her husband in the palm of her hand, we might wonder where she was while all this money was being spent (and if any of it was hers. . .). Are we to envisage Nero spending every waking moment closeted with architect and engineer, while Poppaea wandered the half-finished corridors, wondering if she was ever to be asked for her opinion? It is tempting to wonder whether the level of her enthusiasm matched his; however since she is never mentioned as co-designer, or even mildly curious onlooker, this cannot be claimed with any certainty.

Nonetheless, the *Domus Aurea* – and part of its forerunner, the *Domus Transitoria* – existed for almost the entirety of Poppaea's relationship with Nero: from c. 60 CE (when the *Transitoria* is thought to have been built) until her death, five years later. Both were spectacular in design and decoration, and both influenced architecture for centuries following.

As with much of her life, it is to be regretted that we cannot know how much influence, if any, she had over them, what consideration she might have given to the expenditure involved, or even whether she liked them.

*

An intriguing image, which appears from time to time in historical records, is that of Poppaea as Businesswoman. A number of sources seem convinced that she was the owner of a brick- or pottery works (*figlina*) in the vicinity of Pompeii. These include:

Miriam Griffin:

> . . . *a wax tablet found at Herculaneum refers to brick works in the territory of Pompeii owned by the Empress herself* . . .

Elizabeth Meyer[13], quoting part of the inscription mentioned earlier concerning the sale of a male slave:

> *Done on the Pompeian estate in the Arrian pottery of Poppaea Aug(usta) on the eighth day before the Ides of May when C. Memmius Regulus and L. Verginius Rufus were consuls.* [i.e. 63 CE]

For reasons not immediately apparent, women were actively involved in the production of bricks:

---

[13] *Legitimacy and Law in the Roman World: Tabulae in Roman Belief and Practice* (2004), Cambridge University Press, Cambridge, UK

> . . . *the example of the activity of females in brick and tile production shows that there were sectors* [of the workforce] *where the proportions of men and women could be almost equal.*[14]

Records suggest that women often inherited these businesses from their fathers. Eumachia, daughter of Lucius Eumachius (see Chapter 8), owed her wealth, in part, to the yards her father owned (the rest is thought to have come from a wealthy husband who predeceased her).

As suggested by De Caro, this points once more to the *gens Poppaea* as a possible source of inherited property passing down to Poppaea through her mother, though again we are without definitive proof.

While Romans cannot perhaps lay undisputed claim to the invention of bricks, it must be acknowledged that building materials in use today benefit greatly from their mammoth contribution. Furthermore, stamps habitually engraved onto Roman bricks provide archaeologists and historians with precious information: not only of the owner/resident, but also the dating of the buildings made from them.

Inscriptions were not of course confined to bricks. Pompeii, in particular, is a rich source of messages of all

---

[14] P Berdowski, *Some Remarks on the Economic Activity of Women in the Roman Empire: A Research Problem* (2007), University of Rzeszów Faculty of Ancient History and Oriental Studies, Rzeszów, Poland

kinds left for posterity by her citizens (see also Appendix II). They range from declarations of loyalty to the Emperor and Empress to, as mentioned earlier, proclamations from slaves that they were, possibly for better or worse, a part of that household, and wanted to say so. Others see prostitutes advertising their services, alongside politically minded citizens encouraging others to vote for a particular candidate. Lovers declare their amorous intentions to their beloveds, and mothers encourage votes for their sons. We can hardly wonder at Della Corte's fascination with the field, and that he spent so many years dedicated to it. It is a source of continuing fascination that cities buried for so long can provide such a rich vein of information about those who lived, and died, there.

It is noteworthy that in the innumerable dedications to Emperor Nero – and to his Empress – found in inscriptions in the region, there are none that could be described as negative.[15] While Romans decried and condemned Nero's outrageous behaviour, the citizens of Campania openly declared their allegiance, though sometimes remaining anonymous:

> *Three cheers for imperial decrees; three cheers for the decisions of the Emperor and the Empress. Long live Empress Poppaea.*[16]

---

[15] Rebecca R Benefiel, *Rome in Pompeii: Wall Inscriptions and GIS* in *Latin on Stone: Epigraphic Research and Electronic Archives* (2010), ed. Francisca Feraudi-Gruénais, Lexington Books, Lanham, MD, USA
[16] Quoted in *Heinemann Ancient and Medieval History: Pompeii and Herculaneum* (2005), Louise Zarmati, Pearson Education Australia

> *Good fortune to the judgements of Augustus, father of his*
> *country, and to Poppaea Augusta.*[17]

We might be forgiven for assuming that 'Augustus' here must mean the original one, Octavian; Nero's good judgement – in any respect – is not something that sources are generally at pains to record.

It is also a mark of Campanians' affection for their former daughter that Poppaea did not even have to be present to earn such acclamation. As noted at Chapter 8, when Nero is said to have visited Pompeii in 64 – albeit two years after its earthquake – she was not thought to have been with him. The reason is unknown, though it could have been connected to her health in her second pregnancy.

The name 'Sabinus' is common in inscriptions on both dwellings and commercial establishments in Pompeii. Della Corte would have had these belonging to Poppaea's extended family; others in the field would take care to point out that they could have been inscribed by household slaves who had taken the name of their owners, as already mentioned – in other words 'employees' rather than 'owners'. Even inscriptions thought to have been left by those slaves or freedmen or freedwomen, though, give an indication of the potential numbers who could read and write: they are more than might be supposed,

---

[17] Quoted in *Pompeii and Herculaneum: A Sourcebook* (2004), Cooley and Cooley, *op cit*

although of course the illiterate could have used scribes to mark their messages for them.

Though not for the same reasons, Poppaea as a woman of property made as long-lasting a mark on the records of antiquity as her character with all its alleged defects. These fragments of information about, for instance, the Villa Oplontis allow us tantalising glimpses of how women of rank lived in the Imperial era, outside Rome.

We know by now that relatively little is known about Poppaea herself. However, it is gratifying that the body of work on the lives of women in antiquity is growing. Almost *any* detail of those lives hitherto close to invisible is to be treasured. Still, the foregoing illustrates that much is still unknown.

Ongoing excavations that allow us to build on those pictures of Imperial life as it pertained to other high-status women will continue to generate both interest and excitement. They might be saying 'If you want to know about us, this is how we lived.'

CHAPTER 7

Marriage: "I am Gaia"[1]

Marriage for Roman women of high status was more than an expectation. From the time of the onset of the principate in 27 BCE, it was nearer to a royal command.

The Emperor Augustus enacted stringent laws in 18-17 BCE governing celibacy, marriage, intermarriage between classes, adultery, and the production of children. Known as the *lex Iulia*, this was moral legislation thinly disguised.

That he himself was far from a moral ideal – having divorced his second wife Scribonia within days[2] of their daughter's birth – did not, apparently, prevent him from laying down the law for the rest of Rome. Transgressors could be harshly punished, as Augustus did even against that same daughter, Julia (see Chapter 5). No one, particularly not wayward daughters, argued with the *Princeps*.

---

[1] Part of a woman's pledge at an ancient Roman marriage ceremony
[2] Cassius Dio (*Roman History*, Book 48.34.3) wrote that it was the day after – he was clearly not a fan.

Although the ceremony itself was brief, marriage brought significant life changes for daughters of high-ranking families. It drew a clear line under childhood at an age when girls might still have been playing childhood games (marriage required the ritual putting away of toys), their bodies not yet finished growing. A daughter was passed out from under the legal 'ownership' of her father's house to that of her husband.

Finally, it was a decision taken by parents, usually the father, with the intended bride's feelings towards the other party being of no account; no Roman élite married for love – or presumably died of it either. Prospective husbands were judged on such important criteria as rank, political and financial status, and any resulting advantages for the bride's family. A daughter could refuse a candidate only if he could be shown to be morally objectionable.

As already noted, Poppaea was around thirteen years of age at her first marriage, in 44 CE. It seems likely that her stepfather, the aristocratic Scipio, brought to bear his influence over the choice of husband who, unknown to all concerned, would be the first of three.

*

(i)   *Rufrius Crispinus* (?-66 CE)

Poppaea's first husband was a Knight of the *ordo equester* (order of knights). An esteemed élite, they were seen as "... *nonpolitical member*[s] *of the privileged class*". (*Encyclopaedia Britannica*) While a considerable sum was required to qualify for the *ordo*, it was less than half that required of a senator. Despite this disparity, which made clear his 'middling' status, Crispinus would have been seen by both mother and stepfather as a good match for the young Poppaea.

Nothing is known of Crispinus' origins or early life, including his date of birth or the source of his wealth. Ancient tradition often saw sons following fathers into a military career, but lacking information on his family background, we cannot know if this was the case for him.

The satirist Juvenal wrote of a Crispinus in withering terms, claiming that his origins were Egyptian; Juvenal held all things eastern in contempt and exercised no restraint in saying so. However, the 'Egyptian fish-merchant' (clearly tantamount to a term of abuse) of whom he wrote was connected to the much later court of the Emperor Domitian – obviously the wrong one.

Writing on Juvenal, Barry Baldwin mentions Crispinus as "... *a man* fated [emphasis added] *to be the first husband of Poppaea* ...".[3] He does not elaborate on this, and no further mention is made of her throughout the entire text, surprising after such a loaded comment. It is

---

[3] *Juvenal's Crispinus* in *Acta Classica* (1979), University of Calgary, Calgary, AB, Canada

not easy to see it as a positive reference to her, but at least it was the right Crispinus.

At all events, Crispinus' career seems not to have suffered. Along with Lucius Lusius Geta, he was appointed co-Prefect of the Emperor Claudius' Praetorian Guard, possibly in 43, before his marriage to Poppaea. Prefects were the commanders of the Guard, as high as an *eques* (equestrian) could go. Such a creditable leap in Crispinus' career can only have enhanced his prospects in marrying the daughter of a distinguished woman of rank and the stepdaughter of a patrician senator.

On the face of it, this promotion was unlikely to have been bestowed on a nonentity from the ranks. The possibility must exist that the appointment of either Crispinus or Geta, or both, stemmed from recent events: either the assassination of Claudius' predecessor Caligula by his guards in January 41 (though no sources name either as a co-conspirator); or their support of the Empress Messallina and Britannicus, her son with Claudius, born in February 41, within weeks of Claudius' elevation to Emperor. If the latter, Crispinus had unwittingly set himself up for a fall.

Sandra Bingham suggests that Prefects were likely to have been quartered in the Imperial palace rather than the *Castra Praetoria*, the barracks north-east of the city, in readiness to receive the Emperor's orders.[4] Modern excavations of the barracks site confirm this, since thus far housing for Prefects is not indicated.

Unconfirmed estimates of Crispinus' age from what is known of his career indicate a birth date of c.10 CE – some 20 years before Poppaea; this would have had him born under the reign of the Emperor Augustus. Both Tacitus (*Annals*, VIII.44) and Suetonius (*Lives of the Caesars*, Otho [1]-[3]) suggest that among the attractions for Poppaea of Marcus Salvius Otho (see (ii) below) were his 'youthfulness', 'extravagance' and general fashionable aspect; he was also of similar age to her. Crispinus the military careerist, however, was unlikely to have possessed such traits, supporting a lengthier age gap between the two, common among Romans of high rank.

Bingham notes that recruits normally entered the Guard between eighteen and twenty, and were required to be "... *men of free birth and Roman citizens*". Marriage was officially restricted (though not for those of equestrian rank[5]), however 'unofficial' marriages were apparently

[4] *The Praetorian Guard: A History of Rome's Elite Special Forces* (2013), I B Tauris & Co Ltd, London
[5] W Scheidel, *Marriage, Families, and Survival: Demographic Aspects* in *A Companion to the Roman Army* (2011), P Erdkamp (ed), Blackwell Publishing Ltd (John Wiley & Sons), Oxford, UK

allowed. Sara E Phang suggests that Praetorians married after completing their 16-year term.[6]

Scheidel further states: "*In AD 44, Claudius granted soldiers the conventional legal privileges that Augustus had reserved for married citizens.*" These concerned such matters as dowries and inheritance rights for both wives and children should a soldier die intestate. We do not know whether or not this change of rules affected Crispinus, and ultimately Poppaea, although their marriage in the same year is a striking coincidence. Phang notes further that Claudius' intention was unclear, though his gratitude was a likely factor – see below.

Furthermore, Praetorians' service could sometimes be considerably longer than sixteen years[7], which cannot always have been popular with them, even though extensions might have followed creditable promotions.

This may well have been the case for Crispinus. An estimated career path, accepting his approximate birth date as above, would have him joining the Guard in c. 28 CE, serving sixteen years, and marrying Poppaea close upon release, that is in 44. However this is at odds with his earlier elevation to co-Prefect around 43, and his dismissal by Agrippina in 51 (see below); it makes his service term some twenty-three years. No source appears

---

[6] *The Marriage of Roman Soldiers 13 BC–AD 235* (2001), Brill Academic Publishers, Leiden, Netherlands

[7] See R Cowan, *Roman Guardsman 62 BC-AD 324* (2014), Osprey Publishing Ltd, Oxford, UK

to find him sufficiently interesting or noteworthy to clarify the matter. Indeed, the facet of Crispinus' character most often mentioned by the sources is his loyalty to Messallina and her son Britannicus.

Appointment of the Guard's Prefects did not necessarily rely on military skills, as might be supposed. Of greater importance were the primary requirements of closeness and loyalty to their Emperor. Bingham notes that an emperor required trustworthiness beyond question:

> ... *for the greatest danger he could potentially encounter would come from the armed men who had sworn to protect him.*

The appointment of Crispinus can thus be taken to demonstrate a significant degree of trust on the part of his Emperor, though what might have inspired that trust is less clear. Moreover, Claudius perceived himself to be heavily indebted to the Guard for his elevation to Emperor. His reign was therefore marked by generous rewards to them, from which Crispinus was to benefit.

In around 47 CE the Imperial court was enmeshed in drama and intrigue centred around one Decimus Valerius Asiaticus: enormously wealthy, cultivated, and twice appointed consul. Claudius, said to be constantly in terror of potential plots against him, was convinced by courtiers, possibly under Messallina's influence, of Asiaticus' potential for political troublemaking. He was suspected of having had a minor role in the assassination of Caligula, whom he disliked. (Asiaticus is famously said to have denied involvement in the assassination, but that he wished he had been: no doubt a heartfelt comment, but a most unwise one.)

Messallina had her own reasons for wanting Asiaticus gone. She believed that he was a former lover of Poppaea Sabina the Elder; allied to that was a belief that the elder Poppaea had been involved with Mnester, an actor and supposedly one of her court favourites. Finally, Messallina was said to have coveted the luxurious pleasure gardens of Lucullus which Asiaticus had acquired (see Chapter 4 on this point). A hefty dose of salt is needed to give any weight to such a bizarre and convoluted story.

Messallina set out to remedy matters, using her henchman Suillius effectively as Imperial bully. An extraordinary string of charges was brought against Asiaticus *in absentia* (he was holidaying in Campania). Crispinus was sent south to bring him back with enough troops, in Tacitus' opinion, to quell the heaviest opposition. After a mock trial – he was not permitted a formal one – Asiaticus was found guilty. Having been offered the opportunity to commit suicide as an alternative to execution, he duly complied.

Tragically, Poppaea's mother was the other victim in this drama. Terrified beyond endurance by Messallina's henchmen, her suicide followed. Messallina had succeeded in destroying her supposed rival.

According to Tacitus, Claudius was unaware of this incident of collateral damage. On asking Poppaea the Elder's husband Scipio why she was not present at a dinner held a short time after, he was told that her death prevented it.

However Claudius' apparently innocent query was later to prove suspect. He was noted as having been similarly *laissez-faire* about the circumstances of his own wife Messallina's death[8] a year later, when it was reported to him while he dined. Both incidents suggest a disingenuous distancing of himself from unpalatable events to which he had clear connection, and an impressive level of denial.

Crispinus was awarded the astounding sum of one and a half million sestertii[9], and a prestigious promotion, to reward a job well done in delivering up Asiaticus to face trial. In considering the lone target, the trumped-up charges against him, and the suggested size of Crispinus' accompanying troops, the entire operation seems, to say

---

[8] Courtiers fought hard to convince Claudius that her outrageous behaviour deserved her being put to death. Claudius' famous dithering and inconsistency seemingly smoothed the way.

[9] Virtually impossible to value with any degree of accuracy. One estimate makes one gold coin worth 100 sestertii; another that a family of four could live on 400 sestertii for a year; yet another that a day's pay for a labourer was 1.25 sestertii, with a year's pay for a legionary thought to have been 900. By any calculation it was a staggering amount of money.

the least, disproportionate. Bingham suggests that the reward was undeniably excessive for something so straightforward as a single arrest.

Steven H Rutledge agrees that such a sizeable award for doing so little would have been uncommon. Examining the reasoning behind it, he suggests that a contributory factor was Suillius' elimination of two brothers named Petra.[10]

Tacitus reports that *"The cause of their death was really that they had provided their house as a meeting place for Mnester and* [the elder] *Poppaea* [to conduct their alleged affair]." Even given the Romans' propensity for swift reprisals based on flimsy evidence, such a punishment seems particularly severe.

Rutledge questions Tacitus' recording: *". . . it is far from clear for what Crispinus was rewarded."* He continues: *". . . it is more likely that he* [Crispinus] *was simply involved in some capacity with Suillius in the Petrae's prosecution and remunerated accordingly."*

Whatever the reasons for it, the Emperor's hand must be suspected in such an exceptional display of generosity. That hand may well have been guided by Messallina, who would doubtless have had in mind the loyalty of both co-Prefects to her and her son.

---

[10] *Imperial Inquisitions: Prosecutors and Informants from Tiberius to Domitian* (2001), Routledge, London

Crispinus' finances must now have looked rosy indeed. Poppaea would become similarly wealthy alongside him, but at the cost of her mother's life; can she have thought it worth the loss? Aged seventeen, she now had only her husband of three years and her stepfather to protect her interests.

Whether Crispinus was any support to her in all of this cannot be known. His was a tricky position: Poppaea the Elder, Messallina's second target, was of course his mother-in-law, married to a high-born senator of no small consequence. However ultimately his loyalty would have been to his Emperor, not to his own wife – or her mother.

Lightman and Lightman[11] make a series of theatrical accusations concerning Poppaea's behaviour and motives following her mother's death. Clearly her plight, lacking now both mother and father, and aged less than twenty, warrants no sympathy.

They claim that she ". . . *avenged her* [mother's] *downfall at the hands of Valeria Messallina.*" The meaning here is unclear, aside from the implied addition of 'vengeful' to the list of Poppaea's defects. In what way did the daughter, aged seventeen, avenge the mother's downfall? They do not say.

Crispinus is ". . . *the man who had accused her mother of adultery* . . . ". Though a supporting player, it is a simple

---

[11] *A to Z of Ancient Greek and Roman Women* (2008), Infobase Publishing, New York, NY, USA

matter to establish that Crispinus' status hardly allowed him the role of sole accuser of a charge of adultery against the wife of a patrician senator. Indeed we might wonder at the effect on his relationship with the woman who was his mother-in-law had he done so. Furthermore, Bingham disputes the centrality of his role: *". . . there is no evidence that the prefect actually took part in the proceedings."*

The authors go on to accuse Poppaea of making a fool of her husband Crispinus, but with no elucidation. If it is meant that she allegedly had an affair with Marcus Salvius Otho (see (ii) below) while still married to Crispinus, then Rome was awash with fools – almost to the exclusion of all else – such was the rumoured incidence of extramarital activity within high-ranking society (though sources are not in general agreement on this[12]). Poppaea's character is summarised thus:

> *She has been accused of duplicity, promiscuity, and* sundry other vile acts [emphasis added] *as she moved through two marriages prior to her marriage with the emperor . . .*

The "vile acts" are not explained, nor is any attempt made to clarify or justify the allegations against her.

These salacious 'facts' are indicative of the tenor of the common portrayal of Poppaea the Younger, with high drama accentuated and evidence lacking throughout. In

---

[12] See, for example, Catharine Edwards' *The Politics of Immorality in Ancient Rome* (1993), Cambridge University Press, Cambridge, UK

considering again the issue of historians and education, students of ancient Rome require some discernment to recognise this pejorative material for what it is: more redolent of a frivolous blog than a document purporting to be an encyclopaedia of classical history. No reader benefits from melodramatic and speculative criticism offered as fact.

Following Messallina's death in 48 CE, Claudius' niece Agrippina the Younger became his fourth wife the following year, a change in the law being necessary since the marriage was otherwise considered incestuous.

Crispinus' career must have felt relatively safe – by Roman standards – in Messallina's hands due to his ongoing loyalty to her and her son. However the ground shifted on Claudius' marriage to Agrippina, and Crispinus was to fall victim to her political manoeuvrings within two years.

In 51 Agrippina engineered his dismissal as co-Prefect of the Praetorian Guard with the spurious notion of the Guard being more effectively controlled by one man – hers – than two. Claudius seemed convinced; so Geta and Crispinus went, and Sextus Afranius Burrus[13] came in.

Miriam Griffin[14] records:

---

[13] He went on to become one of Nero's tutors/advisers, along with the philosopher Seneca.
[14] *Nero-The End of a Dynasty* (1984), B T Batsford Ltd, London

> *Lusius Geta was elevated to the post of Prefect of Egypt and Crispinus was consoled with consular insignia.*

Crispinus' feelings on these blatantly political events go unrecorded. Though he had served his emperor(s) loyally, as far as is known, for more than twenty years, no record shows the next step, if there was one, in his career. However a footnote to Tacitus' *Annals* suggests that at some point he was elevated to the equivalent of 'senatorial rank' (not the same as 'senator') by virtue of his property, that is wealth, qualification – boosted by Claudius' extraordinary payment for his role in the Asiaticus affair.

Poppaea and Crispinus went on to produce their only child, named after his father. Young Rufrius Crispinus is not often mentioned in the historical record, even with such an infamous mother, so that most of his short life is shrouded in mystery. Though it might be assumed that, married at thirteen or fourteen, Poppaea would have given birth to him well before she was twenty, other factors call this into question.

His birth date can be estimated by working back from a possible date of death, 66 CE, mentioned by several sources.[15] The suggestion by Griffin that he may not have reached puberty at his death is helpful. If he died aged ten or eleven, he would have been born c. 55 – a decade after his parents married.

---

[15] For example V Rudich, *Political Dissidence under Nero: The Price of Dissimulation* (1993), Routledge, Oxford, UK; J Malitz, *Nero* (2005), Blackwell Publishing Ltd, Oxford, UK; Griffin, *Nero, op cit*

Given the considerable legal and social pressure on high-ranking daughters to marry and reproduce, and the early age at which they were obliged to start, the birth of only one child in a decade is surprising. It suggests the possibility of Poppaea having suffered stillbirths and/or miscarriages before her son was finally born.

The same reasoning might also apply to Poppaea herself having apparently been an only child. Another possible example was Nero, born nine years after his mother Agrippina married Ahenobarbus (see (iii) below).

This would suggest that miscarriages and/or stillbirths may have been common, but gone unrecorded. Babies were of relatively little account until they could be seen to survive; the likelihood of early death was too great.

Other explanations could apply:

• The marriage might have been an unhappy one, with conjugal relations kept to a minimum. In addition, Scheidel suggests that up to three-quarters of the average 25-year military career might be spent on active duty, possibly outside Rome. If soldiers at Prefect level were not quartered in the *Castra Praetoria*, it is not clear where the couple *would* have lived in the perhaps brief periods when Crispinus was not elsewhere on active duty.

- Poppaea may have been knowledgeable about contraception, which was certainly familiar to ancient Egyptians and Greeks. Pliny the Elder, a whizz at natural history and all things scientific (but see also the previous chapter) would doubtless have been familiar with the herb *silphium*, a member of the fennel family, used in contraception and abortion. Did Poppaea know of it too?

- Her enthusiasm for repeated attempts at pregnancy might understandably have been curbed if she *had* suffered stillbirths or miscarriages.

Intriguingly we know nothing of Poppaea's life with Crispinus, in a marriage of some twelve-plus years. (Were they such an uninteresting couple?) We might wonder if sojourns at the Villa Oplontis south of Rome would have been an enjoyable part of it, at least for her and, eventually, their son.

With *equites* (members of the *ordo equester*) spending lengthy intervals away in the course of their duties, Poppaea is likely to have spent long periods left to her own devices. How did she spend her time? Was it in educating herself (see Chapter 3)? Or attending parties? Or giving them? If the latter, Crispinus' attendance would have been required, since women customarily invited female guests to their homes on social occasions, and men invited men. She had her mother only for the first three years of marriage before the latter's suicide, not long to learn the habits of a respectable *matrona*. Tacitus, always disdainful of Poppaea's character, would have scoffed at the image of her days being spent spinning and weaving.

It seems that Poppaea and Crispinus divorced – at whose instigation is rather less clear – in order to advance Nero's cause with her (though see *Marcus Salvius Otho* (ii) below). In 58, the generally agreed start of the Nero/Poppaea affair, she was about twenty-seven, and had been married to Crispinus for more than a decade. The actual divorce date, however, can only be estimated from the timing of surrounding events.

It should be borne in mind that children belonged to their father under Roman law; it was therefore customary for them to live in the paternal house following divorce. No records indicate how such laws applied to the young Crispinus, a small child when his parents parted.

We can only speculate about whether the child's father had been in a position to protect him after the death of his mother in 65 (see Chapter 9), though his father went on to die only a year later. In whose care had the boy been placed? How much time had he spent with either parent, and where? Might any of the statues of young boys found in the vicinity of the Villa Oplontis conceivably have been of him? While we know little of his young life, it was clearly a damaged one, and in that, cruelly, it mirrored that of his mother Poppaea.

Increasingly fearful and distrustful of those around him following Poppaea's death the year before, Nero is said to have brought about the boy's death in 66 by having him drowned. Rudich posits that, rightly or wrongly, Nero perhaps perceived the child to be some kind of potential threat to his position; he therefore had to go. (See Appendix I for an alternative theory concerning this 'threat'.)

Some sources, Suetonius among them, suggest that Nero was warned about the risk inherent in the child's enjoyment of playing at being general and emperor – not unusually, one would have thought, for a young boy with a soldier for a father, and living on the fringes of Imperial circles. Reflecting on Nero's character, both possibilities seem somewhat spurious, although the overactive imagination of the sources can never be discounted.

We are reminded of Caesarion, the young son of Cleopatra and Caesar, whose unfortunate circumstances seem remarkably like those of young Crispinus, and for similar reasons. He was seen as a potential threat to Octavian's (later Augustus) position, since his parentage provided the direct blood link to Caesar that Octavian did not have. Like young Crispinus, Caesarion's death followed that of his detested mother.

The possibility is suggested, perhaps unsurprisingly given Nero's Hellenism and artistic bent, that young Crispinus' fate mirrors that of Palamedes, son of Nauplius, of Greek myth: both were said to have been deliberately drowned while out fishing. Nero supposedly sang at the theatre of Nauplius' 'misfortune' in killing his son by drowning.

R M Frazer Jr claims that all three ancient sources, Cassius Dio, Tacitus and Suetonius, believed Nero to have been guilty of contriving to dramatise his crimes.[16] He suggests that the same scenario might apply to Nero and his stepson, with the attempt at its heart to 'justify the unjustifiable', behaviour that certainly resounds with Nero's known self-deluding character.

Aside from any possible theatrical resonance, the death of Crispinus (II) is poignant indeed. By 66 his mother was already dead at the hand of his stepfather Nero and in dramatic circumstances, whatever the truth of the matter. (No source tells us how, or from whom, he might have learned of her death; any imagined scene of the telling is heart-rending.) We have no hint of where he was living at the time of his drowning, or where it took place; it is distressing to think that it was in the sea at Campania, a place where, like both mother and stepfather, he would have felt safe. The Imperial palace at Antium, though, suggests itself. Nero's whereabouts when the alleged drowning occurred are unknown.

In 65, Crispinus (I) had been exiled to Sardinia, a common place of banishment, by the Emperor's order. The

---

[16] *Nero the Artist-Criminal* in *The Classical Journal* (Classical Association of the Middle West and South), Vol. 62 (1966), Monmouth, IL, USA

ostensible reason was his suspected participation in the Pisonian conspiracy.

*

This was an unsuccessful coup against Nero led by senator Gaius Calpurnius Piso. Executions and exiles followed, one of which latter victims was said to be Rufrius Crispinus.

No source mentions Poppaea being aware that Crispinus was among those exiled. Whether or not he was actually guilty of co-plotting with the rest is a matter for conjecture; the evidence seems thin.

However the focus of Nero's dislike of him was said to have been closer to home. Nero's character easily suggests an inability to tolerate a man of lowly rank – when compared, that is, to an emperor – who had possessed his beloved Poppaea before he did. (See Appendix I for further discussion of Nero and Crispinus.)

The timing of the surrounding events is uncertain. Piso's plot was thought to have been exposed on 19 April 65; recriminations would have followed soon after. However, exactly when Crispinus was banished is not known. No source names him as being among the major conspirators, which would point towards his exile following later rather than sooner; the main culprits would surely have been the first to be despatched.

Sources write of a 'second wave' of persecutions of suspected conspirators in 66. That Crispinus was still alive then, a year after his exile, further makes it doubtful that he was a major player.

It seems likely that Poppaea was alive at Crispinus' banishment; she may well have had a hand in the lesser fate of exile. However the order for his execution seems to have followed her death. If so, it was an act of abject cowardice on the part of Nero, though we might be forgiven for suspecting the hand of co-Prefect Tigellinus, Nero's Imperial exterminator, at work (see Chapter 9 for his role in events).

Having learned in Sardinia that his banishment was now an order for execution, Crispinus is said to have committed suicide in order to pre-empt it.

We do not know the identity of the messenger bringing the news of Nero's final order for execution, though sadly it is likely to have been a member of the Praetorian Guard, of which Crispinus had once been co-Prefect. Likewise it is not known if he was buried in Sardinia, or his body brought back to Rome; nor is it recorded who was witness to his suicide. No details are known of his burial. By custom, soldiers formerly under his command were likely to have ensured him a respectable grave, but records do not reveal who among them even knew of his distant death.

*

As noted, evidence of Crispinus' part in the conspiracy is scant. Aside from Nero's jealousy, however, a further possible reason for banishment existed. Was this Nero's belated punishment for Crispinus' earlier support of Messallina (along with his co-Prefect Geta), and by default the popular young Britannicus, her son and Nero's competition as future emperor? If so, Nero's resentment of Crispinus would have been smouldering for well over a decade.

Though it is to be hoped that young Crispinus (II) did not hear of his father's cruel fate, it is thought that the order for his drowning followed on from it – Nero at his most heartless. In his manic state, and with the political clouds gathering, he gave the appearance of 'clearing the decks'; his vengeance was frightening. One matter seems clear: if the story of the child's drowning is true, Nero would never have had the courage to carry out this deplorable act while Poppaea was still alive.

As with the deaths of Sejanus and Poppaea's father Ollius, closely connected and dying in the same year of 31 CE, effectively at the hand of the Emperor Tiberius, the year of 66 had its own similarly shocking outcomes. Both Rufrius Crispinus (I) and (II) were to die at the hand of Nero, now in the throes of advanced paranoia and out of control. Poppaea was the former wife of one, the mother of the other. Did Nero think of her as he gave the orders for their deaths?

*

(ii)   *Marcus Salvius Otho* (32-69 CE)

Otho was born near Viterbo, north of Rome in present-day Lazio. His mother, Albia Terentia, was from a distinguished family, and Otho was her second son.

His father was Lucius Otho, whose own father Marcus Salvius Otho was claimed by Suetonius to have grown up in the household of Livia Augusta. He further claimed that, through Livia's influence (the reasons for which are unclear), the elder Otho became a senator, though not rising any higher than a praetorship (senior magistracy).[17] More important than Livia's influence, though, would have been the one million sestertii that would-be senators needed to qualify.

Still more surprising was the rumoured suggestion that Tiberius was Lucius' father, so close was their relationship and the physical resemblance between them.

Speculation is hard to resist. Did Livia *know* that her son was said to be Lucius' father? (It is difficult to believe that there was much going on that Livia did *not* know.) If so, those rumoured family ties would be stronger than even the gossip-prone Suetonius was suggesting. And how much of all of this was known to the young Otho? The implications for him of Tiberius being his grandfather would have been monumental. Remarkably, though, sources appear to skate over them.

---

[17] *Lives of the Caesars* – Otho [1], Oxford University Press, UK (trans. Catharine Edwards, 2000)

Aside from the above, Otho's personal contribution to the Imperial landscape is rife with gossip and speculation, due largely to his close association with Nero in their youth. Common portrayals of them are fairly unflattering: a pair of profligates cutting a swathe through the streets of Rome.

Otho's own youthful reputation was unedifying, according to the best-known sources:

Suetonius (*Lives of the Caesars*):

> *From his earliest youth he was extravagant and wild to such a degree that his father often beat him with a thong* [a punishment usually inflicted on slaves].

Tacitus (*Histories*):

> *Otho had led an irresponsible boyhood and a dissolute youth, and endeared himself to Nero by aping his sybaritism.*

Tacitus (*Annals*):

> *. . . Marcus Salvius Otho, an extravagant youth who was regarded as peculiarly close to Nero.*

Cassius Dio:

> *. . . a certain Marcus Salvius Otho . . . had become so intimate with Nero through the similarity of their character and their companionship in crime . . .*

Plutarch:

> *Marcus Otho, now, was a man of good lineage, but from*
> *his very childhood corrupted by luxury and the pursuit of*
> *pleasure as few Romans were . . . because of Otho's*
> *prodigality Nero made an intimate friend of him.*

What gave shape to such reckless behaviour in his early years is nowhere clarified; why was he "corrupted by luxury and the pursuit of pleasure"? No hint is forthcoming of what might have spawned such degenerate behaviour. Nonetheless, such was Otho's youth: a series of dissipated escapades in the company of Nero, marked by outrageous and licentious conduct.

Of all the recorded 'facts' concerning Otho's later life, one stands out as questionable: his 'marriage' to Poppaea, variously described as 'sham', 'fake', 'ruse' (*nuptiarum specie*). But in the innumerable references to it in the sources, no marriage date, even an approximate one, is given. Why is this? Otho was, after all, much the more high profile of Poppaea's first two relationships, becoming Emperor in 69 CE, albeit briefly. Her first marriage, to Crispinus, could be dated (at 44 CE), but Otho's apparently not.

Could this be because this 'marriage' never actually took place? Was it simply a story officially circulated in order to embellish the dramatised narrative of Nero's intense desire to end up with Poppaea?

Molly Pryzwansky questions the recording of the Nero-Otho-Poppaea interaction: ". . . *the accounts*

[Plutarch, Suetonius, Tacitus' *Histories* and *Annals*, Cassius Dio] *differ over how "real" Otho's and Poppaea's marriage was."*[18] She offers a scenario for this dubious marriage that is quite plausible:

> *Otho, a close friend of Nero, was supposed to keep Poppaea near the emperor, but far away from Agrippina, who disliked her son's mistress: the implication . . . is that if Agrippina believed Poppaea to be Otho's wife, she would not take action against her.*

If this claim has any foundation, then what better way to protect Poppaea from Agrippina's wrath than to put it about that she was married to Otho? Even such a determined force as Agrippina might have paused before acting against the wife of a close friend of her son's, whatever she thought of any of them.

But all did not go according to plan – *anyone's* plan. Otho is said to have fallen in love with Poppaea himself, refusing to countenance even Nero as a rival, and refusing to give her back. This extraordinary tale has now begun to resemble a soap opera:

➤ Who met whom first: was it Otho who met Poppaea before Nero did, or the reverse?

➤ Who fell in love with whom first: was it Otho with Poppaea first, or Nero with Poppaea?

---

[18] *Feminine Imperial Ideals in the "Caesares" of Suetonius* (2012), ProQuest, New York, NY, USA

➢ Who instigated Poppaea's divorce from Crispinus: was it Poppaea herself, Otho or Nero[19] (or the by now almost superfluous Crispinus, under some heavy Imperial pressure)?

➢ Was that divorce intended to allow Poppaea to live with Otho, or to pave the way for her, eventually, to marry Nero?

Tellingly, Poppaea appears almost to be taking a back seat in all of this. It is about the men in her life, and who came first; or who is thought to have come first, and who actually *did*. In his *Annals* (XIII.44) Tacitus, greatest of her detractors, surprises by coming to her defence – almost – if only by inference:

> *While married to a knight called Rufrius Crispinus . . .*
> *she was seduced by Marcus Salvius Otho . . .*

His antipathy towards Poppaea was undisguised. That she is not named as the instigator of that seduction, given her reputation – for which he was in large measure responsible – is unexpected.

Plutarch[20] joins the fray with an interesting take:

---

[19] It is thought doubtful that such power lay within the remit even of an emperor.
[20] *The Parallel Lives, The Life of Galba* (19.4), Loeb Classical Library, Vol. XI (1926), Harvard University Press, Cambridge, MA, USA

> *. . . as for Poppaea, Otho corrupted her with hopes of Nero's favour and seduced her first himself, and persuaded her to leave her husband* [Crispinus].

Suetonius[21] does not necessarily agree:

> *Nero induced her to leave her husband and entrusted her for the time being to Otho. Otho himself, however, seduced her . . .*

Where, though, is the promiscuous, ruthless schemer who used her much-vaunted feminine wiles to entrap the Emperor? It seems that her time had not yet come, since Poppaea is painted throughout these muddled events as passive, passed around like a chattel.

The contrast between these two distinctly different Poppaeas is striking, though neither the sources nor later historians appear to consider it worthy of note. However we might be permitted to wonder: at what point did she become the sinister, power-crazed virago so commonly portrayed?

These differing versions of the Nero-Otho-Poppaea triangle are acknowledged by modern historians as leaning towards the farcical: "*. . . the story of the Otho-Poppaea-Nero triangle survives in five accounts, none of which agrees with any other.*"[22] We cannot, it seems, look to the major sources to agree on the sequence of events, let alone

---

[21] *Lives of the Caesars, op cit*
[22] Cynthia Damon (ed), *Tacitus: Histories Book 1* (2003), Cambridge University Press, Cambridge, UK

the rationale behind them. This must therefore remain one of the most intriguing affairs, in every sense, ever to enthrall students of the Neronian era.

From the questionable Poppaea/Otho marriage follows their obviously questionable 'divorce'. Most would, on reading of such an event, assume that a marriage had preceded it. This is not proof that such a marriage ever took place. The fact remains that, however strong the assumptions, from whatever quarter, no one provides a date for it.

*

One figure receded into the background while this farcical manoeuvring was going on: Rufrius Crispinus, the divorced husband. His reactions to the alleged swapping around of his wife are nowhere mentioned; indeed his personality overall remains frustratingly elusive. Was he perturbed, or angry, or saddened by events? Was the loss of Poppaea a cause of regret? Certainly his hands would have been tied; a knight did not warn an emperor – or an emperor's best friend – to stay away from his wife.

Given the invective roundly directed at Poppaea, it further surprises that she does not attract the charge of being a terrible mother to her only child, too busily engaged in contriving to have men fight over her. This is a missed opportunity for her detractors if ever there was one. In fact, throughout the entire charade her son is never mentioned.

This could simply be an indicator of the status that Roman children were customarily afforded: that is to say, very little. That they wore smaller versions of adult clothing is telling. We have only to look at those Imperial children depicted on Augustus' monument in Rome, the *Ara Pacis*. Clearly they were dressed in togas as soon as they could hold one up. They were adults in miniature, awaiting their destiny.

*

So many questions remain unanswered, not least the whereabouts of young Crispinus (II) – and, for that matter, his divorced father, no longer a co-Prefect of the Guard following his dismissal by Agrippina a number of years earlier. Where did the two of them disappear to?

As for Otho, we are told that on incurring, in whatever sequence of events, the apparent displeasure of his Emperor over Poppaea, he was first sidelined in the court, followed by a posting to Lusitania (present-day Portugal/Spain) in 58 CE.

Though of insufficient rank (he was only twenty-six), and without the requisite qualifications, he remained there as governor for ten years. Surprising to all, his term was carried out, in Suetonius' words: ". . . *with notable moderation and restraint.*" A new Otho had seemingly emerged – we can only wonder why. Speculation as to the advent of these new-found talents is noticeably absent in the sources.

Alexis Dawson is among those who explore alternative explanations for Otho's banishment[23], generally ascribed to Nero, possibly at Seneca's suggestion, removing his competition for the hand of Poppaea to that usefully far-flung place.

She rightly points out that a 10-year exile seems excessive for what is little more than a love-quarrel between two men over the same woman. Emperors had ordered swift executions for less, and the image of Nero the Disciplinarian wondering, after year five, or six, or seven, if the recalcitrant Otho had yet learned his lesson before being allowed home is ludicrous; they knew each other too well for that. Tacitus' *Histories* and *Annals* provide two entirely different explanations of the whole affair, ruling him out as a credible source.

Furthermore, Suetonius lets slip a detail that adds further confusion, which Dawson claims he had no reason to invent. He has Otho arranging a banquet on the proposed date of Agrippina's murder by her son, early in 59: the means by which she could be enticed to the required location in order for the matricidal deed to be carried out. However this does not fit with Tacitus' claim that Otho was sent to Lusitania the year before. One or other has to be in error.

---

[23] *Whatever Happened to Lady Agrippina* in *The Classical Journal* Vol. 64, No. 6 (1969), Northfield, MN, USA

In examining the lead-up to Agrippina's death, Dawson dissects Tacitus' version, likening it rather more to an over-spiced melodrama, or a play, than to a rendering of history.

J C Yardley, Tacitus' translator, adds: *". . . the topography of Tacitus' account of Agrippina's final days is hopelessly confused . . ."*.[24] David Shotter agrees; in writing of her death, he points up *". . . a complex set of inconsistencies in the surviving sources . . ."*.[25]

Put simply, if Otho was involved, then he cannot have gone to Lusitania when the sources have him doing so; he would still have been around, organising (and attending?) the sinister banquet in Campania.

These conflicting 'facts' about the timing and justification of events make no sense at all, for which the ancient sources must share full blame; nor should modern historians escape their share of responsibility in attempting to provide clarification, or at least proper scrutiny. Dawson describes the reproduction of ancient texts by later historians as *"sheeplike"*, a claim that appears to have some merit.

Otho's known character does not often show him driven by malice, or spite, or vengeance (though Tacitus

---

[24] *The Annals-The Reigns of Tiberius, Claudius, and Nero*, Oxford University Press, Oxford, UK (trans. 2008)
[25] *Nero Caesar Augustus: Emperor of Rome* (2008), Routledge (Taylor & Francis), Abingdon, UK

would doubtless disagree – see further below). Suetonius provides a rare example, though hardly one of unalloyed evil:

> *When he finally had the chance of revenge, he was the first to support Galba's* [Nero's successor, reigned 68-69 CE] *attempt to seize power.*

Nero's treatment of his former friend and playmate in the Nero-Otho-Poppaea debacle, including the initial distancing from court circles, might qualify as one justifiable reason for resentment. Otho's 'promotion' (for which read banishment) to Lusitania, which must have seemed the Roman equivalent of the ends of the earth, rivalled only by Britannia, is another. Lastly, there was Nero's responsibility for Poppaea's death. No mention is made of Otho and Nero exchanging a civil word, or any other kind, in the wake of all of this. We can fairly assume Nero's lack of enthusiasm for a meeting; Otho's thoughts can only be imagined.

It is hard to believe that Nero gave Otho no thought during his lengthy governorship of Lusitania, nor that he was unaware of Otho's apparent success in the job. Yet no records show any acknowledgement of this, or any sign of commendation or reward to his old friend. Indeed, Nero's failure to recall Otho to Rome after Poppaea's death, aside from a whiff of cowardice, might be said to have rubbed salt into this particular wound. With its lack of charity, given the closeness of their early life, it exemplifies Nero's consuming self-interest.

Following Nero's forced suicide in 68, Otho briefly became Emperor – the second of four – in 69, and a number of acts redeemed him. Overturning his predecessor Galba's order, he reinstated the statues of Poppaea that had been removed from public display.[26] Who is to dispute that he did so as a mark of his former affection for her? Even Tacitus succumbed to the possibility: "[Otho] . . . *even found time to remember his old amours, and passed a measure through the Senate restoring Poppaea's statues".*[27] (Notably these "amours" do not appear synonymous with wives; was this another clue that as far as Otho was concerned, Poppaea never was one?)

He also earmarked a generous sum for Nero's monument to self, the *Domus Aurea*, since Nero had not lived to complete it. Sources are sceptical on the question of how he intended to pay for such munificence, Plutarch expressing notable concern about the level of his debts.

Even for Rome, the procession of four emperors in a year must have shaken its foundations. What shape Otho's principate might have taken had it lasted longer than three months invites speculation. Shotter, for example, wonders if it might have ". . . *demonstrated that lessons had*

---

[26] He is said to have restored those of Nero too, for reasons which were no doubt more politically charged.

[27] *The Histories* (78), Oxford University Press, Oxford, UK (trans. W H Fyfe/D S Levene, 1997)

been learnt from Nero's failings." So blatant were these that Otho would have been hard pressed to ignore them.

Certainly records generally do not attribute to Otho any of the more objectionable qualities of other notorious emperors. Plutarch, however, seemed disinclined to let the issue slide: Otho was *". . . loaded with debt, and besides he was vain, unprincipled, and without self-restraint"*. Once again, these might be said to be relatively minor sins in the great Roman scheme of things.

Had Otho been inclined to introspection, though, he might have admitted charges of extravagance, and bribery; nor was ambition absent either. He appeared shrewd enough to recognise the need to gain the support of the people, even if his methods might have been objectionable to some. Likewise, if his early days were marked by respectful and considerate dealings with the Senate, as Plutarch claimed, this was a canny move on his part.

As to his soldiers, even with excessive generosity as primary tool, he had successfully ensured their loyalty. Indeed, it is suggested that his election to the throne could have been attributed to the Praetorian Guard. Overall, he can be said to have attempted to be all things to all people, which set him apart from the majority of those emperors who did not much care what anyone thought of them.

As for Poppaea, marriage or no-marriage, he plainly had some part in drawing her away from her marriage to

Crispinus. The utter confusion of the sources on exactly when, and how, he brought this about is of no assistance.

Tacitus displayed a similar dislike of both of them, though his usual inconsistencies prevailed. Otho ran the gamut from "... *a man of action and the most distinguished of Galba's officers in the war ...*" to one of " ... *the two men in the world who were most notorious for immorality, indolence, and extravagance ...*".

As was the Tacitean habit, he put the following unambiguous claim into the mouth of Piso, Galba's adopted son: "*His* [Otho's] *mind is full of seductions and debauchery and intrigues with women . . . in his eyes the rewards of the throne.*" Once again, self-indulgence attracts greater opprobrium than Imperial bloodlust. One might imagine Poppaea posthumously sending some words of comfort to her former 'amour' with a world-weary roll of her eyes and a well-placed jab in the ancient historian's direction: "*Yes, that sounds like him. Take no notice.*"

For someone said to have shared most, if not all, of Nero's worst vices, the circumstances of Otho's death in 69 stood in stark contrast to that of his former dissolute playmate only the year before. It appeared quiet and dignified: he died alone, at his own choice and by his own hand.

His final words, as reported by the ancient sources, suggested that he was content to die in order that the Empire might live, to secure 'peace and concord'.

Similarly modest, his monument was constructed, as custom required, by his soldiers; it said simply *"To the memory of Marcus Otho."*

Plutarch, in a somewhat backhanded compliment, declared: *"For though he lived no more decently than Nero, he died more nobly."*[28]

*

(iii)   *Nero* (37-68 CE)

Lucius Domitius Ahenobarbus was born in Antium (modern Anzio), south of Rome, to Julia Agrippina (15-59 CE – also known as Agrippina the Younger), daughter of Germanicus Caesar and Vipsania Agrippina.

His father, Gnaeus Lucius Ahenobarbus[29], was a man, according to Suetonius, *". . . loathsome in every respect."*[30] Most descriptions of Ahenobarbus' character being similarly derisory, it is hard to imagine the 13-year old Agrippina thrilling at the idea of marrying him; he was also more than twice her age.

More significantly, perhaps, the proud father allegedly laid what amounted to a curse on his son's head at birth: that any offspring of his and Agrippina's was

---

[28] *The Parallel Lives-The Life of Otho,* 18.2
[29] A theory exists that Ahenobarbus was sterile, therefore not Nero's birth father. It may or may not be helpful to note that busts of the two do not look at all alike.
[30] *Lives of the Caesars, op cit*

bound to "*. . . inspire loathing and bring disaster for the state.*" What prompted this ominous statement is not explained, though he had clearly missed his calling as an augur.

Ahenobarbus died from illness when his son was three years old. Early in 50 CE the boy was adopted by the Emperor Claudius, whom his mother had married the year before, and took the name of Nero Claudius Caesar Augustus Germanicus: such a weight of Imperial lineage would have gone to anyone's head. He was twelve years old.

Nero's first wife (Poppaea was his second) was his stepsister Claudia Octavia, daughter of Claudius and Messallina. Their arranged marriage in 53, seemingly not embraced with enthusiasm by either, was not a success (see further below).

At Claudius' death in 54, Nero was proclaimed Emperor, aged sixteen. His mother stepped into the unofficial role of regent/chief adviser to compensate for his youth and inexperience. Whatever her faults – and she sits higher in the pantheon of evil than Poppaea, no mean feat – Agrippina's determination and clearsighted political skills were never in doubt.

As far as can be ascertained, Nero had become infatuated with Poppaea around 58; he was twenty-one to her twenty-seven. She was still married to Rufrius Crispinus, with a young son; he to Octavia, whom he did not care for, and with no heir in sight. Part of Poppaea's attraction was undoubtedly her proven fertility, which stood to highlight Octavia's apparent lack of it.

As already noted, one of the most well-worn accusations against Poppaea is that she applied a deal of pressure on Nero to eliminate his mother, in order to clear the way to marrying her son. Agrippina preferred her daughter-in-law Octavia over any mistress of Nero's, more likely for political reasons than any other. Both mother and wife thus constituted barriers to be swept aside before the marriage to Poppaea could proceed.

Nero did finally bring about his mother's death in 59, after more than one attempt, in circumstances that ought to have given him cause to die of shame. Annelise Freisenbruch describes her end, as most historians have accepted it: "... *Agrippina's final moments were of eloquent defiance.*"[31]

We might wonder, though, at Agrippina's ability to utter the now (alleged) immortal request to her (alleged) assassins to be stabbed in the womb that had borne her monstrous son. She was said to have been struck on the head with a blunt instrument immediately before by one of the execution squad, presumably no gentle tap. Most of us would have been stunned, if not incoherent, or at worst unconscious, certainly incapable of calling forth our bravest and best mordant wit. Agrippina's known

---

[31] *The First Ladies of Rome: The Women Behind the Caesars* (2011), Vintage Books, London

character traits, which she in general took no pains to hide, do not remotely suggest that theatricality was among them.

Alexis Dawson offers an alternative scenario in her incisive and painstaking deconstruction of Tacitus' version of Agrippina's death[32], attributed to ". . . the whole anti-Nero legend" to which he was clearly wedded. Significantly, she disputes Nero's murder of his mother, suggesting instead that Agrippina committed suicide.

Whatever the truth of her demise, Nero displayed considerable chutzpah in assuring the Senate[33] that he had acted in response to Agrippina's treacherous plotting against him, therefore against the state.

However it seems that guilt plagued him as he tossed and turned on his bed. The omens were not good; had all support for his mother died with her? Could he sleep easily while attempting to convince himself that his popularity was greater than hers? The sources suggest that he could not sleep at all.

Poppaea's marriage to Nero did not take place until three years later; innumerable sources mention this delay. It belies both her alleged impatience to bring on the nuptials at the first opportunity, and her oft-mentioned

---

[32] *Whatever Happened to Lady Agrippina, op cit*
[33] In a letter, said to have been written for him by Seneca and stuffed with additional charges against his mother reaching back to the reign of Claudius and beyond.

power over the besotted Nero, ensuring his granting of her every wish. Three years is a long time to wait to metaphorically cut the cake.

Political considerations undoubtedly lay behind this lengthy gap: primarily Nero's fear of the consequences of divorcing Claudia Octavia, daughter of the now deified Claudius. Her lineage was impeccable – as his was not – inspiring strong support among the people. Nonetheless, Nero had become used to getting his own way; even someone as strong-willed as his mother had been unable, finally, to control him.

His star began sinking lower. Having finally managed to rid himself of Octavia in shocking circumstances – divorce, exile, murder – he married the pregnant Poppaea in (probably) May 62, allegedly twelve days after the first of those lamentable events. As earlier noted, Augustus had only just beaten him to the dishonourable record by divorcing his wife Scribonia within days of daughter Julia's birth.

Since most sources link Poppaea to it as evidence of her thoroughgoing wickedness, Octavia's eventual death, horrendous by all accounts, is deserving of mention.

*

At ages sixteen and thirteen respectively, Nero's dynastic, and doomed, marriage to Claudia Octavia in 53 CE was overtly political. One of Octavia's marital burdens was Nero's early affair with Acte, a household slave, later freedwoman, thought to have begun within two years of the marriage. Worse still, Octavia was insufficiently cooperative in producing Nero's heir, reason enough in ancient Rome for divorce.

As the only daughter of Claudius and Valeria Messallina, Octavia's credentials were unimpeachable. She was Claudia for her father and Octavia for her great-grandmother, sister of the Emperor Augustus. Whatever the other reasons for his dislike of her, we might reasonably assume Nero's resentment of this lineage that so outstripped his own.

Nero's relationship with Poppaea allegedly began around five years after this marriage. Octavia had already endured his dissolute and uncaring behaviour and extramarital relationships, Acte being a longstanding one. We can only imagine her feelings concerning her inability to produce an heir. As for Nero, it merely gave him more reason, in his terms, to treat her harshly; she had not done what was expected of her. Along with his mother, Octavia became the focus of Nero's plotting. He wanted Poppaea; these two tiresome women stood in his way.

He divorced Octavia on the legitimate ground of barrenness. The much-desired marriage to Poppaea could then take place.

However support for Octavia among the citizenry was solid, and Nero's treatment of her caused outrage. In response he levelled trumped-up charges of adultery against her, and eventually banished her to the island of Pandateria, off the Campanian coast. Finally, he ordered her execution by her guards in gruesome fashion: her severed head was brought to Rome.

Poppaea features large in renditions of this final macabre outcome:

> *Nero's henchmen . . . cut off her head and paraded it through the streets of Rome. Much to the delight of Poppaea.*[34]

> *As a final atrocity her head was cut off and taken to Poppaea.*[35]

> *Her head, dispatched to Nero, served as a trophy for his new wife: Poppaea Sabina.*[36]

The tone of these comments makes for distasteful reading. Aside from the inconsistencies, however, there may be a level of historical inventiveness at work.

As triumphant rival to the virtuous Octavia, Poppaea could not have avoided coming off badly. However, no authoritative sources record her 'delight' at the sight of

[34] M Owen and I Gildenhard, *Tacitus, Annals, 15.20–23, 33–45: Latin Text, Study Aids with Vocabulary, and Commentary* (2013), Open Book Publishers, Cambridge, UK

[35] R Bauman, *Women and Politics in Ancient Rome* (1992), Routledge, London

[36] T Holland, *Dynasty: The Rise and Fall of the House of Caesar* (2015), Little Brown, London

Octavia's severed head, nor that she ordered that it be brought to Rome for her inspection (so that she could gloat over it . . .).

In their evident enjoyment in describing this shocking event, these three male authors join the ranks of those dedicated to exposing Poppaea's alleged despicable and cold-hearted nature. They fit the by now familiar pattern of portraying her as matching Nero at his most monstrous. Her already unfavourable reputation sinks still lower.

Decapitation of an 'enemy' was not without historical precedent. However Eric Varner[37] notes that it was reserved almost exclusively for men; he lists no fewer than six emperors subjected to this *poena post mortem* (punishment after death). Freisenbruch mentions only one woman's decapitation: Lollia Paulina, one of Caligula's wives, who had run up against Agrippina. Varner suggests that it ". . . *may have provided a precedent for that of Octavia,*" though without elaboration.

However the ancient sources' recordings of Lollia Paulina are revealing. Cassius Dio (*Roman History*, Book LXI) reported her decapitation, not the only example of his fondness for excessively gory detail; Tacitus (*Annals*, XII) mentioned only her enforced suicide – once again, one or

---

[37] *Mutilation and Transformation-Damnatio Memoriae and Roman Imperial Portraiture* (2004), Koninklijke Brill NV, Leiden, Netherlands

other had to be in error. Suetonius mentioned neither possibility.

This appalling treatment of women's corpses is so rare that its description by sources as a 'blatantly political act' does not tell us much, and is indeed a grossly insensitive understatement. Both instances are implied to have been ordered by a woman: Agrippina the first, Poppaea the second. Predictably, these two 'executioners' were both reviled in the writings of antiquity, which should tell us much of what we need to know about their veracity.

The heavy-handed implication is that these two detestable women doubtless revelled in such hateful behaviour, encouraging us to think the worst of them at every opportunity. According them responsibility for the beheading of another woman can hardly be bettered as a reason.

*

Whatever was thought of Nero's character by most sources, all agree on his great love for his new wife. His devotion to Poppaea lasted until his death, and could be said to have been one of the few constants in his life. What is less clear, however, is the depth of Poppaea's feelings in return.

Tacitus steps in here to assist: Poppaea was ". . . *insensible to men's love, and herself unloving. Advantage dictated the bestowal of her favours.*"[38] He might have wondered what on earth they saw in her.

One thing, as already noted, was her fertility: first, son Rufrius Crispinus (II), secondly daughter Claudia in early 63 at Antium, birthplace of her father. Nero, overjoyed, had promptly named both mother and child 'Augusta'. It is thought that the entire Senate travelled to Antium to celebrate, presumably no small logistical operation. Although he would doubtless have preferred a son, his daughter's designated position in Imperial history would have been assured:

> . . . *although she could not succeed Nero as emperor she was intended to take her place amongst the imperial women and have her role to play in dynastic strategies.*[39]

In short, Nero would already have been thinking about advantageous marriages for his Imperial daughter. However the child died less than four months later; Nero's grief was said to have been as excessive as his joy at her birth. The infant was deified, and a coin issued in her honour inscribed *'DIVA CLAUDIA NERONIS FILIA'*. A temple was also decreed, but it is not clear that this plan ever came to fruition.

No sources seem inclined to mention Poppaea's feelings about her daughter's death. None mentions her

---

[38] *Annals*, XIII.44 (trans. Michael Grant, 1956-96)
[39] Beryl Rawson, *Children and Childhood in Roman Italy* (2003), Oxford University Press, Oxford, UK

mourning; might this have sat uneasily alongside the favoured negative image of her? However Roman tradition may also have played a part, even for the wife of an emperor. Rawson notes:

> *In formal terms, mourning for infants was expected to be briefer than that for older persons: there was no formal mourning for an infant less than a year old . . .*

Nonetheless, no one would have known better the importance of the Emperor's wife producing children – and what happened to those unfortunate wives who did not. Poppaea was doubtless aware that a lot was riding on her producing an Imperial infant whom the gods might permit to survive, and flourish.

She had of course already produced a child – and a son at that. Perhaps unsurprisingly, no mention is made of young Crispinus (II) having acquired a half-sister. Since no records indicate where he lived out his short life, we can only speculate as to how he felt about it, or even whether he ever saw his baby sister Claudia. As an eight-year old boy, he was unlikely to have been impressed.

Following the death of baby Claudia, Poppaea disappears from the record. Nothing is known about where she spent her time, or her whereabouts at the time of the great fire of Rome in the summer of 64, the year after Claudia's death. The Imperial residence at Antium seems a likely place, since Nero is thought to have been there when the fire started. Fantasy dictates that they might have consoled each other for their loss.

Nero was much involved in the building of his *Domus Aurea* following the great fire, but we read nothing of Poppaea's contribution to its planning and design, if any. It was as if Nero went full steam ahead, designing an enormous, extravagant pleasure palace for himself alone – along with, presumably, an army of slaves. As noted in the previous chapter, even in her notoriety Poppaea warranted no mention in the proposed plans.

Records indicate that the *Domus Transitoria* on the Palatine Hill preceded the *Domus Aurea* as Rome's Nero/Poppaea Imperial property. Thought to have been built around 60 CE, it stretched from the Palatine to the Gardens of Maecenas on the Esquiline Hill.

It was destroyed in the 64 fire, and the *Domus Aurea* built on top of it – as on much else. The scant known details of the original building suggest a sumptuous residential property, lavishly decorated with gold, marble and semi-precious stones. Excavations indicate that much of the original design was incorporated into the *Domus Aurea*, suggesting that Nero's architectural extravagance was already well established – with or without Poppaea's involvement. It seems likely that the *Transitoria* was where they spent their early years, perhaps alternating with the Imperial residence at Antium.

As with Poppaea and the *Domus Aurea*, no mention is ever made of her presence at any of Nero's theatrical appearances. Indeed we have no hint of whether or not she thought her husband was possessed of any talent. The historical silence on the subject may, unusually, speak in her favour.

Wherever she spent her time, Poppaea became pregnant again towards the end of 64; her fertility was proving durable. It can be assumed that Nero would again have rejoiced, his strong desire for children seeming never in doubt.

Poppaea's death in 65, and that of his unborn second child, must have impacted severely on Nero's mental stability, unsteady at the best of times. If we believe that he suffered from guilt on the death of his mother, for which he was entirely responsible, then it follows that the death of his wife Poppaea, and their child, would have caused even more anguish (and guilt). He loved Poppaea throughout; no sources, however hostile to either or both, suggest otherwise. However his feelings towards Agrippina at her death were rather more ambiguous.

A footnote to Nero's unseemly demise in 68 was his burial by Acte, his former mistress. Having by now amassed considerable wealth, she paid for a generous interment in the Ahenobarbi family tomb on Rome's Pincian Hill. Aside from the absence of a 100ft statue in gilded bronze to mark it, Nero would probably have approved.

We might imagine a sphinx-like Poppaea watching in silence from the heavens as her predecessor Acte had what was, in effect, the final word.

*

Poppaea's three marriages, including the questionable central one, have garnered much negative opinion, ancient and modern. The sexually voracious (but unloving) scheming and manipulative siren is by now very familiar.

How might she have envisaged the life that began with the first of her marriages at around fourteen? Her perception of herself as wife and mother is, regrettably, entirely unknown to us. (This is when we wish for that diary.) The true circumstances affecting the decisions she made, the influences on them, and the feelings behind them can only be matters for conjecture.

Yet we have sufficient evidence to say with some certainty that she secured the strong affections of both Otho and Nero. (Crispinus, disappointingly, remains an unknown quantity.) What did she think of the three men in her life – did she love any of them, or not?

Once more her legacy invites comparison with Cleopatra VII. Though there were differences too, the similarities between portrayals of the two cannot be denied. The men in their lives were infatuated with them. What was it about them both that drew to their sides men whom disapproving historians might like to suggest should have known better?

As much as we might wish it otherwise, no possible answers to these questions are likely to surface. However contradictory the portrayals of her, the enigma that was Poppaea Sabina remains.

CHAPTER 8

A politician's wife

Power and ambition, when applied to the women of antiquity, seem almost synonymous. Allied to that is the common conjunction of looks, ambition, and immorality – again pertaining only to women. Anthony Barrett[1] notes:

> . . . *ambitious women are invariably described as beautiful, and beautiful women are stereotypically associated with vice.*

Such women in the Roman landscape are likely to include the usual suspects, as mentioned at Chapter 5: Fulvia, Livia, Messallina, Agrippina.

Political power in Rome was without question a male preserve. Trouble lay in wait for any woman so bold as to attempt to breach those walls. Ambition, though, could not operate in a vacuum; it could be fulfilled for women only through their men. Any woman showing signs of such impropriety laid herself open to vilification. Tacitus set the tone, with Barrett noting his " . . . *unshakeable*

---

[1] *Agrippina-Sister of Caligula-Wife of Claudius-Mother of Nero* (1996), B T Batsford Ltd, London

conviction that the ambitious woman was evil incarnate".[2] The threat embodied in "evil incarnate" suggests that both *fear* and contempt were alive, in equal measure.

Much is made in the sources of Poppaea's quest for power. It is a claim easily made – not just of her – and predictably carries with it all manner of negative connotations:

> *Power-seeking women . . . elicit feelings of moral outrage, including contempt, anger, and disgust.*[3]

Coupled with that is the age-old link, in texts both ancient and modern, between power and sexuality. The claim that this is what women use to get their way needs no explaining; we do not have to look as far back as ancient Rome for that. Butterworth and Laurence[4] nonetheless manage to capture both points in the same sentence:

> *. . . if the unsentimental Poppaea had inherited a taste for power from her father, it was from a mother who had been praised as the most beautiful woman of her day that she derived the means to achieve it.*

(Aside from the clichéd comment about women and their looks, how do they know she was unsentimental?)

---

[2] Quoted in A A Barrett's *Livia-First Lady of Imperial Rome* (2002), Yale University Press, New Haven, CT, USA
[3] Kristin J Anderson, *Modern Misogyny: Anti-Feminism in a Post-Feminist Era* (2015), Oxford University Press, Oxford, UK
[4] *Pompeii: The Living City* (2006), Phoenix (Orion Books), London

Her father Ollius' aspirations were unknown, since he had reached no higher than a quaestorship, the lowest ranking magistracy, before dying around the time of his daughter's birth. She was therefore prevented from sitting at his knee and absorbing the rudiments of power. His role model was hardly helpful; had Poppaea aspired to it, she would have died before reaching any higher than the bottom rung of the Ladder of Success.

Nonetheless, the sources would have Poppaea's character, and her alleged ambition/power-seeking, established at an early age. As discussed at Chapter 2, she is commonly claimed to have taken her grandfather's name over that of her disgraced father some time after the former's death – which occurred when she was around five years old. At her mother's death in 47 CE, she is already being accused of seeking vengeance, aged seventeen and with no known allies to assist in any sinister plans she might have entertained.

Most sources highlight her ruthless ambition to head for the sky in the Imperial court. She might have emerged from the womb with her sights on the Emperor – any emperor – and a commitment to attaining the title of Empress at any cost. Along the way we see again the link between female ambition and immorality: *"A woman of*

Poppaea's ambition, who sought to advance her position by promiscuity . . . ".[5]

Butterworth and Laurence go on to assert that in this she reaches the heady heights of comparison to a star (despite significant differences in background): *"Ambition was in Poppaea's blood as much as it was in Agrippina's."* This is a telling comment on her character, but once again without elucidation or evidence to support it.

Finally, an astonishing earlier claim:

Nero had just married his mistress, the beautiful and profligate Poppaea Sabina, to satisfy whose ambition [emphasis added] *he had first divorced his long-suffering wife Octavia . . .*[6]

This is an extraordinary rationalisation of Nero's behaviour. Are we to believe that he divorced Octavia and married Poppaea only because she wanted it?! While sources concede his infatuation with her, the implication that Poppaea alone was driving the marriage plan, with Nero simply trotting along behind, is a fatuous distortion of events. We need only remember the three-year gap between when he *could* have married Poppaea – after the

[5] E Mary Smallwood, *The Alleged Jewish Tendencies of Poppaea Sabina* in *The Journal of Theological Studies* (1959), Oxford University Press, Oxford, UK

[6] G Edmundson, *Church in Rome in the First Century* (1913), Christian Classics Ethereal Library, Grand Rapids, MI, USA

death of his mother, supposedly a major obstacle – and when he did.

This small, illustrative sample of the scholarly claims of Poppaea's overweening ambition helps to build the image of her that is so prevalent. Barrett injects some balance:

> *The preoccupation of the ancient writers with the evils of female ambition all but blinded them to any admirable qualities they might have possessed.*

He was in fact writing here of Agrippina. However, the same might be said for Poppaea – or any other high-ranking woman of unsavoury reputation – such is the negativity attaching to a perceived ambitious woman in ancient Rome.

Before examining the subject of power more closely, it is instructive to revisit an important issue, noted at Chapter 5: the historian's habit of attributing the vices of the more unpopular of Imperial Roman men to their women.

This is a likely result of sources resorting to handy stereotypes in the absence of solid detail about Rome's 'disreputable' women. Any negative depiction of a man can easily be extended to encompass his female partner-in-crime – whether or not evidence exists to show that she actually *was* one. This is another manifestation of Tacitus' known practice of 'putting words into her mouth' in order to better illustrate her character. (See Chapter 10)

It can also be seen as deriving from the difference in how the sexes are viewed: man the driving force, woman the accomplice – without, presumably, the wit to govern her own actions. It produces another paradox: either she is the quintessential Wicked Woman (no driver required), pushing her own wicked agenda, or she is the appendage, following along behind. She cannot be both.

As the men referred to here are usually in positions of power, this issue is of relevance to the discussion at hand.

*

We need look no further than the present subject. Character assassinations of Poppaea and Nero illustrate the common accusation of the sharing of vices, of evil intertwined. One might simply narrate the story of Nero's detestable behaviour, changing the name throughout.

In the absence of substantial proof, the implication that their relationship was founded on a host of shared (unattractive) character traits is suspect at best. Was it simply a dual case of 'Nature versus Nurture', with nature winning out? Or two personifications of evil, locked together and driven by their hormones?

Livy offered an opinion on the matter generally: *"Evil was drawn to evil, but the woman took the lead."*[7] (We might have known – those hormones again.) In fact he was discussing Tullia, from the 6th century BCE, and her attempts to see her equally despicable husband, Tarquinius Superbus, on the throne. However the message is unambiguous: any amount of appalling behaviour can be counted on, being part of the makeup of an ambitious woman.

Another example comes from an unexpected source:

He [Gessius Florus-see further below] . . . *brought along with him his wife Cleopatra, (by whose friendship with Poppea, Nero's wife, he obtained this government,) who was noway different from him in wickedness.*[8]

The implication here is laughably unsubtle. Cleopatra, wicked wife of the wicked Gessius Florus, was friend to the wicked Poppaea, who was married to the wicked Nero – there was a lot of it going around. Even Josephus of Jerusalem, author of the above extract and seemingly the only historian friend Poppaea had, could not resist. Unhelpfully, he explained neither the nature of Cleopatra's crimes nor the origin or basis of the women's alleged friendship; a number of sources mention the latter issue, though none provides any clarification. While

---

[7] T Stevenson, from *Women of Early Rome as* Exempla *in Livy* (2011), *Ab Urbe Condita*, Book 1 (trans. Benjamin O Foster)
[8] *The Works of Flavius Josephus*, Armstrong & Plaskitt, Baltimore, MD, USA (trans. William Whiston, 1835)

Josephus held Poppaea herself in high regard, the implied shared wickedness hangs in the air.

Livia, wife of Augustus and much maligned by ancient sources, suffers similarly. For Tacitus she was ". . . *a real catastrophe, to the nation, as a mother and to the house of the Caesars as a stepmother"*.[9] Patricia Watson locates this devastating description in Tacitus' ostensible reporting of criticisms of her *husband* following his death.[10] How easily does the poison pen slip . . .

Though fortunately not involving marriage, Poppaea and Tigellinus, co-Prefect of Nero's Praetorian Guard, attract this historical attribution of shared wickedness (see also the chapter following). Tacitus lumped them together as some kind of devilish duo, immoral and uncontrolled. Here Poppaea is linked to someone perceived to be evil personified. His worst qualities – and there is no shortage in the record – are therefore unquestionably assigned to her. Thus the label of 'cruel', while attaching with apparent accuracy to Tigellinus, is one that Poppaea cannot escape, and it follows her everywhere.

Sources mention the issue of *consilium* in connection with the Poppaea/Tigellinus link. It is defined as both advice and a group of advisers, and reaches back to early

---

[9] *Annals*, I.9-11 (trans. Michael Grant, 1956-96)
[10] *Ancient Stepmothers: Myth, Misogyny and Reality* (1995), E J Brill, Leiden, Netherlands

Roman tradition: no decisions should be made alone by those men in positions of responsibility.

Barrett[11] notes that *muliebre consilium* (advice offered by a woman) is a term of disparagement, which should not surprise. However examples of *consilia* in the literature demonstrate just how loosely constituted such a body might have been on any given occasion. Steven Rutledge[12] clarifies the meaning of *consilium*:

> . . . [it] *did not exist as a formal institution . . . it is a term of convenience that modern scholars use to refer to the emperor's friends and advisors . . .*

It could range from a small number of close friends to a body almost as large as the Senate, with any number of permutations in between. John Crook mentions, for example, ". . . *the decision of a praetor taken after consulting a consilium of at least thirty-three members.*"[13] Clearly almost any kind of advisory grouping might qualify:

> . . . *Nero convened the special* consilium, *consisting of Poppaea and Tigellinus, that sat with him when he bypassed his regular advisers in order to cut loose.*[14]

---

[11] *Livia, op cit*
[12] *Imperial Inquisitions: Prosecutors and Informants from Tiberius to Domitian* (2001), Routledge, London
[13] Consilium Principis: *Imperial Councils and Counsellors from Augustus to Diocletian* (1955), Cambridge University Press, Cambridge, UK
[14] R A Bauman, *Crime and Punishment in Ancient Rome* (1996), Routledge, London

The hint of disparagement here, in the mention of 'cutting loose', is unmistakeable. (The "regular advisers" might also have helpfully been named for purposes of comparison alongside the devilish duo.)

This is apparently what Tacitus meant in his *Annals* (XV.58-9) in describing Poppaea and Tigellinus as ". . . *intimate counsellors of the emperor's brutalities.*" Other sources have interpreted this to mean that the two regularly counselled, even encouraged, Nero to do his worst (to "cut loose"), such were their own sinister inclinations.

However it stretches the imagination to see the pair – in particular Poppaea – behaving in the more formal manner required of members of a *consilium*. This involved writing their individual opinions on events under discussion, then handing them to the *Princeps* for consideration alongside his own thoughts on the matter, so that judgements could be passed, decisions made, and action taken.

It is harder still to imagine Poppaea being familiar enough with, for example, the characters of the alleged parties to the Pisonian conspiracy to assassinate Nero (see Chapter 7) to enable her to 'counsel' Nero on how he should deal with them. The key question is: how well did she understand the machinations of court politics, in the absence of training coming from family background to assist her? No records, ancient or modern, enlighten us, though there may be no shortage of assumptions.

Tigellinus would have had no such problems. Nero was alarmed, even frightened, by the reach of the conspiracy. Tigellinus would have stood ready to advise him, and to commit without question whatever acts of retribution his Emperor ordered – that was his job. This was 'men's work', in the truest sense of the term. In the midst of such complex and dramatic events Poppaea, one suspects, is likely to have been somewhat out of her depth.

Despite being Nero's wife, then, Poppaea's *political* position in the court looks to have been a fairly solitary one. Miriam Griffin[15] speculates:

> *Poppaea's actual position could only distantly approximate to Agrippina's. She was far inferior in birth, and she had not the time, nor probably the skill, to build up a nexus of political support.*

The suggestion that, unlike Agrippina, Poppaea was lacking in political skills is likely to contain some truth. Agrippina was unquestionably a savvy political operator – few could have competed with her in this. Major differences in family history and upbringing would have greatly influenced the ways in which the two operated within the court. Agrippina had the family background, the position and the political instincts to operate alone, when necessary calling on those she had placed in key positions to assist her. Poppaea, as far as we know, did not.

---

[15] *Nero-The End of a Dynasty* (1984), B T Batsford Ltd, London

Whether or not her skills were at issue, the picture of Poppaea drawn above challenges the stereotyped unscrupulous, unstoppable schemer that records portray. Though intelligent, beautiful and quick-witted, without that "nexus of political support" these would not have been enough. She could not benefit from that powerful baggage attached to the royal lineage of the Julio-Claudians. As already noted, had she not married Nero she might well have remained no more than a footnote in the record, whatever her ambitions are assumed to have been.

Sources describe Tigellinus as Nero's favourite of his two co-Prefects: an intimate adviser encouraging him in depraved and licentious conduct – Tigellinus being no stranger to either. Nowhere is it claimed that he was Poppaea's favourite too. Indeed we have no hint of her opinion of him (or vice versa), allowing all kinds of assumptions as to their true relationship. However we do know that he and Nero shared early history, whereas he and Poppaea did not. The likelihood is therefore that she was possessed of sufficient native intelligence to be capable of reading his character to a degree that Nero, beholden to him, could not; his need of Tigellinus was by far the greater. (Tacitus can be heard harumphing in disgust; he would have had none of that.)

Poppaea's lack of natural allies within court circles is likely to have included the Praetorian Guard generally. While historically a useful support system, of sorts, they –

or at least their officers – needed to be kept sweet. Imperial donatives from the Emperors Tiberius, Claudius and Nero would have achieved this, ensuring their loyalty. However matters were not always so straightforward, and events could bring about swift changes in fortune. Finally, and crucially, their orders came from Nero, via his favoured Prefect Tigellinus – not from Nero's wife.

It is inarguable that Poppaea was well placed to influence Nero. However no source compares Nero's trust in her in political matters with that of Augustus' notable trust in Livia; the two relationships appear very different in this regard. Furthermore, as the Emperor's wife it is questionable whether Poppaea herself possessed the power to carry out what might be termed 'acts of cruelty' – even supposing she wished to – or to order others to do so on her behalf.

Unlike Agrippina, there is no sense of Poppaea operating alone, confident in her position and her own individual skills and effectiveness; we need only keep in mind her apparent lack of close supporters within the court. She undoubtedly had legions of slaves, but they lacked political clout and the freedom to manoeuvre when necessary; we know of none who might have claimed otherwise.

In fact, Poppaea's earliest entry into Imperial circles came about only by her marriage in 44 CE to Rufrius

Crispinus, co-Prefect of Claudius' Praetorian Guard – a decision that would not have rested with her.

It should also be borne in mind that the primary allegiance of Prefects of the Guard was to their emperor, not his wife. Agrippina was an exception in this, but she had employed a great deal of skilled effort in shoring up her position in this regard, which paid off (though insufficient, in the end, to save her life). No evidence suggests that Poppaea contrived to do the same, or even saw the need for it.

What is known of the natures of both Tigellinus and Poppaea makes it improbable that either could successfully have influenced the other in the commission of misdeeds. Yet both ancient and modern writers commonly link them: Poppaea the Wicked Witch, Tigellinus her cruel, unprincipled henchman.[16] As long as they are connected, her reputation will remain at the same base level; and given *his* awful reputation, that is very low.

In this light, the claims that the two plotted and schemed to manipulate the weak and frightened Nero for their own criminal ends serves merely to ramp up the levels of suspense and drama; we are back once more in the realm of soap opera. With the image of Poppaea, gliding between Emperor and Prefect, eyes glinting as she hatched evil plots and dispensed liberal doses of

---

[16] Poppaea is not alone in this scenario. Messallina, Claudius' wife, was another 'immoral Imperial woman with cruel, unprincipled henchmen': the makings of a stereotype.

sinfulness and vice to be shared between them all, we might wonder how she found time to eat and sleep.

The reality is likely to have been rather different. However she might be depicted, Poppaea was perforce locked out of the two-man power team that was Nero and Tigellinus. The relationship between emperor and prefect was one of political Rome's strongest: for mutual benefit, and to get things done, it had to be. Ascribing the capabilities of a Prefect of the Guard to Poppaea is to misrepresent the roles of both.

Put more crudely, cold-blooded ruthlessness was a major component of any emperor's job description. Nero could, and did, order his favoured Prefect to eliminate anyone considered troublesome or threatening, whether proven or not. The role of eliminator, however, was never one that could realistically have been assigned to the Emperor's wife. In short, her presence was not necessary for Nero's orders to be carried out. He had loyal subordinates for that – and Poppaea was not one of them.

In a fantasy scenario Poppaea could well have gone marching into her husband, complaining that a soldier of the Guard had insulted her, and that he should lose his head for it. However she herself did not possess the power to order that that head be removed.

*

'Power', that most oft-used word in the historical narrative of ancient Rome, preoccupied everyone, including Tacitus. His *Histories* (2.38) confirmed:

> *The old ingrained human passion for power has matured and burst into prominence with the growth of the empire.*

We can safely assume that "human passion" here refers to the male one. This is not to suggest that no Imperial Roman woman ever showed an interest in attaining power. However, with Agrippina perhaps the best example, the price to be paid for any such attempt was a heavy one.

Access to emperors was naturally of paramount importance in the pursuit of power – as was location. Annelise Freisenbruch[17] compares the Palatine's Imperial residence to 'powerhouses' of today such as the White House and 10 Downing Street. So for Imperial Rome:

> . . . *women now presided over a household that also served as the headquarters of government, bringing them closer than ever to the epicentre of political power.*

The whirring sound over the everyday racket in the Forum would have been Cato the Elder (see below) spinning in his grave.

The importance of power in the Empire cannot be overstated. However Roman men's fear of Roman women

---

[17] *The First Ladies of Rome: The Women Behind the Caesars* (2011), Jonathan Cape, London

achieving it is not easily admitted – at least by Tacitus. Cato, however, felt no such restraint. He nailed the crux of that fear in his emotional speech against the repeal of the *lex Oppia* in 195 BCE (see also below). Livy's *History of Rome* (34.3) summarised his argument with these examples:

> As soon as they [women] begin to be your equals, they will have become your superiors.

> . . . more disgrace upon us if we have to submit to laws being imposed upon us through fear of a secession on their [women's] part . . .

Heaven forfend.

Never did a man fight so hard to retain his 'power over' (see Marilyn French[18] below) as Cato did. He was possibly even more wedded than Tacitus was to Republican Rome, the good old days, when men were men, and women – and the rest – knew their place. Rome's relentless descent into degeneracy, lawlessness and immorality must have given both of them cause to weep.

In a wide-ranging look back over millenia, French questions the inevitability of the power of the few over the many. She argues compellingly for the existence of two primary strands: 'power to' (shape events) and 'power

---

[18] *Beyond Power: On Women, Men and Morals* (1986), Jonathan Cape Ltd, London

over' (other people by, for instance, ownership of slaves). She concludes that such totalitarian power is not, nor ever has been, the natural order. We can assume that neither Tacitus nor Cato would have agreed. An imagined 3-way debate on the subject in the Forum is likely to have caused the Senate to spontaneously combust.

The possession and retention of power was therefore problematic for Roman men, at least when it came to their women. Most attractive to the ruling élite was the ability it gave those possessed of it to shape political events. Compounding this was the fervent belief of that same ruling élite that men should have it and women should not. Cato's sustained outburst in the Forum might have laid out the matter more clearly, certainly more heartfelt, than any man before or since. Had any woman dared to argue, it would have been maintained that the gods had so decreed.

The modern equivalent justification is that it is bound up in 'tradition' – but the same rules apply. This situation was not, of course, peculiar to the Romans. Any male 'ruling élite' from any period fought, and fights still, to remain in the seat of power once having seized it – and who would not?

As became increasingly apparent, high-status Roman women resented their exclusion from the political arena, at least when they had substantive complaints – which Cato maintained should properly be made quietly, at home, to their husbands, not publicly and loudly in the

Forum. While women could claim senatorial status alongside their senator husbands, they were denied entrance to the Senate itself; these were not the days of a public gallery for female observers.

A noteworthy example of bending the rules was Livia, Augustus' wife and another skilled political operator. Expert in seeming to be doing very little while actually doing quite a lot, she successfully maintained a delicate balance between private and public personas: the 'power behind the throne' in action, in a marriage of more than fifty years' duration.

By the time Poppaea had reached her early thirties, she had a husband possessed of the ultimate power of Emperor, and who was enamoured of her, from beginning to end. Whether he actually indulged her every wish, or it is simply assumed that he must have done, given his besotted state[19], is ripe for conjecture. She was wealthy and beautiful, Empress of Rome, the owner and resident of grandiose properties. On the face of it, there seemed nothing more to wish for. Had she reached as high as she wanted to go? Yet to both ancient and modern writers she was still suspiciously similar to her (deceased) mother-in-law Agrippina: ambitious, eager for power, ruthless in her determination to have it.

---

[19] Nero's besottedness did not appear to extend to fidelity: a number of sources, Tacitus among them, suggest that he was involved in a relationship with his third and final wife, Statilia Messalina, while still married to Poppaea.

But power to do what? Did she want to be Emperor, and address the Senate (or even be allowed in)? Or stand on the *rostra* in the Forum and proclaim? Wear yet more jewellery and fine clothes, or groom her children to take over the throne? What, in short, did she really want? Sadly, and frustratingly, we cannot know.

Élite Roman women were unlikely to have seen their overstepping of boundaries as a crude search for power. More likely they simply chafed at the restrictions over their lives, and unlike their Greek sisters, were not constrained in attempting to circumvent them. They broke rules, ignored laws that mistreated them, and stretched the patience of the ruling élite beyond endurance. Two famous examples illustrate how far they could go when pushed: the first resulting from the *lex Oppia*, enacted in 215 BCE, the second the impressive oratorical performance of Hortensia.

(i)   *lex Oppia*

This law restricted the permitted clothing and jewellery of high-born Roman women, and their methods of travel. Presumably these outward signs of conspicuous consumption were thought to set a bad example to the citizenry. When it remained in force more than a decade after the rationale behind it had become redundant, they took to the streets in protest. The like of such conduct cannot have been seen before; it broke every rule of proper behaviour that well-born Roman women were expected to hold dear.

In his impassioned plea for its retention, though, Cato was neither particularly honest nor consistent. While proclaiming his respect for the modesty and dignity of (certain) Roman women, he also accused them of wanting unrestricted freedom – with the swift descent into Hades that would doubtless follow. Despite his dread of the intolerable consequences, the law was repealed in 195.

(ii)   *Hortensia*

Daughter of Quintus Hortensius Hortalus (114-50 BCE), Hortensia was well educated and grew up in an intellectual household. Her father was a renowned orator (a rival to Cicero); she may well have picked up her talents from him.

In 42 BCE the Second Triumvirate[20] (Octavian, Marc Antony and Marcus Emilius Lepidus) levied a heavy tax on 1,400 of Rome's wealthiest women to fund the war against Caesar's assassins. Hortensia spoke eloquently from the *rostra* in the Forum on behalf of the enraged women, demanding to know why they should pay for something in which they had had no say: 'No taxation without representation' indeed.

Somewhat surprisingly, guards did not halt their progress through the Forum, and men as well as women showed their support. (Was this a not-so-silent protest

---

[20] A political alliance that formally ended the Roman Republic and was ratified a year after Caesar's assassination

against the law, or against the war with Caesar's assassins?) Their numbers were reduced to 400, and men of a certain level of wealth were taxed alongside them. Although the Triumvirate were incensed at the women's behaviour, Hortensia had won the day.

Poppaea was unlikely ever to have needed to take to the streets to get what she wanted – though the fantasy is a nice one! Given the constraints on their public activities, the above examples show that Roman women did what they could, and what they believed they could get away with. It is difficult now to imagine their courage, and the risks they perceived themselves to be taking. Neither should be underestimated; punishment was not lightly meted out in ancient Rome.

The only Roman women permitted any kind of formal political role were the Vestal Virgins (see also Chapter 5), whose persons were so sacred that they had no need of such outrageous behaviour. Competition was fierce for this coveted role as keepers of home and hearth, and keeping alive the sacred flame, for the goddess Vesta. They had the authority to grant leniency to any convicted criminal applying directly to them, and were the official holders of the wills of wealthy Romans. If that could be called power, then they had it.

Informally, however, the *ordo matronarum* (= order of matrons – see the chapter following) could well have played a part in Hortensia's oratorical triumph in the Forum. A group of wealthy, high-status and forthright women gathering to air their grievances and organise protests certainly sounds like the *ordo*. Employing Hortensia to speak on their behalf indicates the presence of influence, organisation and commitment.

Roman women also engaged in what we know as lobbying. Examples exist of high-ranking women banding together (the *ordo* again?) to protest at their menfolk contemplating war, and successfully dissuading them. They well knew the cost of losing their sons, brothers, husbands and fathers in battle. However honourable the profession of soldiering, such women were not wedded to a brutalising activity in which they had no part, and no say. Those who dared to come even close to military activities were pilloried; this was as 'unwomanly' as it was possible to be. As mentioned at Chapter 5, Fulvia was an example.

Married three times, Fulvia's last husband was Marc Antony. She was said to have been very ambitious for him, even as he began his relationship with Cleopatra. In his *Roman Lives* (10), Plutarch wrote of her with undisguised disdain: ". . . *she cared nothing for spinning or housework.*" How in the name of the gods did anyone bring themselves to speak civilly to her?

As a woman who took on the might of Octavian in support of her husband, she was no shrinking violet. However, like other women who dared approach the battleground, she was vilified for her 'manly' behaviour in a world that was male-centred to its very core.

Conduct so flagrantly in breach of boundaries carried a price. She felt the full onslaught of Octavian's ferocious propaganda machine, directed at her personally (Cleopatra suffered likewise); Antony later repudiated some of her activities on his behalf that he had formerly approved. She died of illness in Greece, largely unappreciated by her husband even having staunchly supported him throughout their marriage.

Other Imperial women famously intervened in their men's affairs, convincing them to temper their inclinations to war. Octavia, Octavian's sister, was one, stepping in more than once to broker peace between Marc Antony and her brother. Agrippina the Elder (Nero's grandmother) created more of a stir by accompanying her husband to the field of battle. Though this caused the expected reaction, her husband being the military 'golden boy' Germanicus allowed her to get away with it.

A women of Poppaea's intelligence could hardly have failed to be aware of her influence as mistress, or wife, of the Emperor. A number of examples illustrate this: for instance her support of Jewish causes, and her likely intervention following the altercation between Pompeii and Nuceria at the former's amphitheatre.

In 59 CE – she and Nero were not yet married – the citizens of these two cities came to blows, fuelled by fierce rivalry between their competing gladiatorial teams. Salvatore Nappo suggests that their animosity was exacerbated by Nero having founded a colony in Nuceria two years earlier[21], allowing the settlement of veteran soldiers, along with a bonus payment per head of population.

Colonial status clearly bestowed special privileges on residents, something that Nucerians could now boast of, and Pompeians could not. After a battle leaving both dead and injured, and the Pompeians victorious, the Senate decreed that gladiatorial contests be banned, and the amphitheatre closed for a decade, as punishment.

Having suffered the worst injuries and deaths the Nucerians, unusually, complained of their treatment direct to the Emperor rather than the Senate. This illustrated further the benefits of colonial status: they could expect preferential treatment, and their wrongs to be righted, since their Emperor had bestowed on them this elevated status.

Inscriptions show that colonial status was subsequently conferred on Pompeii at some point after January 63. This coincided with the birth of Claudia, the short-lived Imperial child. It seems plausible that Nero's decree was in recognition of Poppaea's connection to the city. The gladiatorial ban was lifted by 65, four years early; was this Poppaea's influence at work?

Roman patronage was already established long before Poppaea's lifetime, and for some time after:

---

[21] *Pompeii* (2004), White Star S.r.l., Vercelli, Italy

> ... *over 1200 individuals* [as patrons of communities]
> *are known from the epigraphical record and can be dated*
> *to the period between 50 B.C. and A.D. 327 ... as many*
> *as twenty-one cases have been noted in which the* patron
> *is actually a* patrona.[22]

Both communities and individuals (always of lower status) could benefit. Community patronage in the provinces might include political and/or legal interventions with the powers-that-be in Rome; individual patronage could have either political or cultural focus. Had market research been a feature of Roman life, it would doubtless have demonstrated that 'wicked' women were proponents of political support, and 'virtuous' women of cultural. A few examples:

- ✓ **Livia** (30 BCE-29 CE), wife of Augustus, whose interests were political rather than literary. She supported public building, the restoration of temples, and philanthropy;

- ✓ **Octavia** (c. 69 BCE-11 CE), sister of Octavian, was a *patrona* of literature and learning. She dedicated a library to her much-mourned son Marcellus, who died in 23 BCE as a young man; and

- ✓ **Eumachia** (1st century CE), wealthy *patrona* of the Pompeian guild of fullers (cleaners, dyers and

---

[22] J Nicols, *Gender and Civic Patronage* in *Studies in Latin Literature and Roman History V* (1989), ed. C Deroux, Latomus Revue D'Etudes Latines, Brussels, Belgium

clothing makers), used her own funds to build a large prominent building by the Forum for public use.

It can be seen that the rules governing 'what kind of women did what' apply.

Poppaea is on record as assisting in Gessius Florus (a Roman, of Greek extraction) obtaining the governorship of Judea from 64-66 CE through her alleged friendship with his wife Cleopatra (see above). However his term was marked by his cruelty and greed, along with favouring Greeks over Jews, and he was much hated.

Jewish historian Josephus is the main source; his reading of Florus' character is predictably hostile. He is said to have left more than one account of the tragic events that took place, and to have been contradictory and tendentious in them.

How Poppaea's involvement came about is unclear. However, she can hardly be held responsible for Florus' disastrous tenure. It is reasonable to suppose that had his true character been known, she would not have used her influence with Nero to facilitate his appointment. In addition, her suggested sympathy with Jewish causes does not chime with encouraging the appointment of someone who might conceivably have inclined towards persecuting Jews, in their home territory or elsewhere.

Josephus appears again as the best-known example of Poppaea's overtly political activities. Her assistance in freeing Jewish prisoners held in Rome is noted at Chapter 3. He could be said to have benefited from her patronage in that the mission was successful, and he received gifts from her to take back to Jerusalem.

The bestowing of gifts has been misconstrued by some sources, but Emily Hemelrijk notes the benefits "... *not only money, but also gifts in kind, appointments, privileges and immunities . . .*"[23] to be had from the Emperor in the role of *patron* – or his wife as *patrona*.

William den Hollander[24] posits that the meeting between Poppaea and Josephus concerning the Jewish prisoners is likely to have had more significance for him than for her, in her role as 'Lady Bountiful'. Poppaea's gifts to him, as well as using her influence to favour his request, should not therefore be seen as any more significant than the normal and expected behaviour of a *patrona* towards her client.

Josephus also claimed that Poppaea influenced Nero in a dispute with King Agrippa II in Jerusalem, thought to have taken place around 60-62 CE in the term of the

[23] *Matrona Docta: Educated Women in the Roman Elite from Cornelia to Julia Domna* (1999), Routledge, London
[24] *Josephus, the Emperors and the City of Rome: From Hostage to Historian* (2014), Koninklijke Brill NV, Leiden, Netherlands

Procurator[25] Porcius Festus. This concerned the building of a wall in the temple, intended to block the King's view of (presumably) sacred activities within. Both the King and Festus objected, wanting the wall dismantled. The priests petitioned to Nero who granted the preservation of their wall in order, Josephus believed, to gratify his Empress.

In the world of Imperial politics, much is written about the role of courtiers. In an environment so prone to lightning-swift change, politicking required a great deal of skill, clearsightedness, cool judgement and not a little courage if positions within the Emperor's closest circles were to be maintained.

It was also crucial to sustain some measure of stability – no easy task with Nero in the chair – so that the worst disasters could be averted, and the entire Imperial edifice did not topple, bringing everyone down with it.

Courtiers, after all, potentially had as much to lose with a change of management as did their emperors. Taking steps to consolidate their positions, combined with some fancy footwork, might just have allowed the most ambitious and clever of them to keep their heads, in every sense. If they could work things to their advantage, well and good. Would it last? Almost invariably not; the good times would continue only as long as circumstances allowed.

---

[25] Officials appointed to administer provinces, with particular regard to Imperial finances

Courtiers would struggle to see out more than one 'term', serving the emperor who put them there. Any successor to an ousted emperor would in all likelihood have removed existing courtiers with due haste, understandably suspecting their loyalty. Adrenalin levels within innermost circles must have remained alarmingly high.

Though many courtiers may have begun their 'careers' as slaves, progress within the court was not necessarily proscribed. Whether working in the kitchens, looking after Imperial offspring, dressing the hair and person of the Empress, or entertaining dinner guests, the possibility existed to better themselves and move onwards and upwards if they possessed the necessary skills and found favour with those in control – and as long as the gods smiled on them.

Inscriptions are the most helpful sources in mentioning particular courtiers. D C Braund[26] quotes one such:

> *Polytimus, steward of Poppaea Augusta, wife of Nero Caesar Augustus, has fulfilled his vow to Fortune.*

A steward was a senior servant with substantial responsibilities, employed in a landed property. Since Braund notes this inscription at Arna in Umbria, it is

---

[26] *Augustus to Nero: A Sourcebook on Roman History 31 BC to AD 68* (1985), Croome Helm Ltd, London

unclear how it connects to Imperial Rome, some 110 miles south.

Tana Joy Allen[27] mentions another, reflecting Poppaea's connection to Campania:

> *An inscription from a votive relief found at Aenaria* [modern Ischia] *provides another example of a manumission by the wife of the emperor. The text of the name reads:* Argenne Poppaeae Augustae Augusti liberta . . . *Argenne is the freedwoman of Poppea Sabina, the wife of Nero, and of the emperor himself.*

She goes on to plausibly date the inscription to post-63, when Poppaea was crowned 'Augusta'. Argenne is said to have been cured of some affliction by the therapeutic waters of Aenaria but details are scarce, as with Polytimus' unexplained "vow to Fortune".

As Empress, Poppaea would have been surrounded by slaves to do her every bidding. She may have had a particular fondness for some, but without inscriptions to tell us, their names go unrecorded.[28] Personal slaves, akin to a lady's maid, would have been among them; again, no details of any are known. Theirs was a precarious position: one false move, or one tiny error, and they could

---

[27] *Roman Healing Spas in Italy: A Study in Design and Function* (1998), University of Alberta, Edmonton, AB, Canada

[28] We might hope for their eventual discovery, since Livia's columbarium, built during Augustus' reign and containing the remains of, amongst others, c. 90 of her personal Roman slaves, was excavated more than 1,650 years later, and contains a wealth of information on her household.

be banished – if lucky, with their lives. It seems that Argenne was one of the fortunate ones.

Poppaea's power, then, as wife of an emperor, was evident to the extent that the constraints on Roman women allowed. In French's terms, however, she cannot be said to have enjoyed 'power to'; the power to banish a clumsy slave would hardly have rocked Rome's foundations. As noted, her fairly low level on the Imperial Ladder of Power does not compare to Fulvia, Livia, Messallina or Agrippina.

The relatively few instances where she exercised power, and about which we know, do not bear out the attributed levels in the sources, ancient or modern. Rather, they illustrate the contradictory portrayal of Poppaea's character and behaviour that has become so familiar.

As her fantasy diary might have recorded:

Another day doing nothing very special. N. home from the races and to bed, drunk again. Juno, this is tiresome.

CHAPTER 9

The spectacle of death

Pregnant with her third child, Poppaea died in the summer of 65 CE, aged around thirty-four. Much debate has been occasioned, then and since, as to exactly how her death was brought about.

She seems to have receded somewhat in the public eye towards the end of 64. Having suffered the loss of her infant daughter Claudia in the spring of the year before, she had again become pregnant. The Emperor's pleasure at this evidence of the fecundity of his wife can be assumed.

Nero, meanwhile, had devoted himself to the building of his *Domus Aurea* after the great fire in Rome in July 64, taxing whomever he could to fund it, and bleeding dry the state coffers and the provinces in the process.

As opposition to the Emperor grew in intensity, and plots against him gathered strength – though rather more than the *Domus Aurea* could be considered blameworthy – we assume, in the absence of information to the contrary, that Poppaea's pregnancy progressed well. She makes no further appearance in the historical record until her death.

By all accounts she was nobody's fool. A number of intriguing questions therefore arise when considering the impact of events in those final days. How much could she foresee flowing from Nero's increasingly unstable position? If he was incapable of seeing what was coming, it seems hardly credible that the same applied to Poppaea – that both were so self-deluding. Did Nero look to her for support as the ground shifted beneath his feet?

Neronian courage and strong nerves were rarely qualities on display. However, an exception might fairly be conceded of the critical pre-Poppaean period (<58 CE). Nero's relations with Agrippina were increasingly fraught, and must have called for strong nerves; he was engaged in a battle of wills with a consummate politician who was also his mother. However by the time of Poppaea's death he was more than ten years into his reign, with six years in which to indulge himself since Agrippina's death in 59.

As for Poppaea, nothing indicates the existence of anyone in her closest circles in whom she could confide, and speculate as to the future for herself and her unborn child. Both parents were dead; it is probable also that by this time her stepfather Scipio, some thirty years after she met him, was too. No mention is made of any relationship, good or bad, with her half-brother Scipio (II). At this point, then, a realistic assessment of her position within the court is unlikely to reveal any apparent sources of support.

There was, however, Tigellinus.

*

Gaius Ofonius Tigellinus (c. 10-68 CE), though of modest origins, was appointed co-Prefect of the Praetorian Guard by Nero in 62 CE, the year he and Poppaea married. He remained in the post until his death. Though Nero seems to have favoured him over his co-Prefect Lucius Faenius Rufus, no ancient source had a good word to say about him. Miriam Griffin[1] observes:

> *By virtue of their lower social standing, Poppaea and Tigellinus were more dependent on imperial favour than their predecessors. It is therefore not surprising that they gave Nero different advice and used different means to hold his favour.*

The meaning here is unclear, and neither point is elaborated upon; the second is especially intriguing. At all events, they hardly point to the pair being 'thick as thieves', as is commonly recorded. Rather, the implication is that they were following agendas that were by no means necessarily conjoined. This is puzzling, since it might be thought that any kind of devilish duo must surely have needed to be 'reading from the same page' in

---

[1] *Nero-The End of a Dynasty* (1984), B T Batsford Ltd, London

order to successfully carve out, and hold onto, their positions within the Imperial court.

Tigellinus, then, does not seem a natural ally, even supposing Poppaea considered the possibility. His job was to support, and obey, his Emperor.

*

Poppaea's pregnancy was possibly well advanced when matters came to a head in the Pisonian conspiracy to assassinate Nero in early 65. How much she knew of these events is a matter for speculation. Tacitus, however, claimed that she and her alleged partner-in-crime Tigellinus were present when Nero received a report linking his former tutor Seneca to the plot. Tacitus' source is not made clear, nor are any remarks from either of the devilish duo recorded.

Nero's sweep of suspected conspirators was, as might be expected, ferocious and unrestrained, if a little inconsistent. It is less easy to imagine Poppaea also weighing in with a vengeance, encouraging him (again) to do his worst, as her reputation would have had her do. Her primary focus would surely have been her own health, and that of the child she was carrying; the dramatic aftermath of the conspiracy can hardly have helped maintain a calm atmosphere beneficial to pregnancy. As his Empress, however, she would presumably have been expected to be at the forefront of the support that Nero would have assumed.

With her fate, and that of her baby, inextricably tied to the Emperor, the outcome for both had the assassination succeeded cannot be imagined. She was carrying an Imperial child, not something that could easily have been overlooked. Would she have been killed alongside Nero? It is difficult to envisage a queue of soldiers standing ready to carry out an order to murder a pregnant Empress, whatever the prevailing opinions of her. Banishment may have been a more likely option. Her thoughts on her own position, in the midst of such a threatening and unpredictable atmosphere, can only intrigue us.

It is a matter of regret that, of all the high profile Imperial wives, the workings of Poppaea's mind in particular are unknown. As a woman of intelligence, and wife of one of Rome's more controversial rulers, it is inconceivable to picture her living in her own little bubble, oblivious to everything going on around her. However nowhere do we find hints of what she thought of her husband's political skills, and how they might have affected the futures of both herself and their second child, shortly to be born. Did she feel safe and secure alongside him, or nervous and afraid?

Nero, meanwhile, spent his leisure time at the games – where his head was buried firmly in the sand.

Poppaea's relative non-appearance in the record during the term of this pregnancy has a possible explanation that is, once again, none too subtle. It was wickedness, after all, that commonly propelled high-status Roman women into the limelight. So a pregnant Empress, displaying no wantonness, malevolence, or otherwise indecorous behaviour (in stark contrast to the prevailing negative image) simply drops off the historical page.

Such treatment speaks volumes about the focus of her portrayal by writers old and new. Perversely, it would seem that 'unwomanly', that is, unacceptable, behaviour is what guaranteed Roman women coverage, since it was the most heinous of crimes in the eyes of Roman men. Once again we might ask: are unflattering portrayals preferable to none at all?

The innumerable mentions of Poppaea's death propel her back into the headlines, though they are often brief:

Tacitus (*Annals*):

> *She was pregnant, and her husband, in a chance fit of anger, kicked her.*

Suetonius (*Lives of the Caesars*):

> *Yet he killed her, too, by kicking her when she was pregnant and ill, because she had scolded him when he came home from the chariot-races.*

Cassius Dio (*Roman History*):

> *Sabina also perished at this time through an act of*
> *Nero's; either accidentally or intentionally he had leaped*
> *upon her with his feet while she was pregnant.*

Such is the variety of descriptions that a closer look might be instructive.

What seems not in dispute is that Poppaea was pregnant at her death, although Suetonius is alone in suggesting that she was also "ill". This claim may have to be treated with caution since he also suggested that Nero's paternal aunt Domitia Lepida was ill when he brought about *her* death. These may well be instances of Suetonius unable to resist the opportunity to drive home Nero's despicable character: he would kill women who were already physically vulnerable.

In her third pregnancy – that we know of – we might suppose Poppaea to have been in little fear of its effects, or that the pregnancy would not proceed to its expected outcome. It is as well to bear in mind, however, that in Roman terms, at around her mid-thirties she was now no longer a young woman, at least in the matter of child-bearing.

What is remarkable is the insistence by innumerable sources on Nero having 'kicked her to death'. The 2006 BBC TV docu-drama series "Ancient Rome: The Rise and Fall of an Empire", her most recent known screen appearance, depicts a shocking death scene for Poppaea. Nero, clearly enraged and out of control, repeatedly kicks her as she lies on the floor, to the horror of household slaves gathered round. We see no image of the victim, only the close-up face of the perpetrator, but that is enough.

One assumes that the seven male writers and six male directors involved in the series thought this great drama. The brutality of the scene certainly reflects the popular belief in the manner of Poppaea's death (and Nero's explosive character). However it cannot be said that such a graphic depiction – uncontrolled male violence towards a pregnant woman *as entertainment* – shows its producers in a commendable light.

Sources agree that Poppaea was much loved by Nero. He is also generally accepted to have been very desirous of having children. The idea that he should deliberately kick to death the woman who might give him more children is therefore greatly at odds with the historical record; its credibility must be questionable.

In a revealing statement one of the BBC series producers claimed the focus of its storylines to have been historical accuracy, thought not to have been evident in its main competitor of the previous year, the lavishly produced HBO series "Rome". It seems that some kind of credibility contest was in play between the two productions.

The portrait of Nero the Monster, who would viciously attack the woman he loved in a fit of blind rage, and when she was in no shape to defend herself, illustrates the predilection of historians for emphasising his loathsome character. They are perfectly entitled to do so. However it leads towards the trap, which Tacitus fell into on a regular basis, of favouring dramatic impact over any attempt at historical accuracy. Monstrous figures make such good copy – ask any editor of a populist newspaper.

Nero does not even redeem himself by extravagant displays of grief at the loss of his adored wife, and their baby. This is simply Nero playing to the crowds, no more than what is expected. He is Nero the Drama Queen.

Sources suggest that dislike of Nero is a relevant component of the way such incidents are recorded: "[being] . . . *associated with tyrants* [and] . . . *used to discredit those involved for political reasons.*"[2] Caitlin Gillespie agrees that the record: " . . . *likely reflects gossip promoted by Nero's detractors rather than a historical reality.*"[3]

Finally, a connection might be made to other similar attacks in antiquity by husbands on pregnant wives. Deacy and McHardy point out that no less than seven men killing or attacking their pregnant wives can be found in Greek writings. How many of these were

---

[2] Susan Deacy and Fiona McHardy, *Uxoricide in Pregnancy: Ancient Greek Domestic Violence in Comparative Perspective* in *Evolutionary Psychology* 11.5 (2013), Roehampton, London, UK
[3] *Poppaea Venus and the Ptolemaic Queens: An Alternative Biography* in *Histos* 8 (2014), Western Washington University, Bellingham, WA, USA

intended, as the primary focus, to show 'perpetrator as tyrant'?

Little more can helpfully be said on this issue than to bring home the need for caution when examining ancient sources. Tracy Lynn Deline reminds us: *"Moral tales (exempla) reflect idealized behaviour – the truth as the authors would like it to be . . .".*[4]

As noted, Nero was likely to have been watching the games in the Circus Maximus on the day of Poppaea's death. Sources record his particular fondness for chariot races from early youth, and he is said to have shared an early love of horses with Tigellinus.

It can reasonably be assumed that he would not have been sober on returning home. We imagine a possibly heavily pregnant Poppaea, confronting a not-entirely-sober Nero returning, as is often suggested, later than expected. Poppaea, not feeling her best, is upset. She complains about his tardiness, with the implication that she is not being looked after as she should be. They quarrel; Nero, never tolerant of criticism, loses his temper. Does a man, unsteady from drinking, aim a kick *upwards* at his pregnant wife's belly, while she stands, berating him (even supposing he was angry enough to do so)? Can he still remain balanced and upright if he does? Household

---

[4] *Women in Criminal Trials in the Julio-Claudian Era* (Thesis 2009), University of British Columbia, Vancouver, BC, Canada

slaves were never going to be asked to provide witness statements.

Some possible alternative scenarios might be considered:

No. 1: Nero loses his temper at being castigated, perhaps giving Poppaea a shove; she, heavily pregnant, overbalances and falls. A kick may then – or not – have been directed at her, now that she is prone and an easier target. A woman who is only a few months off giving birth is unlikely to take a fall without serious consequences, both to herself and her unborn child. She cries out, Nero sobers in a second. She begins bleeding . . .

No sources mention who ministered to Poppaea and her baby in the intermediate aftermath of the incident. Slaves would presumably have been sent at once for a physician (*medicus*), likely to have been a Greek, given both their acknowledged superior medical skills and Nero's known favour towards Hellenism. Midwives (*obstetrices*), while most likely in the service of Imperial families, might not have been readily available, since these events would have occurred without warning, the household unprepared for them. Still, their presence cannot be discounted since they enjoyed equal status alongside doctors.[5]

---

[5] Valerie French, *Midwives and Maternity Care in the Roman World* in *Helios*, 13(2) (1986), Texas Tech University Press, Lubbock, TX, USA

No. 2: When Nero loses his temper, he perhaps gives Poppaea a shove; she overbalances and falls. This causes the onset of miscarriage; she begins to bleed . . .

No. 3: Nero's late arrival home, having been out enjoying himself, has nothing to do with Poppaea's pregnancy. For reasons we are unlikely ever to know – possibly connected to Suetonius' suggestion of illness – she suffers a late miscarriage which takes both her life and that of her baby.

While never disguising his detestation of Nero, Tacitus explicitly rejected the suggestion – sources are again not named – that Poppaea died from poisoning. This claim is attributed to those unnamed sources' hatred of Nero, and their desire to paint him as sufficiently monstrous to want to despatch his beloved pregnant wife with poison. No doubt with a perfectly straight face, Tacitus accuses them of pandering to emotionalism and dislike rather than striving for historical accuracy.

The general consensus seems to be that the Emperor did not mean to kill his pregnant wife, or their unborn child; in this instance, at least, he was no murderer.

Nero's reaction to the loss of both his wife and baby, and his resulting behaviour, are covered extensively in the literature. Tacitus, though, goes on to negate his previous mildly sympathetic report:

> *Publicly Poppaea's death was mourned. But those who*
> *remembered her immorality and cruelty welcomed it.*

Noticeably, no mention is made of the loss of the baby.

Tacitus is not alone is this omission. In a late miscarriage the sex of the child would have been apparent, yet there is no record of whether it was a daughter or a son lost, or of the fate of the body. Whether or not its disposal would have been affected by embalming as opposed to cremation is unclear. The unborn child is lost somewhere in the mists of perfumes and spices.

We know that, in homage to eastern customs, Nero decreed that Poppaea's body should be embalmed, not cremated, and filled with 'spices'. No details are known of those whose necessary knowledge and skills were employed in carrying out the procedure.

As for the funerary rites, Pliny the Elder, in his *Natural History* (12.41.83), contributed his thoughts:

> [cinnamon and cassia] . . . *are thought to have been*
> *made by the gods for burning with the dead. Those*
> *knowledgeable about the matter have said that more than*
> *a year's supply was burned by the Emperor Nero on the*
> *last day of his wife Poppaea.*

Frankincense and myrrh are also mentioned, though these may be the spices with which the body was stuffed. Strong-smelling spices such as cinnamon were commonly used in antiquity in part to disguise the smell of corpses, which had various rituals to undergo before being finally dealt with, perhaps some days after death.

Without doubt, vast quantities would have been necessary for the tasks of both embalming and burning. Most sources mention the enormous cost – a subject long known to have been of no interest to the profligate Nero. Indeed, given his extraordinary history of immoderation and over-indulgence, it is likely that he saw this expenditure as a public demonstration of the depth of his love, and loss. It may also have been an attempt to assuage his feelings of guilt and remorse.

While cremation was the Roman tradition, embalming was not entirely unknown. Nonetheless it is likely that Poppaea's embalming would have provoked a measure of shock and disbelief. This was a practice undeniably foreign, by definition inferior – barbarous when compared to the civilised Roman cremation.

At the same time, in its ostentation and spectacle, Nero set himself and his Empress apart from the rest of the people of Rome: 'We are who we are. We are different. See how we do things differently?'. Even unconsciously, he cannot have failed to approve of anything that bolstered the perceived distinction he had already established in the public mind by his fervent dedication to theatre, music and Art. It marked him out, for better or worse, as different from any other emperor excepting, perhaps, his Uncle Caligula. At all events, both 'foreignness' and excess were central to the elaborate manner in which Poppaea was sent on her way to join the gods.

Gillespie, among other sources, suggests that Nero's embalming of Poppaea's body was a link to Ptolemaic kings, since in his later life he saw himself as a 'king-god' (and a 'sun-god' – see the *Domus Aurea*). Poppaea was therefore rightly, in his terms, embalmed and honoured as befitted a queen.

It is a short step, once more, to Cleopatra. Poppaea can be linked again, posthumously, to her legendary sister-queen in immodest displays of excess and extravagance, even though they are Nero's doing. She cannot escape the comparison, even in death.

Nowhere do we read of a will requesting that Poppaea's body be honoured with such extravagant treatment – which does not, of course, mean that no such document existed. Harriet Flower[6] mentions Augustus' instructions for his own funeral, left with his will but not part of it, but admits that we cannot know how common such a practice was. In any event, instructions left by a history-making emperor, as opposed to a rather less well known emperor's wife, cannot compare.

---

[6] *Ancestor Masks and Aristocratic Power in Roman Culture* (1996), Oxford University Press, Oxford, UK

The idea that embalming rather than cremating stemmed from the abhorrence of burning a much loved person might well have applied to Nero and his adoration of Poppaea and her beauty. It might also be interpreted as an attempt to keep the beloved deceased 'alive', impossible to achieve if the body has been destroyed by incineration. In this way death might in some measure be manipulated, if not outdone. Immortality, of a sort, is achieved.

Nero gave Poppaea a state funeral (*funus imperatorium*), but the underlying sniffs of disapproval are everywhere in the record: she had still not earned such a royal fuss, they seem to be saying.

Roman funerals followed elaborate procedures, although no record details how this applied to Poppaea's: for instance, the clothing she was dressed in; how and when the body was removed from the Imperial palace; who transported it to the Forum; the presence of household slaves and others. Nero's love of theatrics makes it is hard to believe that he would not have indulged this to some extent, given customary procedures. Ivana della Portella[7] notes of the funeral ceremony that it was:

> . . . *often a lavish display that made use of theatrical representations with a strong emotional impact . . . The ceremony also included musicians, mimes and dancers*

---

[7] *Subterranean Rome* (2002), Arsenale Editrice, San Giovanni Lupatoto, Italy

who-in the case of illustrious persons-accompanied the
procession as far as the Forum.

We do not know if any of this happened (or whether Poppaea might have approved of such high jinks). However, as befitted the occasion, Nero pronounced the eulogy (*laudatio funebris*) from the *rostra* in the Forum, probably the most public platform in Rome. As would be expected, he praised her beauty, her virtues, and the fact that she had recently given birth to a now deified daughter. The reactions of the crowds gathered there can only be imagined.

Scholars and historians are not in accord as to precisely where Poppaea was buried, perhaps further complicated by the fact of her embalming. There are two possible options:

Tumulus Iuliae

This was the *sepulcrum* (= any burial place) where Julia, daughter of Julius Caesar, was entombed. The precise location is unknown, though it would have been in Rome's Campus Martius, historically an honourable place to be buried.

It considerably predated Augustus' own personally designed tomb. Julia died in childbirth in 54 BCE; Augustus did not begin his own monument until more than twenty years later. Lawrence Richardson describes it as " . . . *an impressive and capacious monument and, as a* tumulus [ancient burial mound], *a forerunner of the* Mausoleum Augusti."[8]

Mausoleum Augusti

This was the Emperor Augustus' extravagant shrine to himself and his family and descendants. It was an enormous circular construction topped by his bronze statue. Today's remains sadly reflect neither the significance nor the grandeur of the original, and it has seen many changes of use over the ages.

A theory exists that Augustus chose the site to make a posthumous connection between himself and other illustrious Romans buried in the Campus, for example Sulla and Julius Caesar. (The latter's precise burial details are a matter of considerable debate – see further below.) Another suggestion is that his choice reflected the fact that the area was flat, facilitating the construction of such a large building.

Richardson goes on to claim that Caesar's daughter Julia was not cremated, though no reason is suggested, nor is it clear who made this decision. Rather, she is said to have been buried in Rome to favour the people, with whom she was popular, rather than at her husband's Alban estate in the hills outside the city. Some sources[9]

---

[8] *A New Topographical Dictionary of Ancient Rome* (1992), The John Hopkins University Press, Baltimore, MD, USA
[9] For example Joann Fletcher, *Cleopatra the Great-The Woman Behind the Legend* (2008), Hodder and Stoughton, London

disagree, asserting that the ashes of both Caesar and Julia were buried in the *Tumulus Iuliae*. Richardson further suggests the likelihood of Julia having been buried in a sarcophagus.

Sarcophagi were not in common usage for some two hundred years after this period; nor, however, was the practice of inhumation a common Roman custom in the late Republic. Customary practice would have displayed the body on top of the sarcophagus while the eulogy was read. It would then have been placed inside, and the whole buried in the appointed place.

Richardson goes on to suggest that the *Tumulus Iuliae* is likely to be where Poppaea was also buried. The most probable reason is that Augustus' Mausoleum was not designed to hold sarcophagi – nor would it have been, since cremation was the custom. Sarcophagi naturally needed rather more space than urns filled with ashes, and the labrynthine passageways inside the *Mausoleum* did not provide for this. That the whole was clearly of enormous size in its original form does not assume similarly sized spaces inside it large enough to accommodate multiple sarcophagi; the house of Augustus was not small in numbers.

As with so much of ancient Roman history, the real story of where Poppaea is buried is ripe for speculation, though Richardson's theory seems plausible. To the Emperor she was his queen, and her funerary rites amply demonstrated this.

However even Nero, the supreme megalomaniac, may have baulked at the possible reaction of the Senate and the people had he marched her corpse straight off to the hallowed *Mausoleum Augusti* for burial. Though he could claim, at a remove, connection to Augustus' bloodline through his mother, he may have needed reminding that Poppaea could not. The *Tumulus Iuliae* might therefore have been an acceptable compromise; if so, it would have been a rare instance of Neronian common sense. The precise whereabouts of the *Tumulus* are still unknown in the absence, thus far, of excavations revealing it.

The speculation concerning Poppaea's burial still leaves questions unanswered. If she was finally laid to rest in a sarcophagus, was her body first displayed on top of it, for all the world to see, while Nero delivered his fulsome eulogy in the Forum? Those unknown persons employed in arranging the entire production would doubtless have been familiar with this tradition. However sources are silent on the point. More poignantly still, was the body of the unborn Imperial child placed alongside her?

We know that a temple, the *Temple of Fecunditas*, was decreed after the birth of baby Claudia in 63 CE to honour Poppaea's fertility, but that no sources claim definitively that it was built. However, a further temple was ordained after Poppaea's death. Peter Kragelund[10] notes the relative lack of mention of it in any sources, and comments:

> *According to this passage* [from Cassius Dio-see below], *Diva Poppaea was posthumously venerated in a temple that Nero officially inaugurated in the spring of 68 . . . Poppaea was here receiving homage as 'the goddess Sabina-Venus' . . .*

He concludes that its location was more likely to have been Campania than Rome, supporting the accepted belief that the former was Poppaea's home territory.

Cassius Dio[11] quoted the inscription on the temple, *"Sabinae dea Veneri"*, and stated further:

> *. . . after he completed and adorned the shrine of Sabina he dedicated it brilliantly, having inscribed on it that the women had made it for the goddess Sabina Aphrodite* [Venus]. *And he was truthful in this; for a great amount of the money from which it was built had been stolen from women.*

The 'women' mentioned are not explained; nor the act of 'stealing' from them (although it points to the financially embarrassed Nero as prime suspect, since he would have spent virtually every penny in the Empire on his *Domus Aurea*). One possibility could be the *ordo matronarum*.

*

---

[10] *The Temple and Birthplace of Diva Poppaea* (2010), in *Classical Quarterly* 60.2, Cambridge, UK
[11] 63.26.3-4 in Gillespie, *op cit*

As with the *consilium*, mentioned in the previous chapter, this is another entity that is difficult to define; its Republican origins may have had a religious grounding. Sources suggest a loose grouping of married women of status habitually gathering to represent their interests and give mutual support. Had there not been such a group in existence, the introduction of the *lex Oppia* in 215 BCE, restricting the way wealthy Roman women could dress and travel (see Chapter 8), might well have instigated one.

It is reasonable to assume that any getting together by high-ranking, intelligent and strong-willed women would have been in response to the fact that Roman women had no formal role in public life, and did not like it. That they felt compelled to display 'unwomanly' behaviour – appearing in public and drawing attention to themselves – would have invited considerable opprobrium, and shocked and angered the ruling élite. Such was the strength of feeling abroad that the women manifestly did not care.

Augustus' wife Livia, as already noted, was something of a groundbreaker. A number of sources, for example Kragelund, mention her having had a connection to an *ordo matronarum*. Amongst other matters, the *ordo* spent time, and presumably private money, restoring temples dedicated to goddesses worshipped only by women: for example, the *Fortuna Muliebris* (the Fortune of Women). In addition, in her role as *Romana Princeps* (first female citizen):

> . . . [Livia] *deals with the divinities in whose hands the*
> res publica [the state or the republic] *reposes, on*
> *behalf of the sections . . . with which she is concerned –*
> *the* ordo matronarum *and the family of which she is*
> *mother.*[12]

Aside from any other consideration, if Livia was connected to the *ordo*, funds would not have been in short supply.

*

Though not all sources agree, it would seem that Nero's worst excesses are likely to have surfaced following that summer of 65 in which Poppaea died. This is not to suggest, necessarily, that she had been any kind of restraining influence; his entire life had seen one after another of those, and he had outlasted them all.

In the wake of the final disposal of Poppaea's body, wherever that might have been, events in the Imperial household took a bizarre turn. Much prurient interest, both ancient and modern, has been shown in the 'relationships' in which Nero went on to immerse himself. However, the focus of this work does not warrant delving too deeply into Nero's sexual proclivities in this regard.

However, he seems to have attempted to reproduce Poppaea as a companion and wife, first with a woman

---

[12] N Purcell, *Livia and the Womanhood of Rome* in *Augustus* (2009), J Edmondson (ed), Edinburgh University Press, Edinburgh, Scotland

resembling her, then with Sporus, the young slave who was said to have been castrated and dressed in the style of Empress (see also Appendix I).

All that can charitably be said about this extraordinary behaviour from the grieving widower is that his personality again shone through, reflecting a lifetime's unrestrained egotism and self-indulgence. It also illustrated the gap Poppaea left in his life, though their relationship had lasted less than ten years, their marriage only three.

Regardless of the questions over the manner of Poppaea's death, and the credibility of his demonstrations of grief, Nero's devotion to her memory was very real. It continued (as Dio tells us) up to the spring of 68, two months before his own enforced suicide.

*

Detailed examination of the aftermath of Poppaea's death cannot properly ignore the 2011 translation of a Greek/Egyptian papyrus fragment found at ancient Oxyrhynchus, south-west of Cairo. It has understandably excited a great deal of academic and scientific interest as part of a large collection of papyri excavated in the late 19th century.

This particular text is a poem, written in Greek, telling the story of the deified Poppaea's looming death and her 'journey' to heaven thereafter; it might be subtitled "Poppaea's Lament". The emphasis is strongly on Poppaea as devoted wife and mother, her interaction with Aphrodite, and her unhappiness at leaving Nero still on earth. This is clearly a Poppaea we have not seen before.

Some scholars suggest that it is a love poem; others that it was written some two hundred years after Nero's death, but with no speculation as to purpose or author. Still others posit that it was written after Poppaea's death in 65, but before Nero's in 68. Gillespie makes a reasonable point, which suggests authorship not long after Poppaea's death:

> . . . *the power of the poetic narrative and its laudatory characterisation of Poppaea would have been strongest for an audience with a living memory of the empress, and of Nero's undying devotion to her.*

What is possibly the main controversy in the text is its suggestion of Nero as god-equivalent, and Poppaea's open acknowledgement of this. It also refutes the idea that her death was caused by a kick from him while she was pregnant: if he had caused her death so brutally, she would not love him. Throughout, her devotion to Nero is apparent.

It is difficult to reconcile these two images of Poppaea, and perhaps we should not try; as noted earlier, Poppaea's feelings towards Nero (excluding Tacitus' take on them) are nowhere mentioned. With both timing and authorship unknown, it nonetheless gives us a portrait of the Imperial couple that requires some suspension of disbelief to accept.

In fact, all the devotion is on Poppaea's side; she bemoans her situation, laments, and waits for Nero to join her. Cynics might suspect a late attempt by Nero's propaganda machine to rework if not his image, then Poppaea's desire to bear his children, oversee their welfare for all eternity, and have him join her in heaven, while she sits, patiently waiting for him.

The timing and meaning of the composition are likely to remain under intense discussion. We can only wonder what Poppaea would have thought of it.

If the above third option of the date of its writing is taken as probable – in the interim between their two deaths – then the hand of Nero, devoted Philhellenist, perhaps still mourning and filled with remorse, might easily be seen.

CHAPTER 10

Chroniclers of Ancient Rome

To paraphrase Jane Austen, it is a truth that may well not be universally acknowledged that the 'accuracy' of history must rely to a large extent on who wrote the book. In no other field of endeavour does this apply with more relevance than to the history of ancient Rome.

The ancient sources who wrote about that history were overwhelmingly members of the élite, whose interest lay in recording the stories of their own kind. Only an exceptional historian of senatorial rank – none springs to mind – would have considered recording the lives and habits of lowly plebeians; most would have been naturally disinclined even to admit their existence. So any reading of Roman history is telling the stories of those who, in the main, belonged to the same privileged classes as those who wrote about them.

The consequences of this for the recording of history should not be underestimated. In concentrating on that favoured minority, the focus of those ancient writers was undeniably narrow. It is easy to forget this. A volume entitled "The History of Rome (but no Women, Plebeians or Slaves)" would be no easy sell.

Roman 'history', then, means the stories of those privileged classes. More than that, it is largely the stories of the male members of those same classes.

Of even greater concern is the fact that this narrowed focus has set the standard for the exploration, and discovery, of the lives of *all* ancient Romans. Given that standard, who can we look to for the inclusion, to any degree, of all those who are *not* part of the story? Where can we find particulars of those lives not deemed worthy of inclusion in the historical narrative? Anyone endeavouring to uncover detailed information on the lives of Roman women will discover just how meagre that information is in the majority of standard textbooks.

Whether this narrowed focus is routinely made part of the story for students of ancient Roman history is less easy to establish. Responsibility for ensuring that it is should rightly fall on modern historians, scholars and teachers of history.

History – of any era – cannot of course be assumed to be of universal interest. Any student can attest to the subject being dramatic or uninspiring, interesting or mind-numbing, exciting or unutterably tedious. We can doubtless remember teachers whose lessons encompassed all of these, who thrilled to (some of) their students' enthusiasm, responding in kind, while failing to notice the glazed eyes of the rest. The appearance of 'Ancient Rome' in the syllabus at the start of an academic year might not, therefore, have necessarily been greeted with eager anticipation.

This serves to emphasise the level of influence enjoyed by history teachers. Backed by traditional textbooks, they can paint pictures of antiquity that are 'accurate' (whatever that might mean), speculative, or somewhere in between.

They can also share their biases, supported by those revered ancient texts. An imagined classroom exchange:

> Teacher: So – as far as Imperial wives go, we know that Nero's second wife Poppaea Sabina was a schemer: she was unscrupulous, promiscuous, immoral – not generally a nice lady.
>
> Student: How do we know if that's really true, Sir?
>
> Teacher: Because Tacitus told us. And he was a brilliant historian, unquestionably our best source.

The present text might be described as a brief 'history' of that bias. It is a matter of profound regret that so many examples of such bias exist, and that it takes as many pages as it does to illustrate just a few.

While not losing sight of the importance of challenging that bias, the even-handed exposition of *all* the residents of ancient Rome should be the very least to be aimed for in any volume professing to explore it. Without that affirmative action, competing with the emperors, the 'stars' in the stories of the Roman Empire, will always be a losing game.

The pathway into history books for the women of ancient Rome is not, nor ever has been, a welcoming one. In general, they are not easy to find, hidden in their cloak of invisibility. When they *are* found, portrayals of them are so often brief, so often unnamed, and as often do not flatter.

As has long been acknowledged, historians of any era are firmly rooted in their own present day, regardless of the period in which they work. Under the influence of attitudes conditioned by their own circumstances, it is unrealistic to suppose that their biases and prejudices will never surface. Such is the reality of history and of its writing.

The general exclusion of Roman women from public activities ensured that they were not in a position to influence that history to any substantive degree. Those attached to a major player were mentioned in that context. Francesca Santoro L'Hoir[1] offers an example of how this worked, and its consequences:

---

[1] *The Rhetoric of Gender Terms-'Man', 'Woman', & the Portrayal of Character in Latin Prose* (1992), E J Brill, Leiden, Netherlands

> *Livy's only reason for inserting women into his history is to further or hinder the action taken by men. Consequently, his female characters are shadowy impersonations of womanhood . . .*

Sarah Pomeroy agrees: *"The women* [of antiquity] *who are known to us are those who influenced matters of interest to men."*[2]

The shortcomings in the depiction of the lives of the women of antiquity, and the relative invisibility of those lives, can have even more troubling consequences. If those lives are not generally acknowledged as part of the historical whole, then where, in any telling of their stories, can the detail be found to flesh them out? Anthony Barrett[3] points up a common practice, one that is far from satisfactory:

> . . . *the common tendency of the ancient sources, especially when they are dealing with certain groups (like ambitious women),* [is] *to think in stereotypes and to tailor the evidence to fit some imaginary preconceived type-model.*

In conjunction with this, sources writing of the lives of high-status women seemed happy to fall back on speculation in the absence of known fact. A cursory glance at any depiction of Poppaea Sabina reveals innumerable

---

[2] *Goddesses, Whores, Wives, and Slaves: Women in Classical Antiquity* (1975), Schocken Books, New York, NY, USA
[3] *Agrippina: Sister of Caligula-Wife of Claudius-Mother of Nero* (1996), B T Batsford Ltd, London

examples, none of which is especially positive. She is of course not alone in this.

Stereotypes and speculation as literary devices are objectionable tools with which to teach us, however there is a third problematic theme. As early as the 16th century, gender issues relating to the chroniclers of history were being exposed:

> *Do you really believe . . . that everything historians tell us about men – or about women – is actually true? You ought to consider the fact that these histories have been written by men, who never tell the truth except by accident.*[4]

Four hundred years later Pomeroy rightly saw the value of reiterating the point: ". . . *the extant formal literature of classical antiquity was all written by men.*" No reader of ancient texts, attuned to the politics of gender, is likely to miss the implications of that.

Along with the prohibited public face, Roman women also lacked a voice, at least on tablet, papyrus or parchment. Emily Hemelrijk[5] makes a disquieting claim:

> *No Roman woman is known to have written a work of oratory, or history, or a treatise on some practical subject . . .*

---

[4] Modesta Pozzo (writing as Moderata Fonte) (1555-1592), *Il merito delle donne* (*The Worth of Women*) (1600), Domenico Imberti, Venezia, Italy
[5] *Matrona Docta: Educated Women in the Roman Elite from Cornelia to Julia Domna* (1999), Routledge, London

It seems hardly credible that no women of either the Republican or Imperial eras ever had a word to say, *or wanted to*, about the events of their time. As Hemelrijk and others[6] demonstrate, it was not as if there were none capable of doing so. A number of possible explanations occur:

o   women *did* write on all, or some, of those topics, and their writings have been 'disappeared'[7]; or

o   the writings of women that were produced fell at the first hurdle, that is the difficulties of circulation and publishing, and therefore of preservation; or

o   we have simply not yet found them.

With the exception of Agrippina's memoirs – almost entirely lost – it is greatly to be regretted that the thoughts

---

[6] See, for example, Jane McIntosh Snyder's *The Woman and the Lyre: Women Writers in Classical Greece and Rome* (1989), Southern Illinois University Press, Carbondale, IL, USA

[7] This possibility is not simply paranoia. The 'New Woman' novels of the late Victorian/early Edwardian era, their heroines free-spirited, educated, forthright, disinclined to marry and have children, were published in their dozens in the late 1800s/early 1900s, and eagerly consumed by a shocked reading public. Seventy or more years later, finding copies of them was found to be extraordinarily difficult. All those authors challenging the restrictions on Victorian women's lives, with their strong, funny, brave heroines, seemed to have been largely 'disappeared', exceptions being well-known names such as Thomas Hardy and H G Wells.

of Roman women on their lives are all but unknown to us. Amy Richlin[8] elaborates:

The fact is, of pre-Christian Roman women, almost no writing remains . . . we hardly know what was lost, though the fact that it includes the memoirs of Agrippina gives an indication of its caliber.

To be obliged to accept the fact that we cannot even know what has been lost is cause for both frustration and regret. It also emphasises the fact, already mentioned, that with no interest in recording the lives of women, ancient historians can be said to have produced only one half of the story.

Some few Roman women who did write (though not, as far as is known, on the subjects mentioned above) are included at Appendix II. Notably they are greatly outnumbered by Greek women. It seems that Greek and Roman men held similarly contradictory attitudes towards their wives and daughters. While the physical freedom of Greek women was restricted even within their own homes, there appeared little problem with them being educated, sufficient to be writing poetry that was published (though this was no straightforward matter[9]) and has survived.

---

[8] *Arguments with Silence: Writing the History of Roman Women* (2014), University of Michigan Press, Ann Arbor, MI, USA
[9] See I M Plant (ed), *Women Writers of Ancient Greece and Rome-An Anthology* (2004), University of Oklahoma Press, Norman, OK, USA

Aside from the obvious problem of ancient texts that are so often fragmented, it is therefore no simple matter to paint a balanced portrait of Poppaea Sabina with the most well-known writers of antiquity as primary sources. Balance appears to be the one element regrettably lacking in all of them.

In addition, Poppaea's life, insofar as we know it, seems ripe for dramatic exposition. The common portrayal suggests that she came out of (relative) nowhere, used her lethal mix of beauty, intelligence, unscrupulousness and immorality to aim at the highest circles, and succeeded. Her very existence, according to Tacitus, brought disaster to the state. (He described Livia Augusta in identical terms.) As is already evident, the excessive use of salacious drama in the telling of her story seems impossible to resist. The sources, it seems, do not even try.

*

Given all of this, it is instructive to look at those ancient historians responsible for one of the most negative portrayals of an Imperial Roman woman ever conceived. Their entries are in the main deliberately brief since all are considered to be authorities, and are widely published accordingly. They are listed chronologically by birth date although this should not be taken as indicative of when they wrote, or the period they covered.

It is also enlightening to note the sources they themselves relied on, although only a brief selection is provided in order to give a flavour. The maxim that historical writers, of any era, are 'only as good as their sources' is a crucial element in any examination of the chroniclers of ancient Rome.

The most familiar historians writing of the Julio-Claudian era (27 BCE-68 CE) were Suetonius, Tacitus and Cassius Dio; they have already been widely quoted in the preceding pages.

Other well known names – not an exhaustive list – are Sallust, Livy, Plutarch and Josephus. A further few are not included for various reasons, for example:

←   Herodian (c. 170-240 CE), because he wrote much later than the present period under examination;

←   Velleius Paterculus (c. 19-c. 31 CE); his *Roman History* ended with the death of Livia Augusta in 29 CE, and is therefore earlier than the present period; and

←   Fabius Rusticus, a contemporary, and admired source, of Tacitus. His history was published c. 83/84 CE but the period it covered is unclear.

*Gaius Sallustius Crispus (**Sallust**)*

Sallust (86-35 BCE) was born in central Italy to a plebeian family. Having become tribune of the plebs[10] in

---

[10] A body (*tribunus plebis*) elected primarily to protect the rights of the common people from oppression by those of higher rank, for example consuls, whose decisions they were empowerd to veto.

52 BCE, he was expelled from the Senate two years later – whether for 'politics' or 'immorality' is unclear. He was charged with extortion after returning to Rome from an appointment as governor of Numidia (North Africa) in 46. Although the charge went nowhere, Sallust retired to private life and wrote historical monographs.

While writing of Cato the Younger (descendant of Cato the Censor below) and the Catiline conspiracy of 63 BCE, Victoria Emma Pagán[11] exposes some of his prejudices:

> [his] . . . *representation of Fulvia (and Sempronia for that matter) conforms to the expectations of Roman historical writing, established in part by Cato the Censor*[12]*, who appears to have consistently doubted the moral capabilities of women. He* [Cato] *equates adulterous women with poisoners; he disparages women's ability to keep secrets . . .*

She goes on to suggest that, Sallust being something of a Cato fan:

> . . . *it is not difficult to imagine that he also imports, whether consciously or unconsciously, the rhetoric of Catonian principles in his own writing.*

---

[11] *Conspiracy Narratives in Roman History* (2004), University of Texas Press, Austin, TX, USA
[12] Also Cato the Elder – see also Chapter 5

John C Rolfe[13], who translated Sallust, seems to agree. He claimed that Lenaeus, a freedman of Pompey Magnus[14], called Sallust ". . . *'an ignorant pilferer of the language of the ancients and of Cato in particular.'* "

Among his sources was Lucius Ateius Philologus, a freedman born in Athens. A rhetorician, historian and grammarian, it is thought that he was also Sallust's mentor.

*Titus Livius (**Livy**)*

Livy was born in 59 BCE (some say 64) and died in 17 CE – c. 13 years before Poppaea was born. He wrote in the early principate, that is after 27 BCE. His home town of Patavium (modern Padua) was steeped in strict conservative values in matters of morality and politics; according to the *Encyclopaedia Britannica* he viewed history ". . . *in personal and moral terms.*" Often grouped with Sallust and Tacitus as the three great ancient sources, his history of Rome and its people became his life's work.

Livy's opinions of women reached back to the absolute monarchies of Roman kings and the later

---

[13] *Sallust* (Loeb Classical Library, 1921), Harvard University Press, Cambridge, MA, USA

[14] Gnaeus Pompeius Magnus (106-48 BCE), statesman and general, born into a family of nobility. Frequently compared to Julius Caesar (who was thought to be the more shrewd politician); the two veered between friends and rivals. He was assassinated in Egypt.

Republic. In a chapter entitled *"Rome, Magna Graecia, and Sicily in Livy from 326 to 200 BC"*[15], Kathryn Lomas notes:

> *Female influence is often presented as a sign of moral decadence or lack of integrity. The backstage manipulations by wives and daughters are a feature of Livy's account of both the Tarquins . . . and of the defection of Syracuse in 212 BCE . . . Undue female influence on public affairs is characterized as both un-Roman and as associated with despotic regimes.*

These stereotypes did not end at 200 BC:

> *In the Augustan period, this was a particularly prevalent stereotype, with clear echoes of Antony and his association with Cleopatra.*

One of Livy's main sources was the Greek Polybius of Megalopolis (c.200-c.118 BCE), author of *The Histories*. It has been suggested that he may have largely reworked Polybius' writings.

Josephus (later *Titus Flavius Josephus*)

Josephus was born in Jerusalem in 37 CE (the same year as Nero) and died c. 100 CE. He travelled to Rome in 64, where he met with Poppaea (see Chapter 3).

As noted at Chapter 1, the language used to describe Poppaea in the historical narrative is rarely less than

---

[15] From *A Companion to Livy* (2015), B Mineo (ed), Wiley Blackwell (John Wiley & Sons Ltd), Chichester, UK

disparaging. Desmond Seward's example is revisited in its entirety since it involves Josephus:

> *On being presented to her - if we can accept Tacitus's description of Poppaea - Josephus found himself confronted by not a ferocious slut but a dignified, surprisingly prudish-looking young lady who, as far as he could make out, was staggeringly beautiful . . . She gave him a gracious welcome.*

We have to assume that "ferocious slut", even in loose translation, is unlikely to have been the phrase Josephus himself would have used (or even Tacitus at his worst). But the rest of the text contradicts every other description of Poppaea that can be found to exist. How can such blatant inconsistency be explained?

Josephus ultimately took Roman citizenship under the Flavians (69-96 CE), changing his name as above, and it was during this period that he wrote. Predictably, his focus was Judaism and the Jewish people and their history. Mentions of women therefore appear in that context (though not often).

His position in Roman society has recently been the subject of increased scholarship, as has his reliability as a source. Views differ as to whether he was a lone isolated Jew in a strange environment or a well-received honorary member of the Roman literati.

Whether he was in Rome when Poppaea died in 65 CE is uncertain. Sources suggest that, had he been, he would have mentioned it in his writings, given his gratitude to her in her role of *patrona*.

In the present context, and as noted earlier, Josephus deserves a place at the head of the ancient sources since he alone wrote of Poppaea in positive terms. As the only source who actually met her, as far as is known, this seems a striking coincidence.

While it can reasonably be assumed that his gratitude would have guaranteed positive mention of her, can this have been the only reason for it? Was she in fact closer to the description Seward attributes to Josephus' first impressions of her than is generally allowed? If so, every derisory portrayal of Poppaea – and that is all of them – calls for careful re-examination. We can only assume that she would have been grateful for Josephus' championing of her had she lived to be aware of it.

Plutarch

Plutarch was a philosopher and essayist, born c. 45 CE into élite Greek society. Though later taking up Roman citizenship, he died in Greece around 120-125 CE. In his mid-twenties when Nero's reign ended in 68, he and Josephus were the only featured sources of adult age during Poppaea's lifetime.

Much of his extensive writings were carried out early in the 2nd century CE, and like Suetonius, he considered himself a biographer rather than historian. He is said to have written a number of works specifically addressed to women friends, including his wife Timoxena. His belief that virtue was the same in both women and men was contentious; ultimately he believed that wives should be subordinate to husbands.

His few references to Poppaea come in his life of the Emperor Galba[16], thought to have been written in 75, ten years after her death. They are carefully qualified: "they say", "as some say" routinely appear. Though not especially complimentary, he seemed to guard against criticism by imputing his remarks to rumour; he might have provided a model for Tacitus, who later did the same.

Plutarch appeared alone in implying that Poppaea might have been as happy to be the Emperor's mistress as his wife. Intriguingly, he does not indicate the source of this contention. The point would doubtless have been fiercely debated by his fellow sources, since it challenged all the claims that she was determined, above all else, to be Empress.

In examining Plutarch's attitudes towards women, it appears that he was generally more respectful than his fellow sources. The most well known of these are thought to have been Polybius, Sallust, Cassius Dio and Livy. He is also said to have used the letters of Cornelia, known as

---

[16] The first in the line-up in 69 CE, known as the 'Year of the Four Emperors'

'Mother of the Gracchi' – the most famous of the paragons of virtue mentioned at Chapter 5 (See also Appendix II).

*Cornelius Tacitus (**Tacitus**)*

Tacitus was born in Roman Gaul – exact location unknown – c. 56 CE, early in Nero's reign, and died around 120 CE. He was therefore a young child when Poppaea entered the record. He is the most highly regarded of ancient writers in depicting the Roman Empire, though vast tracts of his writings are lost.

In particular, modern historians mention a gap in his *Annals* covering the several years prior to 58 CE. This is especially important for present purposes since it covers the run-up to the time when it is thought that Poppaea and Nero began their relationship. The loss is unfortunate, since the timing of events might have been further clarified, and Poppaea's character and motives – with the usual caveats – further illuminated.

Significantly, Tacitus' accounts of the Poppaea/Nero interaction differ greatly between his *Histories* (written first, and published c. 109 CE) and his *Annals*. The reasons why are open to conjecture: differing sources may be one explanation.

According to the *Encyclopaedia Britannica*:

> *He underplayed the effect of immediate circumstances and overplayed the personal factor, a tendency that influenced his use of the historical sources.*

Though he professed an intention to name his sources when they differed, it seems doubtful that he generally kept to his promise. They are said to have included Sallust, Livy and Pliny the Elder. Sallust was apparently helpful for the *Annals*: ". . . *in depicting Poppaea* (XIII 45) *Tacitus turns to Sallust for a model of the unscrupulous woman.*"[17]

David Levene, in his Introduction to the *Histories*[18], makes a revealing comment:

> *From what he presumably saw as broadly accurate sources, he selected the information that would enable him to create his desired picture.*

Tacitus' habit, previously mentioned, of disparaging those connected to already-established targets was undeniably damaging to Poppaea. His detestation of Nero is clear enough; Poppaea was therefore unlikely to escape similar treatment – nor does she.

As noted with Plutarch, he often presented 'fact' as 'rumour' in order to avoid charges of hostility. Another common Tacitean habit is recorded by Levene:

> *Today it is usually thought undesirable for a historian consistently and overtly to instil his biases and his*

---

[17] E Walker and B Henry, *The Annals of Tacitus: a Study in the Writing of History* (1952), Manchester University Press, Manchester, UK
[18] Oxford University Press, Oxford, UK (trans. W H Fyfe 1912; revised by D S Levene 1997)

> *interpretations into his narrative . . . by* imputing to characters thoughts and motives for which he presents no evidence [emphasis added].

Poppaea's portrayal presents clear and consistent evidence of Tacitus' guilt in this, and examples are noted throughout the preceding pages. Of greater concern is the likelihood that this habit passed down, largely unchallenged, to those deferential scholars and historians who followed him.

In addition, he commonly enhanced his narrative by composing and inserting speeches in order to better illustrate the characters of his subjects; Cicero, among other rhetoricians, is suggested by Francesca Santoro L'Hoir[19] to have recommended the practice in order to make a point. Marc Kleijwegt[20] provides an example; writing of Nero's changing relationships with courtiers, he mentions, among others, " *. . . an emotional speech by Poppaea Sabina on the topic of her rival Octavia . . .* ".

Putting words into the mouths of characters he disliked bodes ill for all of them. For Poppaea, it served merely to impute all kinds of manipulative and self-serving motives to be added to her already unflattering portrayal. Her objectionable nature is therefore carried down through the ages, providing a character reading

---

[19] *Tragedy, Rhetoric and the Historiography of Tacitus'* Annales (2006), University of Michigan Press, Ann Arbor, MI, USA

[20] *Nero's Helpers: The Role of the Neronian Courtier in Tacitus'* Annals, University of South Africa Pretoria, in *Classics Ireland*, Vol. 7 (2000)

(whether accurate or not) that seemingly proves hard for modern historians to resist.

A speech Tacitus inserted into his *Agricola* (a biography of his father-in-law, published c. 98 CE), purportedly made by Calgacus, Agricola's Caledonian adversary, is another case in point. While not lacking in dramatic impact, caution is advised in accepting what may have been a literary fiction.[21] No such caution seems ever to be recommended in contemplating Tacitus' portrayal of Poppaea.

Quotations from modern writers illustrating Tacitus' attitudes towards women in general, and Poppaea in particular, are many. Below is a fairly typical example:

> *Our main source concerning Poppaea's* vita moresque [life and character] *is Tacitus who does not even want to veil his detestation and contempt towards the Empress* . . . [22]

A handful of factors are regularly cited to explain those attitudes, with one given particular weight:

---

[21] See for example, D B Campbell, *Mons Graupius AD 83* (2010), Osprey Publishing, Oxford, UK

[22] T Grüll and L Benke, *A Hebrew/Aramaic Graffito and Poppaea's Alleged Jewish Sympathy* in *Journal of Jewish Studies* (2011), Oxford, UK

> *. . . in writing history Tacitus was profoundly influenced by the fact that he was a Roman senator living in an imperial regime.*[23]

While not questioning the truth of this assertion, how it should shape so dramatically Tacitus' treatment of women, and so often to negative effect, is not examined. Indeed, the majority of historians generally ignore the issue altogether.

Ronald Mellor[24] is not one. He gives a revealing taste of the thinly-disguised justification of Tacitean practice:

> *Though . . . undeniably hostile to many women, it might be useful to examine more carefully his understanding of the virtues and vices of women.*

Why should this be useful, or necessary? The reader is asked to 'understand' the consistently harsh treatment of women by probably the most lauded writer of antiquity. It is almost as if we are being asked to take into account his traumatic childhood. Might we expect to find a cold, unloving mother in there somewhere, the cause of all of his subsequent difficulties with women? (As it happens, his mother is never mentioned.)

Pomeroy accurately asserts that "*. . . misogyny taints much ancient literature.*" In a rare admission of this, Mellor

---

[23] D C Braund, *Augustus to Nero: A sourcebook on Roman History, 31 BC-68 AD*, Routledge, Abingdon, UK (originally Croom Helm Ltd, 1985)
[24] *Tacitus* (1994), Routledge, New York and London

states: "[T] . . . *has at times been linked with his contemporaries Martial and Juvenal as a misogynist . . .".* Such is the authority of Tacitus' laudatory reputation that modern writers appear noticeably reluctant to agree.

One interpretation of his leanings provides some amusement:

> *The tradition depicts Poppaea Sabina as a sensuous and extravagant hedonist . . . Tacitus halts his narrative to describe her and, unusually for the* Annals, *ushers in a personage with a detailed character sketch – all of which implies that she will be important (and also suggests that the austere historian may be despite himself rather fascinated by this femme fatale!).*[25]

Had the two been contemporaries, it is unlikely that any such feelings would have been reciprocated to even the smallest degree.

Astonishing as it may seem – and it does – Tacitus seemingly espoused impartiality when he wrote in Book I of his *Histories* that ". . . *those who lay claim to unbiased accuracy must speak of no man* [sic] *with either hatred or affection."* The Tacitean definition of "unbiased accuracy" clearly had no place in his depiction of women.

---

[25] G G Fagan and P Murgatroyd (eds), *From Augustus to Nero: An Intermediate Latin Reader* (2006), Cambridge University Press, Cambridge, UK

Those historians and scholars who seem reluctant to question his attitudes towards women would doubtless leap to Tacitus' defence over any charge of fabrication.

John D Clare[26] is a rare challenger. In a 2013 entry on his history blog, he warns his students:

> *You need to be aware that* [T] *is manipulating his language to prejudice you against them. And if he is manipulating the language, you need to ask yourself, to what extent he is also manipulating the facts . . .*

Gaius Suetonius Tranquillus (**Suetonius**)

Suetonius was born in either Italy or North Africa around 70 CE, some five years after Poppaea's death, and died c. 130. A protégé of Pliny the Younger[27] (c. 61-c. 112 CE), he was employed by the Emperor Hadrian as a general secretary, archivist and librarian, giving him ready access to Imperial archives. Sources record that he was dismissed because of his disrespectful attitude towards Hadrian's wife Vibia Sabina; some suggest that they were involved in a relationship.

Although he was a prolific writer, a distinction is made between, for instance, his *Lives of the Caesars* and Tacitus' *Histories*: between biography and history. The former of course concentrated on the emperors, not their

---

[26] *Tacitus's Attitude To Women – His Use Of The Word* 'Muliebris'
[27] A prolific letter writer; also known for his eye-witness account of the 79 CE eruption of Vesuvius.

wives. His references to women generally occur only when they add to the image of the men on whom he was focussed – as with Livy above.

His sources, like Tacitus, included Marcus Cluvius Rufus, Roman consul, senator and historian, a contemporary of the Emperors Caligula, Claudius and Nero; and Pliny the Elder.

Lucius Cassius Dio (**Cassius Dio**)

Dio was born in Bithynia (modern Turkey) around 150 CE and died in 235. He went to Rome in 180. Said to be an arch-conservative, he entered the Senate during the reign of the Emperor Commodus (180-192 CE).

His main work was a history of Rome from its beginnings to 229 CE, thought to have been written c. 210- c. 230 – some one hundred and fifty years after Poppaea's death. His attempts to employ the popular annalistic tradition of recording history were not always thought successful.

His writing style scaled the heights of inconsistency: it could be ". . . *grandiose and bombastic, reflecting the consciousness of mighty events*" (Byzantine author Photius) or, conversely, " . . . *correct and without affectation.*" (*Encyclopaedia Britannica*) An accurate picture of his work is therefore not easily drawn.

Dio's attitudes towards women, or towards Poppaea in particular (he alone described her throughout as

'Sabina'), are not immediately apparent. He is said to have claimed that all the female masks worn by Nero in his Greek stage appearances after Poppaea's death were fashioned in her likeness ". . . *so that she, even though dead, might tread the stage*"[28] – 'Sabina' having expressed no such desire as far as is known.

However Dio's description of Cleopatra, with whom Poppaea is so often paired in like-minded wickedness, as ". . . *insatiable for sexual passion and money*" is not promising. In addition, a number of sources link him to the claim that, like Cleopatra, Poppaea enjoyed bathing in milk (see Chapter 4). This harks back to the connection noted by Annelise Freisenbruch[29] between female extravagance and immorality. Dio presumably thought the two sisters-in-crime served as examples.

His sources are problematic for modern historians; much scholarship cites Livy as a primary one. However, examination of them produces no firm agreement, with Livy's influence said to have been somewhat overrated.

*

---

[28] Cassius Dio's *Roman History*, 63.9.5, quoted in Niall W Slater's *Nero's Masks* in *The Classical World*, Vol. 90, No. 1 (1996), The John Hopkins University Press, Baltimore, MD, USA

[29] *The First Ladies of Rome: The Women Behind the Caesars* (2011), Vintage Books, London

An entire industry has been built around the analysis of the works of both ancient writers and their sources; the above is a small sample of some of the inherent problems.

A comment attributed to Goethe[30], which might have been aimed specifically at ancient Roman sources, hovers over all of them:

> *Not everything that history offers us has actually happened, and what has actually happened has not happened in the way it is presented ...* [31]

The search for a balanced portrait of Poppaea, then, eludes us; the obstacles seem too great, the prejudices too well-entrenched, and the sources too unreliable.

Given their focus, the writers of antiquity had no interest in portraying women as individuals, sufficient unto themselves, capable of their own rational thought. For this, it seems, we must await the discovery of writings not yet come to light.

However Pomeroy makes a claim for which Poppaea could be seen as a standard bearer:

> *... despite the perspective of some 2,000 years the women of classical antiquity evoke an emotional response.*

---

[30] Johann Wolfgang von Goethe (1749-1832), said to be the greatest German literary figure of his era
[31] Quoted in Alexis Dawson's *Whatever Happened to Lady Agrippina?* in *The Classical Journal*, Vol. 64 *(1969)*, Northfield, MN, USA

Though we know so comparatively little of their lives, a more accurate description of the effect of the women of antiquity on historians and scholars would be hard to find.

Likewise, as can be seen from the preceding pages, the portrayals of Poppaea Sabina, in particular, by those acclaimed chroniclers of ancient Rome can certainly be described as 'emotional'.

But we should not overlook the weight of evidence against their reliability since, emotions aside, it throws up considerable doubt as to whether the term 'accurate' can rightly be applied to any of them.

*

APPENDIX I

A very Roman problem with parentage

In the Notes to Chapter 7, mention is made of a 2009 text by David Woods, *'Nero and Sporus'*[1], which contains speculation as to the possible parentage of Poppaea Sabina:

> . . . *the family and political circumstances surrounding the birth of* [Poppaea] *Sabina were such that it was not impossible that she might have been the* [illegitimate] *daughter of the emperor Tiberius.*

Woods' theory is based on Tiberius' penchant in his later years for forcing himself sexually upon women of high rank, amongst his other much-reported sexual proclivities. (Woods makes the point that, although Tiberius' sexual preferences point to oral sex, it would be naive to assume that all other activities could be excluded.) If Tiberius' behaviour can be accepted as true, the following examples will be two of many:

---

[1] *Latomus Collection*, 68, Brussels, Belgium

(1) At Chapter 7, (ii), in examining Marcus Salvius Otho's forebears, a question is put stemming from the writings of Suetonius. Was Otho's paternal grandmother another victim of Tiberius' assaults? His father, Lucius Otho, was said to physically resemble the emperor, hence the possibility that Lucius Otho's unnamed mother was a victim, and went on to produce a son who resembled him. Lucius Otho's father was said to have been brought up in Livia's household. With Tiberius her son, clearly there were family links.

(2) Several sources mention a woman of rank named Mallonia, who refused Tiberius' sexual demands around 26 CE and was put on trial as a result – behaviour not unheard of from emperors whose advances were spurned (see further below). She committed suicide, but not before publicly condemning his disgusting behaviour in forthright terms. The story of Mallonia is not, however, universally accepted; it is dismissed by Edward Champlin, author of *Nero* (2003), for instance, who maintains that she was fictitious.

At all events, Woods posits that Poppaea the Elder may have been another high-ranking woman unfortunate enough to suffer the Emperor's gross behaviour; he was said to choose women of especial beauty, and by all accounts she was certainly that. In order to protect herself from further harm, she submitted. No woman easily refused the Emperor; Mallonia would have been an example of what happened to those who did.[2]

It should also be borne in mind that Poppaea the Elder would have been a very young woman at this point in time. It can be assumed that, like most others of similar rank, she would have married at around thirteen years of age. This would suggest that she was unlikely to have reached the age of twenty.

It is further suggested, given her husband Ollius' close connection to Sejanus (see Chapter 2), and the latter's increasing disfavour with Tiberius, that she perhaps made it a condition of her submission to Tiberius' demands that her husband would not be persecuted because of that damaging Sejanus connection. This would confirm that events were closing in on Sejanus, and that Poppaea the Elder could foresee her husband's position becoming increasingly untenable, requiring remedial action – even if he could not. Since Ollius clearly did not take steps to distance himself from Sejanus even as it became obvious that he sensibly should, his wife might conceivably have tried to do whatever she could to assist him.

Bearing in mind the estimated date of the younger Poppaea's birth, 30-32 CE, these events, if true, would have taken place around 29-30. Tiberius would have been in his late sixties, and had gone to Caprae in 27, never to return

---

[2] Antonia, Claudius' daughter, was another. Nero allegedly had her executed as she refused to marry him after Poppaea's death, though the story is questioned by some sources.

to Rome (though, as already noted, he did come close). It will be remembered that the Villa Oplontis is in Campania, and that it is generally believed to have been owned by members of the *gens Poppaea*. The two locations are less than 30 kilometres apart by sea.

It is perfectly possible, even likely, that Poppaea the Elder would have been fairly sure of the paternity of her child not yet born, especially if sexual relations with her husband were sporadic. In addition, the fact that, like her daughter, she produced only one (living) child in a lengthy marriage means that the child's paternity is unlikely to have been under question.

Woods goes on to make it clear that had Nero been aware of this parental possibility – and it is implied that he would have been – it would have greatly strengthened his plan to marry Poppaea, rather than remain married to Octavia.

Poppaea had already proven her fertility; Octavia, it seems, could not. Poppaea's direct descendancy from the Emperor Tiberius, albeit illegitimate, would have strengthened Nero's position in his claim to the throne, always an ongoing preoccupation for any emperor. More importantly, any future offspring of a Nero/Poppaea marriage would be Tiberius' grandchildren. If they included boys, this would have further cemented the Nero/Poppaea line, and Nero's position in it.

The theory is an extraordinary one. Whether or not it has any credence is open to lively debate, though it is unclear if the text is common currency; it was published in 2009.

As already noted, the basis of the theory extends, via the elimination by Octavian of Caesarion, son of Cleopatra and Caesar, to the elimination by Nero of young Rufrius Crispinus, Poppaea's son, in 66 CE. By virtue of their parentage, both sons stood to have a claim to the throne: Caesarion through his father Julius Caesar, Crispinus (II) through his (illegitimate) grandfather Tiberius. Both were therefore eliminated at a young age to ensure that their possible succession would never eventuate.

Whatever might be thought of this whole hypothesis, one thing is undeniable: no emperor would ever tolerate threats to his position. Regardless of character, none would have had the slightest hesitation in removing any that might be perceived to exist, in as ruthless a manner as was deemed necessary.

The fate of young Crispinus (II) offers a plausible explanation for the banishment and following suicide of his father Crispinus (I). If, as might reasonably be supposed, the elder Crispinus was aware of his son's true grandfather, then Nero could not afford to risk having him around talking about it – whether or not he was inclined to do so.

Crispinus' alleged part in the Pisonian Conspiracy, then, begins to look a little suspect as the reason for his banishment to Sardinia in 66, with its eventual conversion to an order for execution. Indeed, some sources throw doubt on it in any event. (See Chapter 7 for discussion on this point.)

A number of issues need to be considered. First and foremost is the character of Nero. Enough has been written about him to obviate the need to do so at length here. However, in the wake of the deaths of his mother Agrippina and his wife Poppaea, he was manifestly unstable: paranoid, nervous and fearful, and more than capable of lashing out and eliminating anyone whom he suspected of intended wrongdoing towards him – with or without proof. Such is his reputation that he might be accused of almost anything, however heinous, with few historians caring to leap to his defence. Nothing, in other words, should surprise.

A further point, by way of extension of the above, is the broader picture of the behaviour of emperors generally. They were all-powerful, often deluded into believing themselves godlike, and therefore untouchable. Not only unable to dismiss any threat whatever to their position in the seat of power, they would have ignored disapproval of any steps they saw as necessary to secure that seat. No degree of questioning or criticism would ever be tolerated by those who defined the acceptable limits of their own behaviours.

While none of this is in any measure proof of Woods' theory, it could be said to be part of the underlying story behind those who populated Imperial circles early in the 1st century CE. The power that lay in the hands of *any* emperor was frightening, their exalted position now inconceivable. It would be an exceptional young woman who rebuffed the sexual advances of an emperor. Likewise, who would be brave (or foolish) enough to question anything they did, and still expect to live to tell the tale?

A final point can be added to the speculation. Comparison of the bust commonly held to be Poppaea Sabina, from the Palazzo Massimo alle Terme in Rome, alongside that of Tiberius, from the Ny Carlsberg Glyptotek in Copenhagen, undeniably shows a resemblance.

However as already noted at Chapter 4, images of ancient Roman figures varied considerably according to the models that they copied, the tastes of those who commissioned them, and the fashion of the day. In addition, since statues and busts did not commonly include identifying labels, as any visit to a modern museum will attest, suggested identifying marks necessarily came from coinage, with all the attendant difficulties of size, clarity and variety of features involved.

With such a fascinating hypothesis Poppaea continues to intrigue. True or false? The reader must decide.

Poppaea Sabina

APPENDIX II

Women of Antiquity as Writers

A brief mention – that is sadly all it can be – should be made of those relatively few women in ancient Rome who did write, and about whom we know. However, a key point first needs to be made regarding the risks involved:

> . . . *by writing, and even more by publishing, women broke with the traditional female virtues of modesty and reticence . . .*[1]

The problem was further compounded by the fact that ancient poetry, long the forerunner of prose, was very much an oral tradition, often read to the accompaniment of the lyre. Jane McIntosh Snyder[2] notes that such 'writing' "*. . . was intended not for solitary enjoyment but for public occasions – dinner parties, ceremonies, celebrations.*"

---

[1] Emily A Hemelrijk, *Matrona Docta: Educated Women in the Roman Elite from Cornelia to Julia Domna* (1999), Routledge, London
[2] *The Woman and the Lyre: Women Writers in Classical Greece and Rome* (1989), Southern Illinois University Press, Carbondale, IL, USA

The requirements of those two types of public appearances, as opposed to more usual modest activities within the confines of the *domus*, therefore broke the rules of seemly behaviour expected of the Roman *matrona*, and were presumably not to be countenanced.

The abject disapproval of Roman women of rank engaging in public activities, cause enough to bring down the wrath of the gods – to reinforce the wrath of their husbands or fathers – has already been mentioned. The walls around public appearances closed in still further with a third public outlet that excluded women: that of performing on the stage. Jane Stevenson[3] reminds us:

> . . . *religious festivals represent perhaps the only opportunity, other than her wedding day, for a girl of good family to make an appearance in a public place.*

Ian M Plant confirms the literary leanings of the women of antiquity: *"The majority of attested women authors were poets."*[4] Any research on the matter will find similarly; the overwhelming numbers of women writers were Greek, and the vast majority of their work was poetry – Sappho being the undisputed leader in the field.

---

[3] *Women Latin Poets: Language, Gender, and Authority, from Antiquity to the Eighteenth Century* (2005), Oxford University Press Inc, New York, NY, USA

[4] *Women Writers of Ancient Greece and Rome: An Anthology* (1994), University of Oklahoma Press, Norman, OK, USA

Furthermore, a crucial point should be borne in mind when comparing the women of antiquity with women writers of later centuries. We know that male owners of publishing houses rarely jumped at the chance of publishing women authors. It was no simple matter of caprice that women chose to write under men's names in order to be permitted a voice. Who can say how many women in ancient times were the early forerunners, setting the pattern? How many women, writing on matters considered unseemly for a woman, were assumed to be men?

To add to the difficulties, publishing in antiquity was not straightforward. In the absence of anything similar to later commercial establishments, publishing, for *anyone*, was necessarily a private endeavour. It required adequate means to enable copies to be reproduced, along with both encouragement and determination, as well as practical assistance. However if an audience could be found, there was nothing, in theory, to stop an author from circulating copies of her work.

In examining the education of women in ancient Rome (see Chapter 3), Hemelrijk raises some significant questions:

> *What did women write and why is so little of their writing left? Was it somehow lost, or did Roman women actually write so very little?*

Establishing the truth seems a task close to impossible. Snyder notes that although Roman women enjoyed greater personal freedom than their Greek counterparts, this did not appear to extend to the production of literature to anything like a similar degree to Greek women. We can only speculate as to why, although fundamental differences in culture must have played a part. By way of example, she notes that mention of Roman women in a literary context generally occurs when the education of their children – in particular, unsurprisingly, their sons – is under discussion. No similar constraints are shown to have applied to Greek women.

In any event, Roman literary circles, like so many others, were the exclusive preserve of men. Some vestige of light relief might be enjoyed by imagining a horrified Cicero, asked to welcome women members into his writers' group, responding, *sotto voce*, that he would rather eat his sandals . . .

For all her largely unsympathetic reputation, Agrippina the Younger, mother of Nero, can claim a special place in the pantheon of women writers of antiquity. She wrote her memoirs (*commentarii*), at a time unclear, but regrettably they have not survived. Very little is known about them, though they are thought to have been a series of texts, said to number three.

The reasons why she wrote them have occasioned much scholarly debate: each is possibly as accurate as any other of them. In his *Annals* (Book IV) Tacitus gave it as his opinion that they were *". . . memoirs . . . in which she recorded for posterity her life and her family's fortunes."*

He also quoted a story concerning her mother Agrippina the Elder. Lonely in widowhood, she made a plea to Tiberius, then Emperor and her adoptive father-in-law, to be given his permission to remarry. (He refused.) Tacitus noted that this event had not been recorded by historians; he claimed to have found it in the younger Agrippina's memoirs. (See also Chapter 3)

Tacitus is not the only ancient writer who used them as a source; Pliny the Elder is another. Others, not confirmed, include Suetonius, Juvenal and Cassius Dio. That such a number of esteemed ancient names allegedly made use of her writings gives cause for question. If so many of them read her *commentarii*, and presumably used, or at least were influenced by, some of the contents in their own writings, how is it that so very little of this source material survived? It stretches credibility beyond belief that they were *all* so careless as to take what they wanted, and each and every one of them 'lose' the rest. Or was there malevolent work afoot? Clearly Agrippina assumed that posterity would benefit from their existence; who might have thought otherwise?

Anthony Barrett catalogues the generally hostile reactions that Agrippina invites[5], which should be taken into account when examining historians' attitudes towards those memoirs. Given her position, intelligence and astuteness, however, we can assume that she would have taken some care with the contents.

Her upbringing, like her mother's before her, would have instilled into her a strong belief in her rights: that her background paved the way for a position within Imperial circles close to the centre of power and influence. That she was prevented, by virtue of her sex, from reaching those heights to which she felt she rightly belonged must have cost her dearly. It can reasonably be assumed that some flavour of this life disappointment would have found its way into her memoirs.

They have been dismissed as 'women's doings' which should not surprise, given the obvious lack of encouragement of women to write political treatises – or any other kind – and the restricted spheres in which they were permitted to move. The often hostile reception of the memoirs can therefore explain their effective dismissal as being of any use to the historical record. After all, the author was of relatively little account when compared to the emperors or the most well known sources. She was, at bottom, a woman.

---

[5] *Agrippina-Sister of Caligula-Wife of Claudius-Mother of Nero* (1996), B T Batsford Ltd, London

It might be said, then, that Poppaea is in good company. Had she, or any other Imperial woman, written her story, it would more than likely have suffered similar treatment. Given her relatively lowly background when compared to Agrippina, coupled with the widespread disparagement of her character, it can easily be imagined that levels of disapproval might have been even higher: *'Just* who *does this woman – the Imperial whore – think she is?'*.

As for women writers of ancient Rome generally, it is no easy task to find information on the women comprising the list below. Relatively speaking, they are among the most well known:

✓ **Cornificia** (c. 85-c. 40 BCE) – poet and epigrammatist; the fact that her brother Quintus Cornificius was also an author suggests that they came from a well-educated family of high rank. Though her work is said to have survived for four hundred years, and was highly regarded, none survives today. A monument exists in Rome to both her and her brother. (*Wikipedia*)

✓ **Cornelia** (100-190 BCE) – famously known for her eloquent letters to her adult sons Tiberius and Gaius, to whom she devoted her life after losing her husband. Her writings are said to have reflected her own formidable rhetorical skills, with both Tacitus and Cicero complimenting them. There is not complete agreement as to her authorship of them as some fragments did not surface until a century after her death.

✓ **Sulpicia I** – lived in the reign of Augustus (27 BCE-14 CE); a poet whose writings were thought too risqué for a woman, though there is much scholarly debate as to how much of the works attributed to her were actually written by her. She is the Sulpicia berated by Juvenal in his *Satire VI* for, in essence, being too clever by half.

✓ **Sulpicia II** – lived in the reign of Domitian (51-96 CE); a poet known for producing sexually explicit material about marital love, which is said to have been still read in the Renaissance; that both Sulpicias were poets suggests that the *gens Sulpicia* educated their daughters.[6]

✓ **Claudia Severa** (late 1st century CE) – wrote two letters to a friend, one an invitation, discovered in northern England in the 1970s. Though most is written by a scribe, a small part is hers: the earliest existing example of the handwriting in Latin of a Roman woman of the 1st century CE.

✓ **Plotina Augusta** (c. 70-c. 123 CE) – widow of the Emperor Trajan (98-117 CE); wrote an eloquent letter to the Emperor Hadrian petitioning him to allow the relaxing of rules concerning the naming of foreigners

---

[6] Stevenson, *op cit*

as beneficiaries in Roman wills. The inscription was discovered in Athens in 1890.

✓ **Julia Balbilla** (72-post 130 CE) – élite Roman poet, who in 130 CE had a number of poems inscribed on one of the Colossi of Memnon in Thebes, ancient Egypt while accompanying the Emperor Hadrian and his wife Vibia Sabina on a tour. To honour the royal couple thus at a height of 60-plus feet suggests some pre-planning, and a long ladder.

✓ **Vibia Perpetua** (c.182-203 CE) – kept a diary of her imprisonment resulting from her refusal to recant her Christian beliefs. She was put to death and eventually martyred.

Though of unknown size, one further sample of women writing is deserving of mention. It is those women who inscribed graffiti on the walls of buildings in Pompeii. Some undoubtedly were prostitutes advertising their wares – there can be no mistaking these – however, there were others.

Elizabeth Woeckner[7] tells us of a woman, unnamed, whose profession was that of a *tibicina*, a player of a reed instrument (she questions the common assumption that all such women were prostitutes as well as musicians). Her legacy was four lines, in Woeckner's words ". . . *shot*

---

[7] See *Women's Graffiti from Pompeii* in *Women Writing Latin in Roman Antiquity, Late Antiquity and the Early Christian Era* (2002), Routledge (Taylor & Francis, Inc), New York, NY, USA

through with bitterness and irony . . .". Inscribed on a balcony of a Pompeian house, they decry her irritation and disappointment at the loss of a musical competition to a rival.

Describing the work as *". . . a rare first-person statement by a female performer"*, Woeckner suggests that although her profession was generally held to be of low status, she was clearly possessed of sufficient education and literacy to incorporate into her writing both Greek mythological figures – Themis and her daughter Dike – and the gods Apollo and Volcanus. The overall flavour of the inscription is of a frustrated woman, venting her fury at her misfortune in four lines of confident and expressive prose.

Sources[8] also suggest that women as well as men were involved in the production of electoral *programmata* (posters) in Pompeii. These, like their modern counterparts, often remained in place long after the elections for which they were produced had passed. This activity clearly provided those women with a participating role in Pompeii's political life, though perhaps to a lesser extent than men.

It seems that they were not necessarily related to the candidate for whom they were displaying their support, though this was sometimes the case:

---

[8] For example, Liisa Savunen's *Women and Elections in Pompeii* in *Women in Antiquity: New Assessments* (1995) (eds Richard Hawley and Barbara Levick), Routledge, London

> *I, Taedia Secunda, earnestly entreat you to make Lucius*
> *Popidius Secundus aedile. His Grandmother asks this*
> *and she made [the inscription] (CIL[9] IV 7469)[10]*

As noted at Chapter 6, the above examples again suggest a higher degree of literacy in the Pompeian population than might be assumed.

Along with the writings of the women listed above, those graffiti artists deserve inclusion in the catalogue of the 'anonymous voices' of antiquity. Writing forty erudite volumes of the history of Rome was not essential in order to give expression to personal thoughts and aspirations; and at least graffiti did not need to go through the machinations of publication!

If these few snippets can be found by diligent archaeologists – with posthumous thanks to Matteo Della Corte (see Chapter 6) – and historians, then it is imperative that we keep digging to find more. We can confidently assume that they are there, waiting only for us to find them.

Lefkowitz and Fant[11] sum up the end product of the difficulties faced by the women of antiquity in making their mark on the literature of their time:

---

[9] *Corpus Inscriptionum Latinarum*, a comprehensive collection of inscriptions in Latin from throughout the Roman Empire
[10] Quoted in Bonnie MacLachlan's *Women in Ancient Rome: A Sourcebook* (2013), Bloomsbury Academic, London

> *. . . what little remains of women's writings offers eloquent testimony not so much of an informing literary experience, as of a potential never realised.*

*

---

[11] *Women's Life in Greece and Rome* (1992), The John Hopkins University Press, Baltimore, MD, USA

BIBLIOGRAPHY

Primary sources

Cassius Dio, *Roman History*, William Heinemann London and The Macmillan Co. New York (trans. Earnest Cary/Herbert B Foster, 1905-1927)

Flavius Josephus, *The Antiquities of the Jews* (1737), (trans. William Whiston)

Josephus, *The Works of Flavius Josephus,* Armstrong & Plaskitt, Baltimore, MD, USA (trans. William Whiston, 1835)

— *The Life of Josephus (Brill Josephus Project)*, E J Brill, Leiden, Netherlands (trans./ed. Steve Mason, 2001)

Livy, *Ab Urbe Condita libri* (Books from the City's Foundation)

Pliny the Elder, *Natural History*

Plutarch, *Lives of Galba and Otho*, Macmillan and Co, London and New York (E G Hardy, 1890)

— *The Parallel Lives, The Life of Galba*, Loeb Classical Library, Vol. XI (1926), Harvard University Press, Cambridge, MA, USA

— *Roman Lives,* Oxford University Press, Oxford, UK (trans. Robin Waterfield, 1999)

Sallust, *Sallust,* Loeb Classical Library, Harvard University Press, Cambridge, MA, USA (trans. John C Rolfe, 1921-31)

Suetonius, *Lives of the Caesars,* Oxford University Press, Oxford, UK (trans. Catharine Edwards, 2000)

Tacitus, *The Histories,* Oxford University Press, Oxford, UK (trans. W Hamilton Fyfe, 1912, revised by David S Levene, 1997)

— *The Annals of Imperial Rome,* Penguin Books, London (trans. Michael Grant, 1956-96)

— *The Annals-The Reigns of Tiberius, Claudius, and Nero,* Oxford University Press, Oxford, UK (trans. John C Yardley, 2008)

*

General sources

Pauline Allen, Barbara Garlick, Suzanne Dixon (eds), *Stereotypes of Women in Power: Historical Perspectives and Revisionist Views* (1992), Greenwood Press, Westport, CT, USA

Eve D'Ambra, *A History of Women in the West: From ancient goddesses to Christian saints* (1992), Harvard University Press, Cambridge, MA, USA

— *Roman Women* (2007), Cambridge University Press, New York, NY, USA

Kristin J Anderson, *Modern Misogyny: Anti-Feminism in a Post-Feminist Era* (2015), Oxford University Press, Oxford, UK

K W Arafat, *Pausanias' Greece: Ancient Artists and Roman Rulers* (1996), Cambridge University Press, Cambridge, UK

J P V D Balsdon, *Roman Women: their history and habits* (1963), John Day Co/Barnes & Noble Inc, New York, NY, USA

A A Barrett, *Agrippina-Sister of Caligula-Wife of Claudius-Mother of Nero* (1996), B T Batsford Ltd, London

— *Livia-First Lady of Imperial Rome* (2002), Yale University Press, New Haven, CT, USA and London

M Battles, *Library: An Unquiet History* (2004), Vintage Books, London

R A Bauman, *Women and Politics in Ancient Rome* (1992), Routledge, London

— *Crime and Punishment in Ancient Rome* (1996), Ditto

Rebecca R Benefiel, *Rome in Pompeii: Wall Inscriptions and GIS* in *Latin on Stone: Epigraphic Research and Electronic Archives* (2010), ed. Francisca Feraudi-Gruénais, Lexington Books, Lanham, MD, USA

Margarete Bieber, *Ancient Copies* (1977), New York University Press, New York, NY, USA

Sandra Bingham, *The Praetorian Guard: A History of Rome's Elite Special Forces* (2013), I B Tauris & Co Ltd, London

D C Braund, *Augustus to Nero: A Sourcebook on Roman History 31BC to AD 68* (1985), Routledge, Abingdon, UK (originally Croom Helm Ltd, London)

Susanna Braund and J Osgood (eds), *A Companion to Perseus and Juvenal* (2012), Blackwell Publishing Ltd, USA/UK

T Burgess, *Tracts on the Origin and Independence of the Ancient British Church* (1815), Printed for F C and J Rivington, London

A Butterworth and R Laurence, *Pompeii: The Living City* (2006), Phoenix (Orion Books), London

D B Campbell, *Mons Graupius AD 83* (2010), Osprey Publishing, Oxford, UK

Eve Cantarella, *Pandora's Daughters: The Role and Status of Women in Greek and Roman Antiquity* (1987), The John Hopkins University Press, Baltimore, MD, USA

E Champlin, *Nero* (2003), Harvard University Press, Cambridge, MA, USA

Laurie J Churchill, Phyllis R Brown and Jane E Jeffrey (eds), *Women Writing Latin in Roman Antiquity, Late Antiquity and the Early Christian Era* (2002), Routledge (Taylor & Francis Books, Inc), New York, NY, USA

T M Compton, *Victim of the Muses: Poet as Scapegoat, Warrior and Hero in Greco-Roman and Indo-European Myth and History* (2006), Center for Hellenic Studies, Washington, DC, USA

Joan B Connelly, *Portrait of a Priestess: Women and Ritual in Ancient Greece* (2007), University of Princeton Press, Princeton, NJ, USA

Alison E Cooley and M G L Cooley, *Pompeii and Herculaneum: A Sourcebook* (2004, revised 2014), Routledge, Abingdon, UK

R Cowan, *Roman Guardsman 62 BC-AD 324* (2014), Osprey Publishing Ltd, Oxford, UK

J A Crook, *Consilium Principis: Imperial Councils and Counsellors from Augustus to Diocletian* (1955), Cambridge University Press, Cambridge, UK

Suzanne D Dixon, *Reading Roman Women* (2001), Duckworth, London

G Edmundson, *Church in Rome in the First Century* (1913), Christian Classics Ethereal Library, Grand Rapids, MI, USA

Catharine Edwards, *The Politics of Immorality in Ancient Rome* (1993), Cambridge University Press, Cambridge, UK

— *Suetonius-Lives of the Caesars* (2000), Oxford University Press, Oxford, UK

— *Death in Ancient Rome* (2007), Yale University Press, New Haven, CT, USA

G G Fagan and P Murgatroyd (eds), *From Augustus to Nero: An Intermediate Latin Reader* (2006), Cambridge University Press, Cambridge, UK

Elaine Fantham, Helene P Foley, Natalie B Kampen, Sarah B Pomeroy, H A Shapiro, *Women in the Classical World: Image and Text* (1994), Oxford University Press Inc, New York, NY, USA

A Feldherr (ed), *The Cambridge Companion to the Roman Historians* (2009), Cambridge University Press, Cambridge, UK

Joann Fletcher, *Cleopatra the Great-The Woman Behind the Legend* (2008), Hodder and Stoughton, London

Harriet I Flower, *Ancestor Masks and Aristocratic Power in Roman Culture* (1996), Oxford University Press, Oxford, UK

—   *The Art of Forgetting: Disgrace and Oblivion in Roman Political Culture* (2006), University of North Carolina Press, Chapel Hill, NC, USA

P W Foss and J J Dobbins (eds), *The World of Pompeii* (2007), Routledge, New York, NY, USA

J L Franklin Jr, *Pompeis Difficile Est: Studies in the Political Life of Imperial Pompeii* (2001), University of Michigan Press, Ann Arbor, MI, USA

A Fraschetti (ed), *Roman Women* (originally *Roma al femminile*) (1994), G Laterza & Figli S.p.a., Roma-Bari, Italy

Annelise Freisenbruch, *The First Ladies of Rome: The Women Behind the Caesars* (2011), Vintage Books, London

Marilyn French, *Beyond Power: On Women, Men and Morals* (1986), Jonathan Cape Ltd, London

L H Friedländer, *Roman Life and Manners Under the Early Empire*, Vol. IV (1913), George Routledge & Sons Limited, London

R Gervaso, *Nerone* (1978), Editore Rusconi, Milano, Italy

G Giubelli, *Oplontis–The Villa Poppea* (undated), Carcavallo Editore, Napoli, Italy

J M Greer, *Secrets of the Lost Symbol* (2010), Llewellyn Publications, Woodbury, MN, USA

Miriam T Griffin, *Nero-The End of a Dynasty* (1984), BT Batsford Ltd, London

J F Hall (ed), *Etruscan Italy: Etruscan Influences on the Civilizations of Italy from Antiquity to the Modern Era*, Brigham Young University, Provo, UT, USA

Judith P Hallett, *Fathers and Daughters in Roman Society: Women and the Elite Family* (1984), Princeton University Press, Princeton, NJ, USA

R Hawley and Barbara Levick, *Women in Antiquity: New assessments* (1995), Routledge, London

Emily A Hemelrijk, *Matrona Docta: Educated Women in the Roman Elite from Cornelia to Julia Domna* (1999), Routledge, London

B W Henderson, *The Life and Principate of the Emperor Nero* (1905), Methuen & Co., London

J Holland, *A Brief History of Misogyny-The World's Oldest Prejudice* (2006), Constable & Robinson Ltd, London

W den Hollander, *Josephus, the Emperors and the City of Rome: From Hostage to Historian* (2014), Koninklijke Brill NV, Leiden, Netherlands

Sabine R Hübner and D M Ratzan (eds), *Remarriage and stepfathers in the Greco-Roman East,* in *Growing Up Fatherless in Antiquity* (2009), Cambridge University Press, Cambridge, UK

Sandra R Joshel, *Desire, Empire and Tacitus's Messalina* (2013), University of Chicago Press, Chicago, IL, USA

Ann Olga Koloski-Ostrow and Claire L Lyons (eds), *Naked Truths: Women, Sexuality and Gender in Classical Art* (1997), Routledge, London

Mary R Lefkowitz and Maureen B Fant, *Women's Life in Greece and Rome: A Sourcebook in Translation* (1982-92), The John Hopkins University Press, Baltimore, MD, USA

Marjorie and B Lightman, *A to Z of Ancient Greek and Roman Women* (2008), Infobase Publishing, New York, NY, USA

W L Macdonald, *The Architecture of the Roman Empire, Vol. 1* (1982), Yale University Press, New Haven, CT, USA

Elisabeth B MacDougall (ed), *Ancient Roman Villa Gardens* (1987), Harvard University, Cambridge, MA, USA

Bonnie MacLachlan, *Women in Ancient Rome: A Sourcebook* (2013), Bloomsbury Academic, London

J Malitz, *Nero* (2005-English translation), Blackwell Publishing Ltd, Oxford, UK

Annalisa Marzano, *Roman Villas in Central Italy: A Social and Economic History* (2007), Koninklijke Brill NV, Leiden, Netherlands

R Mellor, *Tacitus* (1993), Routledge, New York, USA and Abingdon, UK

Elizabeth Meyer, *Legitimacy and Law in the Roman World: Tabulae in Roman Belief and Practice* (2004), Cambridge University Press, Cambridge, UK

B Mineo (ed), *A Companion to Livy* (2015), Wiley Blackwell (John Wiley & Sons Ltd), Chichester, UK

S C Nappo, *Pompeii* (2004), White Star S.r.l., Vercelli, Italy

M Owen and I Gildenhard, *Tacitus, Annals, 15.20-23, 33-45, Latin Text, Study Aids with Vocabulary, and Commentary* (2013), Open Book Publishers, Cambridge, UK

Victoria Emma Pagán, *Conspiracy Narratives in Roman History* (2004), University of Texas Press, Austin, TX, USA

Sara E Phang, *The Marriage of Roman Soldiers 13 BC-AD 235* (2001), Brill Academic Publishers, Leiden, Netherlands

I M Plant (ed), *Women Writers of Ancient Greece and Rome: An Anthology* (2004), University of Oklahoma Press, Norman, OK, USA

Sarah H Pomeroy, *Goddesses, Whores, Wives, and Slaves: Women in Classical Antiquity* (1975), Schocken Books, New York, NY, USA

Ivana della Portella, *Subterranean Rome* (2002), Arsenale Editrice, San Giovanni Lupatoto, Italy

Modesta Pozzo (writing as Moderata Fonte) (1600), *Il merito delle donne (The Worth of Women) (1600)*, Venezia, Italy

Molly Pryzwansky, *Feminine Imperial Ideals in the "Caesares" of Suetonius* (2012), ProQuest, New York, NY, USA

Beryl Rawson, *The Family in Ancient Rome: New Perspectives* (1993), Cornell University Press, Ithaca, NY, USA

— *Children and Childhood in Roman Italy* (2003), Oxford University Press Inc, New York, NY, USA

L Richardson Jr, *A New Topical Dictionary of Ancient Rome* (1992), The John Hopkins University Press, Baltimore, MD, USA

Amy Richlin, *Arguments with Silence-Writing the History of Roman Women* (2014), University of Michigan Press, Ann Arbor, MI, USA

J C Rolfe, *Sallust* (Loeb Classical Library, 1921), Harvard University Press, Cambridge, MA, USA

V Rudich, *Political Dissidence under Nero: The Price of Dissimulation* (1993), Routledge, Oxford, UK

S H Rutledge, *Imperial Inquisitions: Prosecutors and Informants from Tiberius to Domitian* (2001), Routledge, London

Joyce E Salisbury, *Encyclopedia of Women in the Ancient World* (2001), ABC-CLIO Inc, Santa Barbara, CA, USA

R P Saller, *Personal patronage under the early Empire* (1982), Cambridge University Press, Cambridge, UK

Francesca Santoro L'Hoir, *The Rhetoric of Gender Terms-'Man', 'Woman', & the Portrayal of Character in Latin Prose* (1992), EJ Brill, Leiden, Netherlands

— *Tragedy, Rhetoric and the Historiography of Tacitus'* Annales (2006), University of Michigan Press, Ann Arbor, MI, USA

Liisa Savunen, *Women and Elections in Pompeii* in *Women in Antiquity: New Assessments* (1995) (eds R Hawley and Barbara Levick), Routledge, London

W Scheidel, *Marriage, Families, and Survival: Demographic Aspects* in *A Companion to the Roman Army* (2011), P Erdkamp (ed), Blackwell Publishing Ltd (John Wiley & Sons), Oxford, UK

D Seward, *Jerusalem's Traitor: Josephus, Masada and the Fall of Judea* (2008), Da Capo Press, Cambridge, MA, USA

D Shotter, *Nero Caesar Augustus: Emperor of Rome* (2008), Routledge (Taylor & Francis), Abingdon, UK

Marilyn B Skinner, *Clodia Metelli: The Tribune's Sister* (2011), Oxford University Press, Oxford, UK

Joan Smith, *Misogynies* (1989), Faber and Faber, London

Jane M Snyder, *The Woman and the Lyre: Women Writers in Classical Greece and Rome* (1989), Southern Illinois University Press, Carbondale, IL, USA

J Solomon, *The Ancient World in the Cinema* (2001), Yale University, New Haven, CT, USA

Dale Spender, *Man-Made Language* (1980), Routledge & Kegan Paul, London

R Stark, *The Rise of Christianity-A Sociologist Reconsiders History* (1996), Princeton University Press, Princeton, NJ, USA

G Stern, *Women, Children, and Senators on the Ara Pacis Augustae: A Study of Augustus' Vision of a New World Order in 13 BC* (2006), ProQuest LLC, Ann Arbor, MI, USA

Jane Stevenson, *Women Latin Poets: Language, Gender, and Authority, from Antiquity to the Eighteenth Century* (2005), Oxford University Press Inc, New York, NY, USA

Susan Treggiari, *Terentia, Tullia and Publilia: The Women of Cicero's Family* (2007), Routledge, Abingdon, UK

Jennifer Trimble, *Women and Visual Replication in Roman Imperial Art and Culture* (2011), Cambridge University Press, Cambridge, UK

D L Vagi, *Coinage and History of the Roman Empire, C. 82 BC-AD 480* (1999), Fitzroy Dearborn Publishers, Chicago, IL, USA

E R Varner, *Mutilation and Transformation-Damnatio Memoriae and Roman Imperial Portraiture* (2004), Koninklijke Brill NV, Leiden, Netherlands

E Walker and B Henry, *The Annals of Tacitus: a Study in the Writing of History* (1952), Manchester University Press, Manchester, UK

A Wallace-Hadrill (ed), *Patronage in Ancient Society* (1989), Routledge, London/New York

Patricia A Watson, *Ancient Stepmothers: Myth, Misogyny and Reality* (1995), E J Brill, Leiden, Netherlands

Margaret H Williams, *Jews in a Graeco-Roman Environment* (2013), Mohr Siebeck, Tübingen, Germany

R Winsbury, *The Roman Book* (2009), Gerald Duckworth & Co Ltd, London

Elizabeth Woeckner, *Women's Graffiti from Pompeii* in *Women Writing Latin in Roman Antiquity, Late Antiquity and the Early Christian Era* (2002), Routledge (Taylor & Francis, Inc), New York, NY, USA

Susan E Wood, *Imperial Women: A Study in Public Images, 40 BC-AD 68* (1998), Koninklijke Brill NV, Leiden, Netherlands

A Wright, *Glut: Mastering Information Through the Ages* (2007), Cornell University Press, Ithaca, NY, USA

Louise Zarmati, *Heinemann Ancient and Medieval History: Pompeii and Herculaneum* (2005), Pearson Education Australia

*

Articles, Theses and Websites

Tana Joy Allen, *Roman Healing Spas in Italy: A Study in Design and Function* (1998), University of Alberta, Edmonton, AB, Canada

S Aubry, *Inscriptions on Portrait Gems and discs in Late Antiquity (3rd-6th centuries AD)* in *Gems of Heaven: Recent Research on Engraved Gemstones in Late Antiquity, AD 200-600* (2011), C Entwistle and N Adams (eds), British Museum Company Ltd, London

B Baldwin, *Juvenal's Crispinus*, in *Acta Classica* (1979), University of Calgary, Calgary, AB, Canada

P Berdowski, *Some Remarks on the Economic Activity of Women in the Roman Empire: A Research Problem* (2007), University of Rzeszów, Faculty of Ancient History and Oriental Studies, Rzeszów, Poland

L Bruce, *Palace and Villa Libraries from Augustus to Hadrian* (1986), in *The Journal of Library History*, Vol. 21, No. 3 (1974-1987), University of Texas Press, Austin, TX, USA

S De Caro, *The Sculptures of the Villa of Poppaea at Oplontis* from *Dumbarton Oaks Colloquium on the History of Landscape Architecture* (1987), MacDougall, Elisabeth B (ed), Trustees for Harvard University, Washington, DC, USA

Maureen Carroll, *Exploring the Sanctuary of Venus and its sacred grove. Politics, cult and identity in Roman Pompeii* (2010), Papers of the British School at Rome, 78

Rosaria Ciardello, *The Villa of Poppaea at Oplontis: decorative frescoes from Republic to the Empire* in *Apolline Project Vol. 1: Studies on Vesuvius' North Slope and the Bay of Naples* (2009), eds F de Simone, G de Simone and R T MacFarlane, Napoli, Italy

Alexis Dawson, *Whatever Happened to Lady Agrippina?* in *The Classical Journal*, Vol. 64, No. 6 (1969), Northfield, MN, USA

Susan Deacy and Fiona McHardy, *Uxoricide in Pregnancy: Ancient Greek Domestic Violence in Comparative Perspective* in *Evolutionary Psychology* 11.5 (2013), Roehampton, London, UK

Tracy Lynn Deline, *Women in Criminal Trials in the Julio-Claudian Era* (2009 Thesis), University of British Columbia, Vancouver, BC, Canada

R M Frazer Jr, *Nero the Artist-Criminal* in *The Classical Journal*, Vol. 62 (1966), The Classical Association of the Middle West and South, Monmouth, IL, USA

Valerie French, *Midwives and Maternity Care in the Roman World* in *Helios* 13(2) (1986), Texas Tech University Press, Lubbock, TX, USA

Caitlin Gillespie, *Poppaea Venus and the Ptolemaic Queens: An Alternative Biography* in *Histos* 8 (2014), Western Washington University, Bellingham, WA, USA

Mary L Gordon, *The* Ordo *of Pompeii* in *The Journal of Roman Studies*, Vol. 17 (1927), Cambridge, UK

T Grüll and L Benke, *A Hebrew/Aramaic Graffito and Poppaea's Alleged Jewish Sympathy* in *Journal of Jewish Studies* (2011), Oxford, UK

Wilhelmina F Jashemski, *The Vesuvian Sites Before A.D. 79: The Archaeological, Literary, and Epigraphical Evidence* in *The Natural History of Pompeii* (2002), W F Jashemski and F G Meyer (eds), Cambridge University Press, Cambridge, UK

M J J Johnson, *The Mausoleum of Augustus: Etruscan and Other Influences on its Design* in *Etruscan Italy: Etruscan Influences on the Civilizations of Italy from Antiquity to the Modern Era* (1996), J F Hall (ed), Brigham Young University, Provo, UT, USA

M Kleijwegt, *Nero's Helpers: The Role of the Neronian Courtier in Tacitus'* Annals, University of South Africa, Pretoria, RSA in *Classics Ireland*, Vol. 7 (2000)

Christina Kokkinia, *Survey results in Boubon (Cibyratis, northern Lycia) 2004-2006*, Kera, Institute for Greek and Roman Antiquity, Athens, Greece

P Kragelund, *The Temple and Birthplace of Diva Poppaea* in *Classic Quarterly*, Vol. 60, Issue 2 (2010), Cambridge, UK

Kathryn Lomas, *Rome, Magna Graecia, and Sicily in Livy from 326 to 200 BC*, in *A Companion to Livy* (2015), B Mineo (ed), Wiley Blackwell (John Wiley & Sons Ltd), Chichester, UK

R Mayer, *What Caused Poppaea's Death* in *Historia* 31 (1982), Franz Steiner Verlag GmbH, Stuttgart, Germany

Michele Murray, *Playing a Jewish Game: Gentile and Christian Judaizing in the First and Second Centuries, CE* (2004), Canadian Corporation for Studies in Religion

J Nicols, *Gender and Civic Patronage* in *Studies in Latin Literature and Roman History V* (1989), C Deroux (ed), Latomus Revue D'Etudes Latines, Brussels, Belgium

N Purcell, *Livia and the Womanhood of Rome* in *Augustus* (2009), J Edmondson (ed), Edinburgh University Press, Edinburgh, Scotland

Molly M Pryzwansky, *Feminine Imperial ideals in the "Caesares" of Suetonius*, (2008 Dissertation), Dept of Classical Studies, Duke University, Durham, NC, USA

Alexandra Revell, *Tacitus' Female Tyrants* (undated Thesis), Oxford University, Oxford, UK

W Scheidel, *Updated citation scores for ancient historians in the United States* in *Princeton/Stanford Working Papers in Classics* (2011), Stanford University, Stanford, CA, USA

N W Slater, *Nero's Masks* in *Classical World*, Vol. 90, No. 1 (1996), The John Hopkins University Press, Baltimore, MD, USA

Mary E Smallwood, *The Alleged Jewish Tendencies of Poppaea Sabina* in *The Journal of Theological Studies* (1959), Oxford University Press, Oxford, UK

S E Smethurst, *Women in Livy's* History in *Greece and Rome*, Vol. 9, Issue 56 (1950), Cambridge University Press, Cambridge, UK

T Stevenson, *Women of Early Rome as* Exempla *in Livy*, Ab Urbe Condita, Book 1, in *Classical World*, Vol. 104, N.2 (2011), The John Hopkins University Press, Baltimore, MD, USA

Jenifer M Swindle, *A Rhetorical Use of Women in Tacitus'* Annales in *Studia Antiqua*, Vol. 3 No. 1 (2003), Brigham Young University, Provo, UT, USA

Rena Van den Bergh, *The Role of Education in the Social and Legal Position of Women in Roman Society* (2000), Revue Internationale des droits de l'Antiquité XLVII, University of South Africa, Pretoria, RSA

I Varriale, *Architecture and Decoration in the House of Menander in Pompeii* in *Contested Spaces-Houses and Temples in Roman Antiquity and the New Testament* (2012), D L Balch and Annette Weissenrieder (eds), Mohr Siebeck, Tübingen, Germany

D Woods, *Nero and Sporus* in *Latomus Collection*, 68 (2009), Brussels, Belgium

48818378R00179

Made in the USA
Middletown, DE
01 October 2017